Contents

Cambridge School Shakespeare

Introduction

This *Hamlet* is part of the **Cambridge School Shakespeare** series. Like every other play in the series, it has been specially prepared to help all students in schools and colleges.

The **Cambridge School Shakespeare** *Hamlet* aims to be different. It invites you to lift the words from the page and to bring the play to life in your classroom, hall or drama studio. Through enjoyable and focused activities, you will increase your understanding of the play. Actors have created their different interpretations of the play over the centuries. Similarly, you are invited to make up your own mind about *Hamlet*, rather than having someone else's interpretation handed down to you.

Cambridge School Shakespeare does not offer you a cut-down or simplified version of the play. This is Shakespeare's language, filled with imaginative possibilities. You will find on every left-hand page: a summary of the action, an explanation of unfamiliar words, and a choice of activities on Shakespeare's stagecraft, characters, themes and language.

Between each act and in the pages at the end of the play, you will find notes, illustrations and activities. These will help to encourage reflection after every act and give you insights into the background and context of the play as a whole.

This edition will be of value to you whether you are studying for an examination, reading for pleasure or thinking of putting on the play to entertain others. You can work on the activities on your own or in groups. Many of the activities suggest a particular group size, but don't be afraid to make up larger or smaller groups to suit your own purposes. Please don't think you have to do every activity: choose those that will help you most.

Although you are invited to treat *Hamlet* as a play, you don't need special dramatic or theatrical skills to do the activities. By choosing your activities, and by exploring and experimenting, you can make your own interpretations of Shakespeare's language, characters and stories.

Whatever you do, remember that Shakespeare wrote his plays to be acted, watched and enjoyed.

Rex Gibson
Founding editor

This new edition contains more photographs, more diversity and more supporting material than previous editions, whilst remaining true to Rex's original vision. Specifically, it contains more activities and commentary on stagecraft and writing about Shakespeare, to reflect contemporary interest. The glossary has been enlarged too. Finally, this edition aims to reflect the best teaching and learning possible, and to represent not only Shakespeare through the ages, but also the relevance and excitement of Shakespeare today.

Richard Andrews and Vicki Wienand
Series editors

This edition of *Hamlet* uses the text of the play established by Philip Edwards in **The New Cambridge Shakespeare**.

Cambridge School
Shakespeare

HAMLET

Edited by Richard Andrews
Series editors: Richard Andrews and Vicki Wienand
Founding editor: Rex Gibson

CAMBRIDGE
UNIVERSITY PRESS

CAMBRIDGE
UNIVERSITY PRESS

University Printing House, Cambridge CB2 8BS, United Kingdom

One Liberty Plaza, 20th Floor, New York, NY 10006, USA

477 Williamstown Road, Port Melbourne, VIC 3207, Australia

4843/24, 2nd Floor, Ansari Road, Daryaganj, Delhi – 110002, India

79 Anson Road, #06–04/06, Singapore 079906

Cambridge University Press is part of the University of Cambridge.

It furthers the University's mission by disseminating knowledge in the pursuit of education, learning and research at the highest international levels of excellence.

www.cambridge.org
Information on this title: www.cambridge.org/9781107615489

Commentary and notes © Cambridge University Press 1994, 2014
Text © Cambridge University Press 1985, 2014

First published 1994
Second edition 2005
Third edition 2014
20 19 18 17 16 15 14 13 12 11 10 9 8 7 6

Printed in Spain by GraphyCems

A catalogue record for this publication is available from the British Library

ISBN 978-1-107-61548-9 Paperback

....

Cover image: Baxter Theatre Company/RSC 2006, © Donald Cooper/Photostage

Hamlet dramatises the tragic story of the young prince of Denmark. His country is threatened with invasion by Norway, but Hamlet is obsessed with the recent death of his father and the marriage of his mother, Gertrude, to his uncle, Claudius, who has become king.

Hamlet's first appearance, dressed in black, conveys his isolation from the court. His unhappiness about Gertrude's relationship with Claudius is evident. The outcome will be the destruction of two families: Hamlet's (Gertrude and Claudius) and royal counsellor Polonius's (Laertes and Ophelia).

Hamlet learns the truth from his father's ghost: Claudius murdered old Hamlet. Hamlet desires revenge, but is not sure if the Ghost has spoken honestly.

To test the truth of the Ghost's story, Hamlet puts on 'an antic disposition'. His strange behaviour arouses the suspicion of Claudius.

Claudius sends for Hamlet's old schoolfriends, Rosencrantz and Guildenstern, to spy on his stepson. Hamlet greets them joyfully, but then discovers they are Claudius's agents.

Hamlet plans to discover Claudius's guilt. He orders
a group of players to stage a play showing a king
murdered by his brother, who then marries the queen.

Hamlet's plan
succeeds, and Claudius
acknowledges his guilt as
he prays. Hamlet is about
to kill Claudius,
but decides to wait until
he can choose a moment
when Claudius's soul will
go straight to hell.

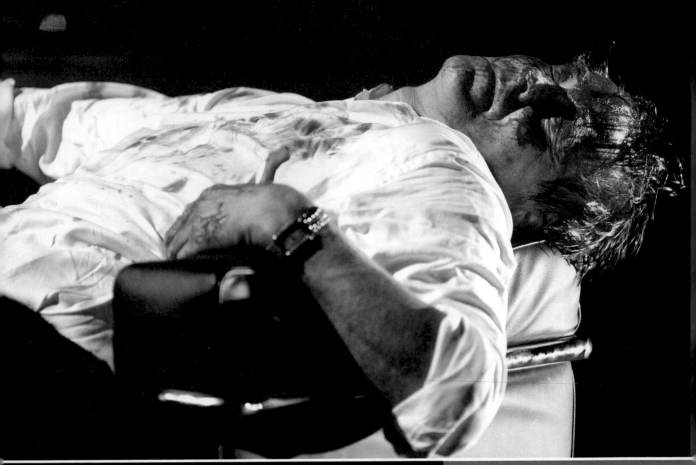

▲ Polonius has concealed himself, wishing to overhear what Hamlet says to Gertrude. But Hamlet mistakes the hidden Polonius for Claudius, and kills him.

◄ Hamlet rages at his mother, begging her to give up Claudius. But Claudius, wanting to be rid of his dangerous stepson, sends Hamlet to England, secretly ordering his execution there.

► (top) Claudius and Gertrude watch appalled as Ophelia's songs recall Hamlet's rejection and his killing of her father, Polonius. Her madness will shortly result in her death.

► (bottom) Hamlet has escaped execution in England, but has sent Rosencrantz and Guildenstern to their deaths there. In the graveyard, the sight of Yorick's skull prompts him to reflect on mortality.

Hamlet duels with Laertes, Polonius's son, who
seeks revenge for his father's and sister's deaths.

Claudius and Laertes have conspired to kill Hamlet by deceit. But their plot
descends into chaos: Gertrude drinks the poison intended for Hamlet,
and Laertes, Claudius and Hamlet are all fatally wounded by the poisoned sword.

List of characters

The Royal House of Denmark

HAMLET Prince of Denmark
CLAUDIUS King of Denmark, Hamlet's uncle
GERTRUDE Queen of Denmark, Hamlet's mother
GHOST of King Hamlet, Hamlet's father

The Court of Denmark

POLONIUS Counsellor to the king
OPHELIA his daughter
LAERTES his son
REYNALDO his servant

OSRIC
LORDS ⎫ Courtiers
GENTLEMAN ⎭
MESSENGER and ATTENDANTS

VOLTEMAND ⎫ Ambassadors to Norway
CORNELIUS ⎭

MARCELLUS ⎫
BARNARDO ⎬ Officers of the Watch
FRANCISCO ⎭

SOLDIERS and GUARDS

Former fellow students of Hamlet

HORATIO Hamlet's friend
ROSENCRANTZ ⎫
GUILDENSTERN ⎭ Sent for by Claudius to inform on Hamlet

Norway

FORTINBRAS Prince of Norway
CAPTAIN in Fortinbras's army

Other characters in the play

First PLAYER ⎫
Other players ⎭ actors visiting Elsinore
English AMBASSADORS
SAILORS
CLOWN gravedigger and sexton
SECOND CLOWN his assistant
PRIEST at Ophelia's funeral

The action of the play is set in and around the Danish royal palace at Elsinore.

Francisco is on sentry duty on the gun platform of Elsinore. It is midnight and freezing cold. Barnardo comes to relieve Francisco. Horatio and Marcellus arrive to join Barnardo.

Stagecraft

To experience the tense and uneasy atmosphere of the play's opening, the best thing to do is take parts and act out the first nineteen lines. As you rehearse, talk together about the following points. Remember, your aim is to make the opening moments of the play gripping and dramatic.

- What will be the first thing the audience sees? For example, is Francisco on sentry duty, patrolling the stage, before the first members of the audience enter?
- Barnardo, the newcomer, challenges Francisco. This is contrary to military practice (Francisco should challenge him). How can you use that error to intensify the nervous atmosphere?
- What effect do the short, staccato ('rapid fire') verbal exchanges have?
- How can you show the audience that the night is bitterly cold?
- Francisco is never seen again in the play, but his remark 'And I am sick at heart' forecasts the troubled melancholy that Hamlet feels when he appears in the next scene. How might Francisco speak and behave during his brief time on stage? What would be the effect if Hamlet and Francisco were played by the same actor?
- In Shakespeare's day, plays were staged in broad daylight. Identify all the words and phrases in the script that help create the impression of night and darkness.

1 Horatio

This is the first time we meet Horatio, who will turn out to be an important character in the play.

- Look at Horatio's lines in the script opposite and on the following page, and start making notes on his character, based on the attitude he takes towards the Watch and the Ghost. Write down the range of emotions he displays. As you progress through the play, your first impressions of his character will inform your notes on Horatio, and the role he plays in relation to Hamlet.

Nay answer me go ahead – answer me

unfold yourself identify yourself, give the password

Long live the king! (the password, which will prove ironic as the play reveals the death of King Hamlet)

most carefully precisely

relief (both 'relief' in the modern sense, and replacement on the watch or guarding of the battlements)

rivals partners

Stand ho! stop and declare yourself

this ground this castle and country

liegemen to the Dane loyal followers of the Danish king

Give you I wish you

A piece of him a characteristically laconic, witty or modest statement from Horatio

Hamlet, Prince of Denmark

Act 1 Scene 1
A gun platform on the battlements of Elsinore Castle

Enter BARNARDO *and* FRANCISCO, *two* sentinels

BARNARDO	Who's there?	
FRANCISCO	Nay answer me. Stand and unfold yourself.	
BARNARDO	Long live the king!	
FRANCISCO	Barnardo?	
BARNARDO	He.	5
FRANCISCO	You come most carefully upon your hour.	
BARNARDO	'Tis now struck twelve, get thee to bed Francisco.	
FRANCISCO	For this relief much thanks, 'tis bitter cold	
	And I am sick at heart.	
BARNARDO	Have you had quiet guard?	
FRANCISCO	Not a mouse stirring.	10
BARNARDO	Well, good night.	
	If you do meet Horatio and Marcellus,	
	The rivals of my watch, bid them make haste.	
FRANCISCO	I think I hear them.	

Enter HORATIO *and* MARCELLUS

	Stand ho! Who is there?	
HORATIO	Friends to this ground.	
MARCELLUS	And liegemen to the Dane.	15
FRANCISCO	Give you good night.	
MARCELLUS	Oh farewell honest soldier,	
	Who hath relieved you?	
FRANCISCO	Barnardo hath my place.	
	Give you good night.	*Exit Francisco*
MARCELLUS	Holla, Barnardo!	
BARNARDO	Say,	
	What, is Horatio there?	
HORATIO	A piece of him.	

Marcellus reports that he and Barnardo have seen the Ghost twice. Horatio doesn't believe them, but is struck with fear and amazement when the Ghost of Hamlet's father appears.

Stagecraft

'Enter GHOST' – dead King Hamlet appears (in pairs)

The entry of the Ghost of Hamlet's father is a thrilling moment in the theatre. Each new production attempts to ensure that the entrance is as electrifying and memorable as possible. Imagine you are directing the play. You will keep a Director's Journal in which you consider stagecraft, how to advise the actors, tone and other features of the production.

a Talk with your partner and write notes on each of the following:

- What does the Ghost look like? Horatio gives a clue in lines 47–9 (and see the pictures in the photo gallery and on pp. 10 and 146).
- Suggest how the Ghost might enter. Slowly or suddenly? From which direction? Decide whether he makes any gestures, what sound effects you might use and how he leaves the stage.
- Sometimes, as the Ghost appears, the bell strikes. Would you have it strike if you were directing the play? Why, or why not?

b In some productions, the Ghost does not appear physically. The audience has to imagine its presence through lighting, sound and characters' reactions. How effective do you think this style of presenting the Ghost would be? Have two groups present the scene, one with the Ghost on stage and the other with him off stage, to compare dramatic effect.

1 An inner ghost? (in pairs)

In a production at the Royal Court Theatre in London in 1980, the actor Jonathan Pryce played Hamlet, with the Ghost appearing to speak from inside him. At times he was bent double with the pain of the Ghost's voice coming through him; at other times the Ghost appeared to speak in a horrible voice that cut through Hamlet's own voice, bubbling up in an uncontrolled fashion. Discuss the following points:

- What are the advantages and disadvantages of having the Ghost come from within a character?
- How could this first scene be presented if the Ghost is an internal rather than an external presence?
- What does an inner Ghost imply about the nature of ghosts, and the purpose of this particular Ghost in the play as a whole?

but our fantasy only our imagination

Touching concerning

entreated requested and urged

apparition vision, ghostly sight

approve our eyes believe our story

Tush, tush (equivalent to a combination of 'sshh' and 'tut tut')

assail your ears tell you forcefully

yond yonder (far distant)

pole pole star (North Star)

t'illume to illuminate

scholar student (ghosts were believed to speak Latin)

harrows tortures, tears

usurp'st wrongfully seizes

buried Denmark the dead King Hamlet

charge order

BARNARDO	Welcome Horatio, welcome good Marcellus.	20
MARCELLUS	What, has this thing appeared again tonight?	
BARNARDO	I have seen nothing.	
MARCELLUS	Horatio says 'tis but our fantasy,	
	And will not let belief take hold of him	
	Touching this dreaded sight, twice seen of us.	25
	Therefore I have entreated him along	
	With us to watch the minutes of this night,	
	That if again this apparition come	
	He may approve our eyes, and speak to it.	
HORATIO	Tush, tush, 'twill not appear.	
BARNARDO	Sit down awhile,	30
	And let us once again assail your ears,	
	That are so fortified against our story,	
	What we two nights have seen.	
HORATIO	Well, sit we down,	
	And let us hear Barnardo speak of this.	
BARNARDO	Last night of all,	35
	When yond same star that's westward from the pole	
	Had made his course t'illume that part of heaven	
	Where now it burns, Marcellus and myself,	
	The bell then beating one –	

Enter GHOST

MARCELLUS	Peace, break thee off. Look where it comes again.	40
BARNARDO	In the same figure, like the king that's dead.	
MARCELLUS	Thou art a scholar, speak to it Horatio.	
BARNARDO	Looks a not like the king? Mark it Horatio.	
HORATIO	Most like. It harrows me with fear and wonder.	
BARNARDO	It would be spoke to.	
MARCELLUS	Question it Horatio.	45
HORATIO	What art thou that usurp'st this time of night,	
	Together with that fair and warlike form	
	In which the majesty of buried Denmark	
	Did sometimes march? By heaven I charge thee speak.	
MARCELLUS	It is offended.	
BARNARDO	See, it stalks away.	50
HORATIO	Stay! Speak, speak, I charge thee speak!	

Exit Ghost

Horatio agrees that the Ghost is the exact image of the dead King Hamlet. He thinks it foretells disasters for Denmark. Horatio begins to explain why there are so many urgent preparations for war.

1 A battle? Or an angry gesture? (in small groups)

Do lines 62–3 tell of Denmark's king defeating the Polish army ('Polacks') in a battle on the ice ('sledded' = on sledges)? Or do they mean that the king, in an angry discussion ('parle') with the Norwegians, struck his battle-axe on the ice like a sledgehammer (= 'sledded'). Sometimes the word 'Polacks' is printed as 'polax' (poleaxe).

- Stage two tableaux (frozen pictures) showing each interpretation. Decide which version is more imaginative and dramatic.

Write about it
Denmark prepares for war (in pairs)

In lines 70–9, Marcellus questions why Denmark is feverishly preparing for war. Guards are mounted everywhere. 'Brazen' (brass) cannons roll off the production line daily. Weapons are bought in foreign countries and imported ('foreign mart for implements of war'). Ships are being built by forced labour ('impress'), working night and day, even on Sundays (unusual in a Christian country).

- Write six additional lines, in Shakespearean verse or in modern prose, listing more of Denmark's frantic war preparations. Use the same urgent style as Marcellus does.

Language in the play
'Doubling' – a feature of the play

In the script opposite there are several examples of a language device that recurs through the play. It is the use of 'and' between two verbs, nouns or noun phrases, or between adjectives, to achieve a 'doubling' effect: 'tremble and look pale', 'sensible and true avouch', 'gross and scope', 'strict and most observant'.

- **a** As you read on, list other examples (there are at least seven in Horatio's lines 80–107). The technical term is **hendiadys** (pronounced 'hen-die-a-dees'). You will find information about its dramatic importance on page 267.
- **b** What is the linguistic and dramatic effect of such doubling?

---

sensible and true avouch evidence

Norway King of Norway

parle exchange of words leading (in this case) to violence

Polacks forces from Poland

jump exactly

martial stalk military stride

In what particular ... work how to think about it

gross and scope general view

bodes ... state is ominous for us and for Denmark

Good now now then (deriving from 'In the name of God' or "For God's sake')

mart market

impress employment

toward in preparation

emulate jealous

sealed compact treaty

ratified confirmed

law and heraldy laws of chivalry

MARCELLUS	'Tis gone and will not answer.	
BARNARDO	How now Horatio? you tremble and look pale.	
	Is not this something more than fantasy?	
	What think you on't?	55
HORATIO	Before my God, I might not this believe	
	Without the sensible and true avouch	
	Of mine own eyes.	
MARCELLUS	Is it not like the king?	
HORATIO	As thou art to thyself.	
	Such was the very armour he had on	60
	When he th'ambitious Norway combated;	
	So frowned he once, when in an angry parle	
	He smote the sledded Polacks on the ice.	
	'Tis strange.	
MARCELLUS	Thus twice before, and jump at this dead hour,	65
	With martial stalk hath he gone by our watch.	
HORATIO	In what particular thought to work I know not,	
	But in the gross and scope of mine opinion	
	This bodes some strange eruption to our state.	
MARCELLUS	Good now sit down, and tell me he that knows,	70
	Why this same strict and most observant watch	
	So nightly toils the subject of the land,	
	And why such daily cast of brazen cannon,	
	And foreign mart for implements of war,	
	Why such impress of shipwrights, whose sore task	75
	Does not divide the Sunday from the week.	
	What might be toward, that this sweaty haste	
	Doth make the night joint-labourer with the day?	
	Who is't that can inform me?	
HORATIO	That can I –	
	At least the whisper goes so. Our last king,	80
	Whose image even but now appeared to us,	
	Was as you know by Fortinbras of Norway,	
	Thereto pricked on by a most emulate pride,	
	Dared to the combat; in which our valiant Hamlet –	
	For so this side of our known world esteemed him –	85
	Did slay this Fortinbras; who by a sealed compact,	
	Well ratified by law and heraldy,	
	Did forfeit (with his life) all those his lands	
	Which he stood seized of, to the conqueror;	

Horatio says that young Fortinbras intends to regain the lands his father lost when killed by King Hamlet. The Ghost's appearance presages violence, just as Caesar's death was foretold by ominous events.

1 Act out Horatio's story (in groups of six or more)

In lines 80–107, Horatio explains why Denmark is preparing for war. The king of Norway (old Fortinbras) had challenged King Hamlet (Hamlet's father) to personal combat. Both men wagered ('gagèd') large areas of land on the outcome of the duel. King Hamlet killed Fortinbras and so took over his territory, which was passed on to his son, Hamlet, when he died. Now young Fortinbras, with an army of mercenaries ('landless resolutes'), seeks to recover his father's lost lands. The Danes are hastily preparing to defend themselves against the imminent invasion.

- Bring Horatio's story to life. One person narrates while the others enact each episode. The lines contain over twenty-five separate actions that can be shown. (For instance, 'Sharked up' is a vivid **image** of a shark feeding indiscriminately.)

Write about it
Predicting disasters

'A mote it is to trouble the mind's eye' says Horatio (line 112): the appearance of the Ghost is an irritant ('mote') to the imagination. It suggests that disasters lie ahead. Shakespeare had written *Julius Caesar* shortly before *Hamlet*. The sinister omens that preceded the death of Caesar were fresh in his mind. Horatio lists them: the living dead, comets, bloody rain, sunspots, an eclipse of the moon ('the moist star'). Horatio uses the language of classical **allusion** (referencing), which gives the speech a lofty, important style.

- **a** Compare Horatio's style here (lines 112–39) with that of his speech at lines 148–56 in this scene. Why does he use the more florid style in the script opposite?

- **b** Find a copy of *The Elizabethan World Picture* by E.M.W. Tillyard (first published in 1943) and write up a paragraph or two of background information on how the Elizabethans and Jacobeans (people living under the reign of James I, 1603–25) saw the universe and its influence on humanity. You could also compare Gloucester and Edmond's lines in *King Lear* (Act 1 Scene 2, 103–33). Present your research to the rest of the class. You might wish to develop these short presentations into a wall display or some other resource that everyone in the group can refer to.

moiety competent equal amount

gagèd calculated, wagered

comart ... design treaty

unimprovèd mettle untested bravery

skirts of Norway edges of the kingdom/edges of the king's influence

a stomach in't courage in it

terms compulsatory forced agreement

post-haste and romage frantic activity and turmoil

portentous with importance and future significance

palmy (literally, with servants waving palm leaves to keep Caesar cool, but also with the suggestion of decadence and corruption)

tenantless empty

trains trails

Neptune's empire the sea

precurse forewarning of doom (pre-curse)

harbingers messengers

climatures territories

Against the which a moiety competent 90
Was gagèd by our king, which had returned
To the inheritance of Fortinbras
Had he been vanquisher; as by the same comart
And carriage of the article design,
His fell to Hamlet. Now sir, young Fortinbras, 95
Of unimprovèd mettle hot and full,
Hath in the skirts of Norway here and there
Sharked up a list of landless resolutes
For food and diet to some enterprise
That hath a stomach in't; which is no other, 100
As it doth well appear unto our state,
But to recover of us by strong hand
And terms compulsatory those foresaid lands
So by his father lost. And this, I take it,
Is the main motive of our preparations, 105
The source of this our watch, and the chief head
Of this post-haste and romage in the land.

[BARNARDO   I think it be no other but e'en so.
Well may it sort that this portentous figure
Comes armèd through our watch so like the king 110
That was and is the question of these wars.

HORATIO   A mote it is to trouble the mind's eye.
In the most high and palmy state of Rome,
A little ere the mightiest Julius fell,
The graves stood tenantless and the sheeted dead 115
Did squeak and gibber in the Roman streets;
As stars with trains of fire, and dews of blood,
Disasters in the sun; and the moist star,
Upon whose influence Neptune's empire stands,
Was sick almost to doomsday with eclipse. 120
And even the like precurse of feared events,
As harbingers preceding still the fates
And prologue to the omen coming on,
Have heaven and earth together demonstrated
Unto our climatures and countrymen.] 125

Horatio five times demands that the reappearing Ghost speak to him. The cock crows and the Ghost vanishes without reply. Horatio says it cannot be harmed, but that it behaved like a criminal summoned to justice.

Characters

Horatio's response to the Ghost (in pairs)

a Look back at Horatio's lines in this scene, and refer to your notes on the activity about Horatio on page 2. Make a list of the different characteristics Horatio has shown, then compare them with a partner and build up a list that includes your combined ideas. Share this list with the class as a whole.

b Try reading out lines 112–25 and lines 126–39, experimenting with different styles of delivery. The two sections are clearly different, but in how many ways could you present each of the sections? Which combination works best?

c Stage an interview with Horatio, questioning him about his different reactions to the Ghost. Questions could include: what was your first reaction to hearing the reports of Marcellus and Barnardo? Have you changed your position since seeing the Ghost? What do you think its presence portends (signifies)?

d Extend your notes on Horatio from the page 2 activity by writing up what you have learnt about his character from the activities on this page.

◀ In what ways does this Ghost match your own conceptions of how he might look?

soft quiet
cross address, confront

privy to knowledgeable about

uphoarded hoarded, hidden
Extorted wrenched out by force

partisan pike, long-handled spear

invulnerable impossible to hurt
vain blows futile attempts to hit

started seemed surprised
a guilty thing … summons an evildoer caught red-handed

extravagant and erring wandering
hies … confine hurries to his prison (cell, place of confinement)
present object apparition (the Ghost)
made probation gave proof

Enter GHOST

But soft, behold, lo where it comes again!
I'll cross it though it blast me. Stay, illusion.
                    It spreads his arms
If thou hast any sound or use of voice,
Speak to me.
If there be any good thing to be done   130
That may to thee do ease, and grace to me,
Speak to me.
If thou art privy to thy country's fate,
Which happily foreknowing may avoid,
Oh speak.   135
Or if thou hast uphoarded in thy life
Extorted treasure in the womb of earth,
For which they say you spirits oft walk in death,   *The cock crows*
Speak of it. Stay and speak! Stop it Marcellus.

MARCELLUS   Shall I strike at it with my partisan?   140
HORATIO   Do if it will not stand.
BARNARDO   'Tis here.
HORATIO   'Tis here.
MARCELLUS   'Tis gone.

                                        Exit Ghost

We do it wrong being so majestical
To offer it the show of violence,
For it is as the air invulnerable,   145
And our vain blows malicious mockery.

BARNARDO   It was about to speak when the cock crew.
HORATIO   And then it started like a guilty thing
Upon a fearful summons. I have heard,
The cock, that is the trumpet to the morn,   150
Doth with his lofty and shrill-sounding throat
Awake the god of day; and at his warning,
Whether in sea or fire, in earth or air,
Th'extravagant and erring spirit hies
To his confine. And of the truth herein   155
This present object made probation.

Marcellus claims that the cockerel crows all night long at Christmas, a time when no harm can be done. Horatio seems to agree. He proposes that they tell Hamlet about the Ghost.

1 Daybreak after darkness: a change of mood
(in pairs)

Dawn is breaking. The mood of fear, tension and apprehension gives way to a different emotional climate. Lyrical, poetic language creates a sense of religious awe and wonder. To experience the atmosphere of these closing moments of Scene 1, try the activities below:

a Talk together about non-verbal ways in which the change of mood could be conveyed in the theatre (lighting, sound, posture and so on).

b Marcellus is a soldier. He may be dressed in armour for his night's vigil, but he speaks eloquently. His words are filled with poetic wonderment, and do not sound like the language of a no-nonsense military man. Experiment with ways of speaking lines 157–64: full of religious awe; bluntly and factually; conspiratorially, as a great secret. Decide how you think the lines should be spoken on stage.

c After Marcellus's eloquent description of how Christmastime prevents any evil, Horatio responds with 'So have I heard, and do in part believe it.' His remark seems tinged with scepticism. Speak line 165, emphasising 'in part'. See if you can agree on whether the actor should use the line to show that Horatio does not really believe what Marcellus says.

Themes
Disorder, death and the afterlife **(in pairs)**

The first scene in *Hamlet* provides us with an atmospheric and dramatic start to the play. The Watch is nervous, having seen the Ghost twice already. There is a tense political situation – Denmark is in dispute with Norway over lands that have been awarded to Hamlet, following the killing of the king of Norway by Hamlet's father. The Ghost's appearance seems to foreshadow a number of disturbing themes.

a Note down as many themes as you can identify in this opening scene. Remember that a 'theme' can be captured by more than a single word. So, as well as 'fear', 'anxiety' and 'politics', for example, you can characterise a theme in a more complex way, such as 'the relationship between reason and the imagination'.

b Arrange the themes you have identified in a diagram that shows how they relate to each other.

ever 'gainst always before (or in expectation of)

our Saviour Jesus Christ

bird of dawning cockerel

stir abroad move around outside

no planets strike (the planets were assumed to crash into each other at times, causing disorder in the world)

takes bewitches, does harm

hallowed holy

russet mantle reddish-coloured cloak

impart tell

spirit (the Ghost)

acquaint him with it let him know about it

most conveniently very easily

12

MARCELLUS   It faded on the crowing of the cock.
            Some say that ever 'gainst that season comes
            Wherein our Saviour's birth is celebrated,
            This bird of dawning singeth all night long,   160
            And then, they say, no spirit dare stir abroad,
            The nights are wholesome, then no planets strike,
            No fairy takes, nor witch hath power to charm,
            So hallowed and so gracious is that time.

HORATIO   So have I heard, and do in part believe it.   165
            But look, the morn in russet mantle clad
            Walks o'er the dew of yon high eastward hill.
            Break we our watch up, and by my advice
            Let us impart what we have seen tonight
            Unto young Hamlet, for upon my life   170
            This spirit, dumb to us, will speak to him.
            Do you consent we shall acquaint him with it,
            As needful in our loves, fitting our duty?

MARCELLUS   Let's do't I pray, and I this morning know
            Where we shall find him most conveniently.   175

                                                        Exeunt

Claudius announces to the court that, although he grieves for his dead brother, he has, with joy, married Gertrude. He turns his attention to the political situation: young Fortinbras is threatening Denmark.

1 Claudius: honest or devious? (in small groups)

King Hamlet has recently died. Claudius, his brother, has become king of Denmark and has married Gertrude. Claudius now possesses his dead brother's throne and his widow. He explains his marriage to his sister-in-law so soon after her first husband's death (lines 1–16), and then turns to political affairs (lines 17–39).

a **Stage the entrance** Explore different stagings of Claudius's entrance. One version could show Claudius respected by the courtiers. Another might show he is feared: his courtiers suspect he may become a tyrant.

b **Honest or devious?** Some critics argue that Claudius's eloquence is appropriate to the occasion. His long, carefully constructed sentences suggest he is self-assured and honest. But other critics argue that the speech reveals his insincerity. Its fluency makes it sound rehearsed and false. His constant references to himself using the royal 'we', 'us', 'our' suggest he is anxious about whether his kingship is legal. Take turns to speak lines 1–39 to show Claudius as, alternately: confident and in control, uneasy and insecure, devious and crafty, honest and sincere. Afterwards, talk together about what you feel Claudius's language reveals about his character.

c **Oppositions** Lines 10–14 display another characteristic of the play's language: **antithesis** (setting words against each other, for example 'defeated' versus 'joy', 'mirth' versus 'funeral', see p. 265). Speak the lines using an action to accompany each antithesis.

see p. 265

Characters

Claudius

a After you have done some or all of the activities above, start making notes on Claudius as a character. There is much in this opening speech for you to include. Collect what you see as the key lines in Claudius's speech. Then annotate each quotation with comments about Claudius's character. As the activities above suggest, you can gauge his character through his actions, his words and his manner of speaking.

b Compare your notes with others to see if you are coming to the same initial conclusions about Claudius.

green young, fresh
us befitted was appropriate
contracted creased

sometime former
imperial jointress joint ruler of the state

auspicious promising happiness
dirge sad song
dole sadness
barred rejected, disregarded

Holding ... worth underestimating us

Colleaguèd linked
dream of his advantage his imagined advantage and rights
Importing concerning
bands of law legally binding agreements

Act 1 Scene 2
The Great Hall of Elsinore Castle

Trumpet Call   Enter CLAUDIUS *King of Denmark*, GERTRUDE
the Queen, HAMLET, POLONIUS, LAERTES, OPHELIA,
VOLTEMAND, CORNELIUS, LORDS *attendant*

CLAUDIUS	Though yet of Hamlet our dear brother's death	
	The memory be green, and that it us befitted	
	To bear our hearts in grief, and our whole kingdom	
	To be contracted in one brow of woe,	
	Yet so far hath discretion fought with nature	5
	That we with wisest sorrow think on him,	
	Together with remembrance of ourselves.	
	Therefore our sometime sister, now our queen,	
	Th'imperial jointress to this warlike state,	
	Have we, as 'twere with a defeated joy,	10
	With one auspicious and one dropping eye,	
	With mirth in funeral and with dirge in marriage,	
	In equal scale weighing delight and dole,	
	Taken to wife; nor have we herein barred	
	Your better wisdoms, which have freely gone	15
	With this affair along – for all, our thanks.	
	Now follows that you know: young Fortinbras,	
	Holding a weak supposal of our worth,	
	Or thinking by our late dear brother's death	
	Our state to be disjoint and out of frame,	20
	Colleaguèd with this dream of his advantage,	
	He hath not failed to pester us with message	
	Importing the surrender of those lands	
	Lost by his father, with all bands of law,	
	To our most valiant brother. So much for him.	25
	Now for ourself and for this time of meeting	
	Thus much the business is: we have here writ	
	To Norway, uncle of young Fortinbras,	

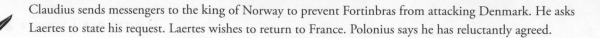
Claudius sends messengers to the king of Norway to prevent Fortinbras from attacking Denmark. He asks Laertes to state his request. Laertes wishes to return to France. Polonius says he has reluctantly agreed.

1 Claudius's manliness?

The king of Norway is, like Claudius, a man who has succeeded to his brother's throne. Claudius describes him as 'impotent and bedrid' (line 29).

- Suggest a way of speaking the line to give the audience an insight into Claudius's character. For example, might he embrace Gertrude as he speaks, to stress his own virility and manhood? Emphasise the linguistic power of his speeches: Claudius's use of imperatives, the royal 'we', his referring to himself as 'the Dane' and the insistent questioning.

2 Social superiority (in eights)

Everyone takes a part: Claudius, Gertrude, Hamlet, Polonius, Laertes, Ophelia, Cornelius and Voltemand. Line up in order of social status in Denmark. You can look back at the character list on page 1 to help you decide. Do you all agree on who is socially superior to whom? Argue any differences in view. As you work through the play, you can use this ranking activity in other ways (order of dramatic importance, or age, or most moral to least moral and so on).

Themes

The political dimension

Old Norway is Fortinbras's uncle, and present ruler of Norway. Cornelius and Voltemand are dispatched to Norway to deliver the 'dilated articles' (clear, full statements) that no doubt concern the matters raised in the first scene: Hamlet and Denmark's right to appropriate lands that formerly belonged to Norway.

- **a** Compare and contrast the first scene with the opening of this second scene. How could they be linked?
- **b** Hamlet is King Hamlet's son; Claudius is his uncle and the former king's brother. What parallels can you see with the situation in Norway, and why do you think Shakespeare is setting up a comparison here?
- **c** Add to the list of themes you began compiling on page 12.
- **d** Look at Laertes's speech in lines 50–6. What impression do you get of his character, and of his position in the Danish court?

impotent powerless (in politics and sex)

further gait herein going further

in that because

levies … lists soldiers

full proportions army necessary for this campaign

subject people

dilated fully open

suit request

the Dane (i.e. Claudius himself, the king of Denmark)

native related

instrumental serviceable

dread feared and honoured

leave and favour agreement and support

bend again turn again

bow them surrender them or subject them

pardon blessing, forgiveness

wrung squeezed

slow leave reluctant permission

laboursome petition persistent asking

sealed confirmed

hard consent grudging agreement

Who, impotent and bed-rid, scarcely hears
Of this his nephew's purpose, to suppress   30
His further gait herein, in that the levies,
The lists, and full proportions, are all made
Out of his subject; and we here dispatch
You, good Cornelius, and you, Voltemand,
For bearers of this greeting to old Norway,   35
Giving to you no further personal power
To business with the king, more than the scope
Of these dilated articles allow.
Farewell, and let your haste commend your duty.

CORNELIUS ⎫
VOLTEMAND ⎭ In that and all things will we show our duty.   40
CLAUDIUS   We doubt it nothing, heartily farewell.

Exeunt Voltemand and Cornelius

And now Laertes, what's the news with you?
You told us of some suit, what is't Laertes?
You cannot speak of reason to the Dane
And lose your voice. What wouldst thou beg Laertes,   45
That shall not be my offer, not thy asking?
The head is not more native to the heart,
The hand more instrumental to the mouth,
Than is the throne of Denmark to thy father.
What wouldst thou have Laertes?

LAERTES   My dread lord,   50
Your leave and favour to return to France,
From whence though willingly I came to Denmark
To show my duty in your coronation,
Yet now I must confess, that duty done,
My thoughts and wishes bend again toward France,   55
And bow them to your gracious leave and pardon.

CLAUDIUS   Have you your father's leave? What says Polonius?
POLONIUS   He hath my lord wrung from me my slow leave
By laboursome petition, and at last
Upon his will I sealed my hard consent.   60
I do beseech you give him leave to go.

1 Hamlet: the listener (in pairs)

You will discover that everything Hamlet says throughout the play reveals his acute alertness to language. He listens carefully to everything that is said to him, and often plays or **puns** on the words he has heard, giving them different meaning and significance (see p. 254).

Hamlet immediately picks up the implications of Claudius's use of 'cousin' and 'son'. He detests the close kinship that Claudius's marriage to his mother has created. His first line puns on 'kin' and 'kind', saying in effect that he feels too closely related, and does not have the same nature as his new stepfather. His second line plays on 'sun' and 'son', again rejecting any close relationship to Claudius.

a Talk together, and then write notes in your Director's Journal (see p. 4) for the actor playing Hamlet about how to speak line 65. Is he speaking to himself? To the audience? In a sardonic tone, or bitterly? Or some other way? The line is an **aside**, not heard by other characters. Also give advice on line 67: which word or words might Hamlet stress to question his kinship to Claudius, for example?

b Read aloud the script opposite, one person as Hamlet and one as Claudius/Gertrude. Play with emphasis and intonation on key words in the short exchanges Hamlet has with Claudius and Gertrude to show how characterisation can be shaped?

▼ **Does this image of Hamlet, from an all-male Japanese production, fit your impression of Hamlet the listener? Why, or why not?**

thy best graces
your good characteristics

nighted dark, gloomy

thine eye your eyes, your entire disposition

Denmark the king (Claudius), as well as the country

vailèd lids downcast eyes

common commonly accepted and understood

nature (a complex term in Elizabethan and Jacobean ideology, but here meaning 'life', all that is natural)

inky black

windy suspiration sighs

fruitful river in the eye tears

haviour of the visage facial expression

denote characterise, define

passes show bypasses or circumvents appearance

trappings clothes

filial obligation a son's duty

obsequious dutiful, as required by funeral rites (obsequies)

persever ... condolement keep up this stubborn mourning

impious unholy

CLAUDIUS	Take thy fair hour Laertes, time be thine,	
	And thy best graces spend it at thy will.	
	But now my cousin Hamlet, and my son –	
HAMLET	(*Aside*) A little more than kin, and less than kind.	65
CLAUDIUS	How is it that the clouds still hang on you?	
HAMLET	Not so my lord, I am too much i'th'sun.	
GERTRUDE	Good Hamlet cast thy nighted colour off,	
	And let thine eye look like a friend on Denmark.	
	Do not forever with thy vailèd lids	70
	Seek for thy noble father in the dust.	
	Thou know'st 'tis common, all that lives must die,	
	Passing through nature to eternity.	
HAMLET	Ay madam, it is common.	
GERTRUDE	If it be,	
	Why seems it so particular with thee?	75
HAMLET	Seems madam? nay it is, I know not seems.	
	'Tis not alone my inky cloak, good mother,	
	Nor customary suits of solemn black,	
	Nor windy suspiration of forced breath,	
	No, nor the fruitful river in the eye,	80
	Nor the dejected haviour of the visage,	
	Together with all forms, moods, shapes of grief,	
	That can denote me truly. These indeed seem,	
	For they are actions that a man might play,	
	But I have that within which passes show –	85
	These but the trappings and the suits of woe.	
CLAUDIUS	'Tis sweet and commendable in your nature Hamlet,	
	To give these mourning duties to your father;	
	But you must know, your father lost a father,	
	That father lost, lost his, and the survivor bound	90
	In filial obligation for some term	
	To do obsequious sorrow; but to persever	
	In obstinate condolement is a course	
	Of impious stubbornness, 'tis unmanly grief,	

Claudius criticises Hamlet's continued grief, declares him next in line to the throne, but refuses him permission to return to Wittenberg University. Gertrude pleads with Hamlet to stay. He agrees to her request.

Stagecraft
Rebuke, assurance and refusal (in small groups)

In an extended speech, Claudius first delivers a long criticism of Hamlet's grief. Next, he briefly pleads with Hamlet to abandon his mourning and declares him heir to the throne. Then, he abruptly refuses Hamlet permission to return to Wittenberg. Claudius's speech offers opportunities for the actor to establish the king's character and his attitude to his stepson. Take turns to speak the three sections:

- **The rebuke** (lines 87–106, to 'This must be so') Use a commanding tone. Emphasise repetitions ('fathers', 'father', 'father'; 'a fault', 'A fault', 'a fault'), and the critical expressions ('persever', 'obstinate condolement' and so on).
- **The assurance** (lines 106–12, to 'toward you') Use a cordial tone, and make much of declaring Hamlet as 'most immediate to our throne' (the next king).
- **The refusal** (lines 112–17) Be abrupt and sharp, but end using a seemingly friendly, reassuring tone.

Do you agree with the division of the speech into these categories? Discuss, then work on how the speech could be delivered on stage.

Language in the play
Key words

So far in this scene, at least three key words have been used: 'nature', 'will' and 'sense'.

- **a** First, scour the pages of the play up to this point, and see if you can identify other key words that have more than one meaning and that seem central to the preoccupations of the characters.
- **b** By yourself or in pairs, research the meanings of these key words in a dictionary and/or on the Internet. In particular, look for past or obsolete meanings that will give an indication of the history of the word. In what ways are these words significant to the play so far?
- **c** Present your findings to the rest of the class in pairs, or play a game of 'Call My Bluff' where each member of a team of three presents one of the meanings, trying to persuade the rest of the class or another team that their definition is the 'right' one.

will self-determination
heart unfortified weak sense of drive, passion and feeling

sense feel, be aware of; it also suggests sensibleness and sensibility, and is thus a complex term in Shakespeare – see the 'Language' box opposite
peevish irritable
fault offence
corse corpse

unprevailing useless

most immediate next in line, heir
nobility of love regard and respect, fatherly warmth

impart offer
intent intention
school university
Wittenberg (one of the top universities in eastern Germany at the time; Martin Luther, the father of Protestantism, taught there in the early sixteenth century)
retrograde opposite
bend you accept the idea

accord agreement
in grace whereof in recognition of the 'divine' agreement
jocund health happy toast in wine
rouse toast
bruit noisily announce

It shows a will most incorrect to heaven, 95
A heart unfortified, a mind impatient,
An understanding simple and unschooled.
For what we know must be, and is as common
As any the most vulgar thing to sense,
Why should we in our peevish opposition 100
Take it to heart? Fie, 'tis a fault to heaven,
A fault against the dead, a fault to nature,
To reason most absurd, whose common theme
Is death of fathers, and who still hath cried,
From the first corse till he that died today, 105
'This must be so.' We pray you throw to earth
This unprevailing woe, and think of us
As of a father, for let the world take note
You are the most immediate to our throne,
And with no less nobility of love 110
Than that which dearest father bears his son,
Do I impart toward you. For your intent
In going back to school in Wittenberg,
It is most retrograde to our desire,
And we beseech you bend you to remain 115
Here in the cheer and comfort of our eye,
Our chiefest courtier, cousin, and our son.

GERTRUDE Let not thy mother lose her prayers Hamlet.
I pray thee stay with us, go not to Wittenberg.

HAMLET I shall in all my best obey you madam. 120

CLAUDIUS Why, 'tis a loving and a fair reply.
Be as ourself in Denmark. Madam, come.
This gentle and unforced accord of Hamlet
Sits smiling to my heart, in grace whereof,
No jocund health that Denmark drinks today 125
But the great cannon to the clouds shall tell,
And the king's rouse the heaven shall bruit again,
Re-speaking earthly thunder. Come away.

Flourish. Exeunt all but Hamlet

Hamlet longs for death but knows that suicide is forbidden by God. He is disgusted that his mother has married so soon after his father's death, but feels he must keep silent. He greets Horatio and Marcellus.

1 A soliloquy

A **soliloquy** is spoken by a character who is alone (or thinks he or she is alone) on stage. It reveals the speaker's true thoughts and feelings. Hamlet's soliloquy exposes his deep depression. In turn he expresses weariness, despair, grief, anger, nausea, loathing and disgust, and resignation. He has no thoughts about political matters, about becoming king, or about being forbidden to return to Wittenberg. His troubled mind is obsessed solely with family matters: his father, his uncle and – above all – his mother.

- First, read the soliloquy to yourself. Then listen to it read aloud by someone else.
- On another copy of the speech, mark what you think are the key breaks (shifts of thought) in the speech.
- Discuss these breaks as a whole class, and agree on what you think are the main breaks – thus defining the structure of the speech.
- In small groups, take a section of the speech each and explore it in detail, teasing out its meaning(s). Also work out how you would deliver the section aloud.
- Each group now speaks their section (using individual and/or choral voices). The whole speech is delivered, section by section.
- In your groups, reflect on what you learnt by dealing with the speech in this way.
- Finally, note down words and phrases in the speech that you think are pivotal to Hamlet's thought and moral development as a character.

HAMLET   O that this too too solid flesh would melt,
Thaw and resolve itself into a dew,   130
Or that the Everlasting had not fixed
His canon 'gainst self-slaughter. O God, God,
How weary, stale, flat and unprofitable
Seem to me all the uses of this world!
Fie on't, ah fie, 'tis an unweeded garden   135
That grows to seed, things rank and gross in nature
Possess it merely. That it should come to this!
But two months dead – nay not so much, not two –
So excellent a king, that was to this
Hyperion to a satyr, so loving to my mother   140
That he might not beteem the winds of heaven
Visit her face too roughly – heaven and earth,
Must I remember? why, she would hang on him
As if increase of appetite had grown
By what it fed on, and yet within a month –   145
Let me not think on't; frailty, thy name is woman –
A little month, or ere those shoes were old
With which she followed my poor father's body
Like Niobe, all tears, why she, even she –
O God, a beast that wants discourse of reason   150
Would have mourned longer – married with my uncle,
My father's brother, but no more like my father
Than I to Hercules – within a month,
Ere yet the salt of most unrighteous tears
Had left the flushing in her gallèd eyes,   155
She married. Oh most wicked speed, to post
With such dexterity to incestuous sheets.
It is not, nor it cannot come to good.
But break, my heart, for I must hold my tongue.

Enter HORATIO, MARCELLUS *and* BARNARDO

HORATIO   Hail to your lordship.
HAMLET   I am glad to see you well.   160
Horatio – or I do forget myself.
HORATIO   The same, my lord, and your poor servant ever.
HAMLET   Sir, my good friend, I'll change that name with you.
And what make you from Wittenberg, Horatio?
Marcellus.   165

Hamlet does not believe Horatio returned to Denmark as a truant or to attend King Hamlet's funeral, but to see Gertrude's marriage. Horatio reports that he thinks he saw Hamlet's father the previous night.

Characters

Hamlet and Horatio (in pairs)

Take parts and read the exchange between Hamlet and Horatio. Try it in different ways:

- with Hamlet as consistently disbelieving Horatio
- with Hamlet changing mood frequently, or once or twice
- as close friends, or as past friends that have moved away from each other and are more cautious about their relationship.

What does your reading of the dialogue suggest to you about the relationship and about the differences between the two characters?

▼ In a production, would you have Horatio consistently 'lower' than Hamlet in staging and positioning, as in the image below, or do you see him as older and wiser (and possibly taking the upper moral ground)?

make you brings you

truant abandoning, wandering, resistant

disposition nature

truster believer

hard upon quickly thereafter

Thrift this is a tongue-in-cheek way of saying 'steady on' or 'be careful'

coldly as cold meats (or leftovers)

furnish forth bring forth

Or ever before

a was he was

   all in all weighing all his qualities

Season your admiration control your amazement

   attent attentive (as in the French attendre, to wait)

MARCELLUS	My good lord.
HAMLET	I am very glad to see you. (*To Barnardo*) Good even sir.
	But what in faith make you from Wittenberg.
HORATIO	A truant disposition, good my lord.
HAMLET	I would not hear your enemy say so,
	Nor shall you do my ear that violence
	To make it truster of your own report
	Against yourself. I know you are no truant.
	But what is your affair in Elsinore?
	We'll teach you to drink deep ere you depart.
HORATIO	My lord, I came to see your father's funeral.
HAMLET	I pray thee do not mock me fellow student,
	I think it was to see my mother's wedding.
HORATIO	Indeed my lord, it followed hard upon.
HAMLET	Thrift, thrift, Horatio. The funeral baked meats
	Did coldly furnish forth the marriage tables.
	Would I had met my dearest foe in heaven
	Or ever I had seen that day, Horatio.
	My father, methinks I see my father –
HORATIO	Where my lord?
HAMLET	In my mind's eye, Horatio.
HORATIO	I saw him once, a was a goodly king.
HAMLET	A was a man, take him for all in all.
	I shall not look upon his like again.
HORATIO	My lord, I think I saw him yesternight.
HAMLET	Saw? Who?
HORATIO	My lord, the king your father.
HAMLET	The king my father!
HORATIO	Season your admiration for a while
	With an attent ear, till I may deliver
	Upon the witness of these gentlemen
	This marvel to you.
HAMLET	For God's love let me hear.

Line numbers: 170, 175, 180, 185, 190, 195

▲ This image is from the 1948 movie of *Hamlet*, starring Laurence Olivier.

1 Creating atmosphere in the theatre

One of the challenges of theatre, as opposed to film, is how to create atmospheric scenes such as the one depicted above.

a Imagine you were the director of a staged play, and you had your choice of setting for *Hamlet*. Would you set it in an actual building that you know, or recreate the scene within a theatre?

b Write notes in your Director's Journal for how you would create an atmospheric setting for the battlement scenes.

dead waste desolation

at point correct in every detail

cap-a-pe from head to foot

march style of walking, gait

oppressed the sight weighed heavily on their eyes

Within his truncheon's length as close to the Ghost as the reach of his military baton

distilled melted

impart they did they told

as they had delivered exactly as they described it

apparition ghostly sight

platform gun emplacement, battlement

address / Itself to motion began to move

writ down in our duty part of our duty to you

Hold you the watch tonight? are you on guard duty tonight?

HORATIO   Two nights together had these gentlemen,
Marcellus and Barnardo, on their watch
In the dead waste and middle of the night,
Been thus encountered. A figure like your father,
Armèd at point exactly, cap-a-pe,   200
Appears before them, and with solemn march
Goes slow and stately by them. Thrice he walked
By their oppressed and fear-surprisèd eyes
Within his truncheon's length, whilst they, distilled
Almost to jelly with the act of fear,   205
Stand dumb and speak not to him. This to me
In dreadful secrecy impart they did,
And I with them the third night kept the watch,
Where, as they had delivered, both in time,
Form of the thing, each word made true and good,   210
The apparition comes. I knew your father,
These hands are not more like.

HAMLET   But where was this?

MARCELLUS   My lord, upon the platform where we watched.

HAMLET   Did you not speak to it?

HORATIO   My lord, I did,
But answer made it none. Yet once methought   215
It lifted up it head and did address
Itself to motion like as it would speak;
But even then the morning cock crew loud,
And at the sound it shrunk in haste away
And vanished from our sight.

HAMLET   'Tis very strange.   220

HORATIO   As I do live my honoured lord 'tis true,
And we did think it writ down in our duty
To let you know of it.

HAMLET   Indeed, indeed sirs, but this troubles me.
Hold you the watch tonight?

MARCELLUS ⎫
BARNARDO ⎭   We do, my lord.   225

HAMLET   Armed say you?

MARCELLUS ⎫
BARNARDO ⎭   Armed my lord.

HAMLET   From top to toe?

Hamlet continues his close questioning about the Ghost. He resolves to join the others on watch that night and to speak to the Ghost. He commands the others not to talk about what they've seen.

Stagecraft

Very fast exchanges? (in fours)

Take parts and speak lines 224–42, in which Hamlet questions the three men. Theatrical convention is that when speeches follow each other in single lines, or when a line is shared between speakers, the dialogue should be spoken very quickly, without pauses (in a staccato or 'rat-a-tat-tat' style).

a Read the exchanges in this manner, then experiment with using pauses. Afterwards, discuss whether the actors should follow dramatic custom here, or use pauses.

b Without knowing what is to follow in the play, what can you gather from the dramatic foreshadowing (suggestion that something is about to happen) that occurs on this page?

Write about it

Choose one of the following activities:

a **Marcellus and Barnardo compare notes** Marcellus and Barnardo have seen the Ghost three times. They have told their news to Hamlet. Imagine they have returned to their quarters. They talk about their sightings of the Ghost and about Hamlet's response. Write the script of their conversation, using your knowledge of Scenes 1 and 2.

b **Hamlet writes about his day's experience** Hamlet's final four lines express surprise, apprehension, suspicion, impatience and the certainty that evil actions cannot remain concealed. As you will discover in Scene 5, Hamlet keeps a notebook ('tables') in which he writes down what he learns. Write Hamlet's notebook entry for this day. It should describe his behaviour at the court, his feelings about Claudius and Gertrude and his own moodiness, what he makes of Horatio's story, and his speculations about why his father's Ghost appears to be haunting Elsinore.

c **A more distanced look** Write a paragraph or two giving your initial impressions of the impact of the Ghost on Horatio, the Watch and Hamlet. Bear in mind the context (Denmark is at war with Norway), Hamlet's position as Prince of Denmark, the nature and form of the Ghost, and the different reactions of the characters. Include quotations in your text.

beaver visor

countenance look

tell count

grizzled grey

sable silvered black with a few white hairs

Perchance perhaps
warrant promise, guarantee
assume take on

concealed not spoken about
tenable held, kept secret
hap happen
Give it … tongue think about it and consider its significance, but do not speak about it
requite reward
loves duty, honour towards me

doubt fear, suspect

Though all the earth … eyes however deeply buried

MARCELLUS BARNARDO }	My lord, from head to foot.	
HAMLET	Then saw you not his face?	
HORATIO	Oh yes my lord, he wore his beaver up.	
HAMLET	What, looked he frowningly?	230
HORATIO	A countenance more in sorrow than in anger.	
HAMLET	Pale, or red?	
HORATIO	Nay very pale.	
HAMLET	And fixed his eyes upon you?	
HORATIO	Most constantly.	
HAMLET	I would I had been there.	
HORATIO	It would have much amazed you.	235
HAMLET	Very like, very like. Stayed it long?	
HORATIO	While one with moderate haste might tell a hundred.	
MARCELLUS BARNARDO }	Longer, longer.	
HORATIO	Not when I saw 't.	
HAMLET	His beard was grizzled, no?	
HORATIO	It was as I have seen it in his life,	240
	A sable silvered.	
HAMLET	I will watch tonight,	
	Perchance 'twill walk again.	
HORATIO	I warrant it will.	
HAMLET	If it assume my noble father's person,	
	I'll speak to it though hell itself should gape	
	And bid me hold my peace. I pray you all,	245
	If you have hitherto concealed this sight,	
	Let it be tenable in your silence still,	
	And whatsomever else shall hap tonight,	
	Give it an understanding but no tongue.	
	I will requite your loves. So fare you well:	250
	Upon the platform 'twixt eleven and twelve	
	I'll visit you.	
ALL	Our duty to your honour.	
HAMLET	Your loves, as mine to you. Farewell.	

Exeunt all but Hamlet

My father's spirit, in arms! All is not well.
I doubt some foul play. Would the night were come. 255
Till then sit still my soul. Foul deeds will rise
Though all the earth o'erwhelm them to men's eyes.   *Exit*

Laertes warns Ophelia against Hamlet's love, saying it is merely youthful infatuation. As a prince, Hamlet is not free to choose his own wife; he must marry in the interest of the state.

1 Advice to a sister (in pairs)

Laertes hands out much advice to his sister. His elaborate style may make him sound pompous, even overbearing.

a **Young love won't last** In lines 5–10, Laertes stresses Hamlet's youth and the fickleness of young love. It won't last, he tells Ophelia, and he makes comparisons with short-lived things: 'fashion' (passing mood), 'toy in blood' (whim of passionate youth), 'violet' (a flower of early spring) and so on. One person reads lines 5–10, pausing at each punctuation mark. In the pause, the other person repeats what has just been said, but with scornful emphasis. How many comparisons with short-lasting love does Laertes make?

b **Maturity comes with age** When Ophelia questions Laertes's assertion that Hamlet's love will be short-lived, he replies very formally: the body ('this temple') does not only increase ('waxes') in sinews and size ('thews and bulk'), but in wisdom too. Take turns reading Laertes's lines 10–14 to each other. Use actions to bring out the meaning.

c **Princes can't choose** Can a prince choose to marry whomever he wants? Laertes doesn't think so. He tells Ophelia that 'his [Hamlet's] will is not his own'. In lines 17–28, he gives reasons why a prince, unlike an ordinary person, is not free to marry anyone he chooses; he must bear in mind the needs and interests of his country. Discuss whether you think what Laertes says was true in past times – and whether it is true for princes and other royalty today.

Language in the play

Laertes's diction

A character's **diction** signifies (among other meanings) a selection of the wider language that the character uses, repeated to the extent that it becomes distinctive.

a Make a note of three or four phrases that typify Laertes's diction. For example, one feature of Laertes's speech is that he uses 'doubling' (see p. 6) frequently, as in 'no soil nor cautel'.

b Make a comparison between Laertes and his father, Polonius, when the latter shortly arrives in this scene. What similarities and differences are there in their dictions?

necessaries luggage

convoy is assistant ships are available

trifling of his favour (Laertes is making light of Hamlet's courting of Ophelia)

the youth of primy nature (the spring; 'primy' is an invention of Shakespeare's, suggesting 'early', 'primitive' or 'immature')

suppliance pastime

crescent growing, ascendant

no soil nor cautel no blemish or deceit

unvalued persons people who are 'lower' than a prince or king

Carve choose

circumscribed limited

peculiar sect and force high status

give … deed turn into action

main voice majority opinion (but also that of the monarchy)

Act 1 Scene 3

Elsinore A private room

Enter LAERTES *and his sister* OPHELIA

LAERTES	My necessaries are embarked, farewell.
	And sister, as the winds give benefit
	And convoy is assistant, do not sleep
	But let me hear from you.
OPHELIA	Do you doubt that?
LAERTES	For Hamlet, and the trifling of his favour,
	Hold it a fashion, and a toy in blood,
	A violet in the youth of primy nature,
	Forward, not permanent, sweet, not lasting,
	The perfume and suppliance of a minute,
	No more.
OPHELIA	No more but so?
LAERTES	Think it no more.
	For nature crescent does not grow alone
	In thews and bulk, but as this temple waxes
	The inward service of the mind and soul
	Grows wide withal. Perhaps he loves you now,
	And now no soil nor cautel doth besmirch
	The virtue of his will; but you must fear,
	His greatness weighed, his will is not his own,
	For he himself is subject to his birth.
	He may not, as unvalued persons do,
	Carve for himself, for on his choice depends
	The sanctity and health of this whole state,
	And therefore must his choice be circumscribed
	Unto the voice and yielding of that body
	Where of he is the head. Then if he says he loves you,
	It fits your wisdom so far to believe it
	As he in his peculiar sect and force
	May give his saying deed, which is no further
	Than the main voice of Denmark goes withal.

5

15

20

25

Laertes continues to warn Ophelia not to trust Hamlet, because young women are vulnerable and face many dangers. She reminds him to follow his own advice. Polonius urges Laertes to leave.

1 Is Laertes pompous, or sincerely caring? (in pairs)

In the script opposite, Laertes uses images of treasure, war, masks and disease to warn Ophelia against losing her virginity to Hamlet. How does Laertes speak all his advice to his sister? Pompously? Lovingly? Imploringly? And how does Ophelia react as her brother lectures her on the briefness of young love, Hamlet's high status and the dangers that face young women?

a   Take parts and experiment with different ways of speaking lines 1–44, and of showing Ophelia's reactions.

b   Afterwards, jointly write a paragraph saying what you think is Laertes's attitude to his sister. For example, is he genuinely affectionate or is he sexist and condescending? Bear in mind what you know about family relationships then and now.

2 First impressions of Ophelia (in pairs)

In lines 45–51, Ophelia agrees to follow Laertes's advice, but then reminds him to practise what he preaches. Is her first sentence (agreeing) spoken ironically or submissively?

*   Experiment with speaking the lines and decide which style best fits your view of Ophelia's character and of the relationship between her and her brother.

▶ **What does this photograph suggest about Ophelia's character?**

credent trustful, believing

list his songs listen to his love talk

chaste treasure virginity

unmastered importunity uncontrolled harassment (Hamlet does not appear to Laertes to be experienced in love-making)

keep you … affection keep your feelings hidden

chariest most modest

prodigal lavish, wasteful

calumnious slandering

strokes lashes, attacks

canker rot, cancer

galls poisons

buttons buds

Contagious blastments infectious diseases and viruses

Whiles whilst

puffed puffed-up

dalliance amorous and frivolous play

recks not his own rede disregards his own advice, doesn't practise what he preaches

the wind … your sail the wind is behind you, ready to drive you on

stayed for awaited

Then weigh what loss your honour may sustain

If with too credent ear you list his songs,   30

Or lose your heart, or your chaste treasure open

To his unmastered importunity.

Fear it Ophelia, fear it my dear sister,

And keep you in the rear of your affection,

Out of the shot and danger of desire.   35

The chariest maid is prodigal enough

If she unmask her beauty to the moon.

Virtue itself scapes not calumnious strokes.

The canker galls the infants of the spring

Too oft before their buttons be disclosed,   40

And in the morn and liquid dew of youth

Contagious blastments are most imminent.

Be wary then, best safety lies in fear:

Youth to itself rebels, though none else near.

OPHELIA   I shall th'effect of this good lesson keep   45

As watchman to my heart. But good my brother,

Do not as some ungracious pastors do,

Show me the steep and thorny way to heaven,

Whiles like a puffed and reckless libertine

Himself the primrose path of dalliance treads,   50

And recks not his own rede.

LAERTES   Oh fear me not.

Enter POLONIUS

I stay too long – But here my father comes.

A double blessing is a double grace;

Occasion smiles upon a second leave.

POLONIUS   Yet here Laertes? Aboard, aboard for shame!   55

The wind sits in the shoulder of your sail,

And you are stayed for. There, my blessing with thee,

Polonius gives Laertes fatherly advice on speech, friendship, quarrelling, judgement, dress, money and consistency. He questions Ophelia about her relationship with Hamlet, saying she has met him often.

Characters

A father gives advice to his son (in pairs)

How does Polonius deliver his advice to his son? So far, his style has been variously comic, authoritarian, lovingly sincere and pompous.

a Try speaking lines 58–81 in these styles, then talk together about what the lines and various modes of delivery suggest about Polonius's character.

b How do Laertes and Ophelia react? In some productions, Polonius's children listen dutifully and respectfully. In others they make faces behind Polonius's back, mocking his advice. In yet others they silently mouth his words, showing they have heard it all many times before. In your Director's Journal, advise Laertes and Ophelia how to react to each sentence of counsel.

1 Ophelia's broken promise

In lines 85–6, Ophelia promises to keep Laertes's advice secret. But three lines later she begins to tell Polonius what the advice was about.

• Suggest to the rest of the class one or two reasons why she so quickly breaks her promise.

Themes

Father/daughter and mother/son (whole class)

We have already seen the beginnings of a relationship between son and father (Hamlet and his father's Ghost); and a very different father/son relationship in Polonius and Laertes. Here, we see the beginnings of a father/daughter relationship – and we have already seen Hamlet's response to his mother (one that will develop further in the play).

a Compare and contrast any two of these inter-generational relationships. Follow them through the play. This particular theme could develop into a piece of extended writing later on.

b Discuss in class the nature of parental relationships. Are sons closer to their mothers and daughters to their fathers? Or do gender divides rule more strongly within families? How do your conclusions apply to this play?

precepts moral principles
character engrave, imprint
unproportioned ill-considered
familiar friendly
adoption tried worthiness tested

dull thy palm
squander your hospitality
courage comrade

censure opinion, criticism
habit clothes
gaudy over-rich, in bad taste

husbandry
good housekeeping, thrift

my blessing … in thee
let my blessing help to embed these precepts in you

touching regarding
Marry by St Mary (a mild oath)

audience time, attention
put on me reported to me

And these few precepts in thy memory
Look thou character. Give thy thoughts no tongue,
Nor any unproportioned thought his act.   60
Be thou familiar, but by no means vulgar.
Those friends thou hast, and their adoption tried,
Grapple them unto thy soul with hoops of steel,
But do not dull thy palm with entertainment
Of each new-hatched, unfledged courage. Beware   65
Of entrance to a quarrel, but being in,
Bear't that th'opposèd may beware of thee.
Give every man thy ear, but few thy voice;
Take each man's censure, but reserve thy judgement.
Costly thy habit as thy purse can buy,   70
But not expressed in fancy: rich, not gaudy.
For the apparel oft proclaims the man,
And they in France of the best rank and station
Are of a most select and generous chief in that.
Neither a borrower nor a lender be,   75
For loan oft loses both itself and friend,
And borrowing dulls the edge of husbandry.
This above all, to thine own self be true,
And it must follow, as the night the day,
Thou canst not then be false to any man.   80
Farewell, my blessing season this in thee.

LAERTES   Most humbly do I take my leave, my lord.

POLONIUS   The time invites you. Go, your servants tend.

LAERTES   Farewell Ophelia, and remember well
What I have said to you.

OPHELIA   'Tis in my memory locked,   85
And you yourself shall keep the key of it.

LAERTES   Farewell.   *Exit Laertes*

POLONIUS   What is't Ophelia he hath said to you?

OPHELIA   So please you, something touching the Lord Hamlet.

POLONIUS   Marry, well bethought.   90
'Tis told me he hath very oft of late
Given private time to you, and you yourself
Have of your audience been most free and bounteous.
If it be so, as so 'tis put on me,
And that in way of caution, I must tell you   95
You do not understand yourself so clearly

Polonius, scornful of Hamlet's love, remonstrates with Ophelia. He orders her not to believe Hamlet's love-talk. She must give up seeing him because of his royal position and his merely lustful desire.

Polonius picks up words Ophelia uses and interprets them differently: 'affection' (love/lust), 'tenders' (offers/look after/make), 'fashion' (manner/pretence). But does he speak harshly and/or affectionately?

behooves is appropriate to

tenders / Of his affection acts that show his feelings

green inexperienced
Unsifted Inexperienced

sterling of true value or currency

Roaming playing with
fool baby, simpleton
importuned addressed, solicited

countenance strength, support

springes to catch woodcocks traps to catch birds
prodigal lavishly
blazes passionate flare-ups

scanter less free, more grudging
entreatments negotiations
command to parley invitation to talk of love
tedder tether (rope)
In few briefly
brokers pimps, agents
investments pun meaning both investment (as in a bond or pledge that can expect handsome returns) and clothes
implorators of unholy suits mischief makers
sanctified and pious bonds true marriage promises
slander any moment leisure do not waste words any further

Characters

Polonius

a Compare Polonius's advice to Laertes with his advice to Ophelia. What are the main points he makes in each case?

b Build a portrait of Polonius from these two speeches. Use it as a foundation to explore his character in more depth as the play progresses. Highlight and collect key quotations from the speeches and from elsewhere in this act, to provide evidence of his character and of his language.

c Compose an entry in Ophelia's diary, written after this advice from her father. How does she feel about the treatment from her brother and father? And how does she feel about Hamlet's 'tenders / Of … affection'?

As it behooves my daughter, and your honour.
What is between you? Give me up the truth.

OPHELIA He hath my lord of late made many tenders
Of his affection to me.   100

POLONIUS Affection? Puh! You speak like a green girl,
Unsifted in such perilous circumstance.
Do you believe his tenders as you call them?

OPHELIA I do not know my lord what I should think.

POLONIUS Marry I'll teach you. Think yourself a baby   105
That you have tane these tenders for true pay,
Which are not sterling. Tender yourself more dearly,
Or – not to crack the wind of the poor phrase,
Roaming it thus – you'll tender me a fool.

OPHELIA My lord, he hath importuned me with love   110
In honourable fashion.

POLONIUS Ay, fashion you may call it. Go to, go to.

OPHELIA And hath given countenance to his speech, my lord,
With almost all the holy vows of heaven.

POLONIUS Ay, springes to catch woodcocks. I do know,   115
When the blood burns, how prodigal the soul
Lends the tongue vows. These blazes daughter,
Giving more light than heat, extinct in both
Even in their promise as it is a-making,
You must not take for fire. From this time   120
Be something scanter of your maiden presence.
Set your entreatments at a higher rate
Than a command to parley. For Lord Hamlet,
Believe so much in him, that he is young
And with a larger tedder may he walk   125
Than may be given you. In few Ophelia,
Do not believe his vows, for they are brokers,
Not of that dye which their investments show,
But mere implorators of unholy suits,
Breathing like sanctified and pious bonds,   130
The better to beguile. This is for all:
I would not in plain terms from this time forth
Have you so slander any moment leisure
As to give words or talk with the Lord Hamlet.
Look to't I charge you. Come your ways.   135

OPHELIA I shall obey, my lord.

Exeunt

Just after midnight. Trumpets and gun salutes are heard. Hamlet condemns the drunkenness of the Danes and reflects that some men have a particular character fault that overwhelms reason and dignity.

1 Danish revelry: a custom best broken?

Hamlet explains that 'A *flourish of trumpets and two pieces goes off*' means that Claudius is celebrating with revelry ('wake'), drinking ('rouse', 'wassail') and wild dances ('swaggering up-spring reels'). As Claudius drinks his draughts of 'Rhenish' (German wine), loud music accompanies his toast ('pledge'). In Scene 2, lines 125–8, Claudius had promised such noisy revelry. Hamlet deplores this tradition of the Danes, saying more honour results from not following the custom ('More honoured in the breach than the observance').

* In your Director's Journal, write down, giving reasons, the tone in which you think Hamlet speaks lines 8–22.

2 Fatal flaw: 'some vicious mole of nature'

In lines 23–36, Hamlet reflects on how a single character flaw ('complexion') can corrupt a person entirely. One way of looking at Shakespeare's plays is to emphasise the destructive effect of such a character defect: Macbeth is destroyed by ambition, Othello by jealousy, Coriolanus by pride. Laurence Olivier began his film of *Hamlet* (see pp. 26 and 276) with lines 23–36 as a voice-over, and added: 'This is the tragedy of a man who could not make up his mind.'

Aristotle, in the *Poetics*, says that the most important element of tragedy is plot, i.e. what happens. But he also mentions four types of tragedy: complex tragedy, depending on reversal and recognition; the tragedy of suffering; the tragedy of character; and simple tragedy. *Hamlet* is probably a tragedy of character, with elements of all the other types woven into the whole. There is reversal and recognition: a straightforward revenge plot, but also a complex interrelationship of the personal and political, the parent–child relationship, and meditations on love, existence and death. For more information about Hamlet as a tragic hero, see pages 258–9.

a Research the nature of classical and Shakespearean tragedy.

b As you read on in the play, keep a record of the types of tragic action that you see emerging. Collect quotations as evidence of the progress of this action

c One key question to think about, and perhaps write about later, is whether Hamlet's tragedy could be avoided or whether he was impelled toward his end.

shrewdly sharply

lacks of is just short of

held his wont is accustomed
pieces pieces of ordnance, i.e. cannon or gunfire

bray make an unpleasant sound, like a donkey's cry

to the manner born accustomed to the practice
breach breaking of it
heavy-headed drunken
traduced and taxed of slandered and criticised by
clepe call
Soil our addition dirty our good name
pith and marrow … attribute essence of our reputation

complexion state of bodily mood or attitude
pales boundaries
o'erleavens … manners unbalances good behaviour

Act 1 Scene 4
The gun platform

Enter HAMLET, HORATIO *and* MARCELLUS

HAMLET	The air bites shrewdly, it is very cold.
HORATIO	It is a nipping and an eager air.
HAMLET	What hour now?
HORATIO	I think it lacks of twelve.
MARCELLUS	No, it is struck.
HORATIO	Indeed? I heard it not. It then draws near the season

Wherein the spirit held his wont to walk.

A flourish of trumpets and two pieces goes off

What does this mean, my lord?

HAMLET   The king doth wake tonight and takes his rouse,
Keeps wassail, and the swaggering up-spring reels,
And as he drains his draughts of Rhenish down,
The kettle-drum and trumpet thus bray out
The triumph of his pledge.

HORATIO   Is it a custom?

HAMLET   Ay marry is't,
But to my mind, though I am native here
And to the manner born, it is a custom
More honoured in the breach than the observance.
[This heavy-headed revel east and west
Makes us traduced and taxed of other nations.
They clepe us drunkards, and with swinish phrase
Soil our addition; and indeed it takes
From our achievements, though performed at height,
The pith and marrow of our attribute.
So, oft it chances in particular men,
That for some vicious mole of nature in them,
As in their birth, wherein they are not guilty,
Since nature cannot choose his origin,
By their o'ergrowth of some complexion,
Oft breaking down the pales and forts of reason,
Or by some habit that too much o'erleavens
The form of plausive manners – that these men,

5

10

15

20

25

30

39

The Ghost appears, interrupting Hamlet's reflections on human nature. Hamlet addresses it as his dead father, asking why it has returned from the grave. Marcellus urges Hamlet not to follow the Ghost.

1 'The dram of eale'

In lines 36–8, the meaning of 'The dram of eale … scandal' might be that a small quantity ('dram') of 'eale' (some kind of rotting agent) corrupts the whole of a noble enterprise, bringing discredit on a man, however good he may be.

a Write about how you might edit these three lines (you can change the words if you think it sensible; for example, 'eale' might become 'evil').

b Think more broadly about editing the script, as some directors do. Is there anything in the first four scenes that you would edit out, to make the play more engaging to the audience? Decide on which lines you would cut, bearing in mind that you need to maintain the flow of the action. Then discuss your selections with the rest of the class.

c As a whole class, discuss whether you think editing of this sort is justifiable, or whether it would be better to leave Shakespeare's script as it stands.

Language in the play
A good spirit? Or an evil goblin? (in pairs)

Hamlet is unsure about what type of apparition he sees. Is it a good spirit from heaven or an evil goblin from hell, tempting him to eternal damnation? He expresses his uncertainty in vivid antitheses (see p. 265):

'spirit of health' versus 'goblin damned'
'airs from heaven' versus 'blasts from hell'
'wicked' versus 'charitable'.

The problem of knowing whether the Ghost is good or bad will preoccupy Hamlet for much of the play. You will find notes on pages 249–50 to help you understand why Hamlet speaks of 'Angels', 'goblin damned', 'heaven' and 'hell' here.

• Take turns to read lines 39–57 to each other. Emphasise the antitheses, and try different pacings: fast, slow, varied. Experiment with different tones: amazed, questioning, fearful and pleading.

---

stamp imprint

livery costume (inheritance)

fortune's star bad luck

The dram of eale … his own scandal the meaning might be that a small quantity ('dram') of 'eale' (some kind of rotting agent?) corrupts the whole of a noble enterprise, bringing discredit ('scandal') on a man, however good he may be

canonised buried in holy fashion

hearsèd coffined

cerements shrouds, grave-clothes

enurned buried

ponderous heavy

complete steel armour

glimpses of the moon moonlight

disposition balanced state of being and consciousness

impartment message

wafts waves

removèd ground remote place

Carrying I say the stamp of one defect,
Being nature's livery or fortune's star,
His virtues else be they as pure as grace,
As infinite as man may undergo,
Shall in the general censure take corruption   35
From that particular fault. The dram of eale
Doth all the noble substance of a doubt
To his own scandal.]

Enter GHOST

HORATIO   Look my lord, it comes!
HAMLET   Angels and ministers of grace defend us!
           Be thou a spirit of health, or goblin damned,   40
           Bring with thee airs from heaven or blasts from hell,
           Be thy intents wicked or charitable,
           Thou com'st in such a questionable shape
           That I will speak to thee. I'll call thee Hamlet,
           King, father, royal Dane. Oh answer me.   45
           Let me not burst in ignorance, but tell
           Why thy canonised bones, hearsèd in death,
           Have burst their cerements; why the sepulchre,
           Wherein we saw thee quietly enurned,
           Hath oped his ponderous and marble jaws   50
           To cast thee up again. What may this mean,
           That thou, dead corse, again in complete steel
           Revisits thus the glimpses of the moon,
           Making night hideous, and we fools of nature
           So horridly to shake our disposition   55
           With thoughts beyond the reaches of our souls?
           Say, why is this? wherefore? What should we do?
                          Ghost beckons Hamlet
HORATIO   It beckons you to go away with it,
           As if it some impartment did desire
           To you alone.
MARCELLUS   Look with what courteous action   60
           It wafts you to a more removèd ground.
           But do not go with it.
HORATIO   No, by no means.

Horatio tries to persuade Hamlet not to follow the Ghost. Hamlet is determined to follow. He threatens Horatio and Marcellus with death if they try to restrain him. He follows the Ghost.

1 Hamlet defends himself

Below is an image of Mel Gibson as Hamlet in a 1990 film by Franco Zeffirelli. A strong tradition has developed of Hamlet following the Ghost while using his sword hilt as a cross to defend himself against evil. That gesture, the ambiguous nature of the Ghost, and Marcellus's line 90 ('Something is rotten in the state of Denmark') create a sense of corruption that grows increasingly through the play.

• Can you think of any other props or gestures that Hamlet could use to try and protect himself at this point in the scene?

a pin's fee the value of a pin

flood sea

beetles hangs

sovereignity the guiding and balancing quality in mankind: reason and a stable consciousness

toys of desperation suicidal thoughts

petty arture drop of blood (little artery)

hardy brave

Nemean lion's nerve terrifying lion's sinews (Hercules strangled the lion terrorising Nemea because weapons could not hurt it)

I'll make a ghost ... lets me I'll kill the man who prevents me

waxes increases

Have after let's follow him

issue end

Something is rotten in the state of Denmark (see pp. 243–5 and 264)

HAMLET	It will not speak. Then I will follow it.	
HORATIO	Do not my lord.	
HAMLET	Why, what should be the fear?	
	I do not set my life at a pin's fee,	65
	And for my soul, what can it do to that,	
	Being a thing immortal as itself?	
	It waves me forth again. I'll follow it.	
HORATIO	What if it tempt you toward the flood my lord,	
	Or to the dreadful summit of the cliff	70
	That beetles o'er his base into the sea,	
	And there assume some other horrible form	
	Which might deprive your sovereignty of reason,	
	And draw you into madness? Think of it.	
	[The very place puts toys of desperation,	75
	Without more motive, into every brain	
	That looks so many fathoms to the sea	
	And hears it roar beneath.]	
HAMLET	It wafts me still. Go on, I'll follow thee.	
MARCELLUS	You shall not go my lord.	
HAMLET	Hold off your hands.	80
HORATIO	Be ruled, you shall not go.	
HAMLET	My fate cries out,	
	And makes each petty arture in this body	
	As hardy as the Nemean lion's nerve.	
	Still am I called. Unhand me gentlemen!	
	By heaven I'll make a ghost of him that lets me.	85
	I say away! – Go on, I'll follow thee.	

Exit Ghost and Hamlet

HORATIO	He waxes desperate with imagination.	
MARCELLUS	Let's follow, 'tis not fit thus to obey him.	
HORATIO	Have after. To what issue will this come?	
MARCELLUS	Something is rotten in the state of Denmark.	90
HORATIO	Heaven will direct it.	
MARCELLUS	Nay let's follow him.	

Exeunt

1 An agent of the devil? (in small groups)

The Ghost hints at the terrors of its suffering. It cannot go to heaven because it died before it could confess its sins. So it must suffer dreadfully in purgatory. According to medieval (Catholic) Christian belief, purgatory is the place where unconfessed sinners experience indescribable remorse as their sins are burnt and purged away before they can see God in heaven (see pp. 249–50). But the Ghost says it is forbidden to tell of its terrifying ordeal ('this eternal blazon must not be').

The majority of Shakespeare's audiences were Protestants, and they would have two reasons for suspecting that the Ghost was an evil agent of the devil. First, because Protestantism had abolished the notion of purgatory. Second, because the Protestant Church judged revenge as a sin, for which the revenger's soul was damned. But the Ghost's words make thrilling theatre.

- Experiment with readings of lines 9–22 that will make the audience shrink back in their seats. The lines are packed with vivid phrases suggesting horrors and torments. Make the most of them! Add sound effects as you think appropriate. You might also wish to construct a tableau to show how the Ghost and Hamlet appear in line 25.

▼ Search in the library or on the Internet for further pictures by Hieronymus Bosch (1450–1516), whose image of Hell is shown here. Bosch painted haunting scenes of the torments of the dead. They will help you imagine what Shakespeare's audience might have pictured the Ghost enduring.

Whither where
Mark me listen to me

My hour daybreak
sulph'rous (hellish flames were thought to be composed of foul-smelling sulphur)
render up myself return

unfold reveal
bound compelled, ready

term period
fast starve, but also held firm

But were it not

harrow cruelly rip
start stand out
combined locks tangled hair

porpentine porcupine
eternal blazon telling of what happens after death
List listen

Act 1 Scene 5
The walls of Elsinore Castle

Enter GHOST *and* HAMLET

HAMLET	Whither wilt thou lead me? Speak, I'll go no further.
GHOST	Mark me.
HAMLET	I will.
GHOST	My hour is almost come

When I to sulph'rous and tormenting flames
Must render up myself.

HAMLET	Alas poor ghost!
GHOST	Pity me not, but lend thy serious hearing 5

To what I shall unfold.

HAMLET	Speak, I am bound to hear.
GHOST	So art thou to revenge, when thou shalt hear.
HAMLET	What?
GHOST	I am thy father's spirit,

Doomed for a certain term to walk the night,   10
And for the day confined to fast in fires,
Till the foul crimes done in my days of nature
Are burnt and purged away. But that I am forbid
To tell the secrets of my prison house,
I could a tale unfold whose lightest word   15
Would harrow up thy soul, freeze thy young blood,
Make thy two eyes like stars start from their spheres,
Thy knotted and combinèd locks to part
And each particular hair to stand an end
Like quills upon the fretful porpentine.   20
But this eternal blazon must not be
To ears of flesh and blood. List, list, oh list!
If thou didst ever thy dear father love –

HAMLET	O God!
GHOST	Revenge his foul and most unnatural murder. 25
HAMLET	Murder?

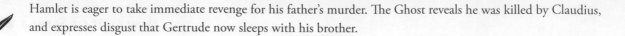

Hamlet is eager to take immediate revenge for his father's murder. The Ghost reveals he was killed by Claudius, and expresses disgust that Gertrude now sleeps with his brother.

Write about it
Family matters again

Like Hamlet (in his soliloquy in Scene 2, lines 129–59), the Ghost seems little concerned with affairs of state. His mind is full of family matters. He expresses revulsion at the thought of Gertrude's sexual relationship with Claudius ('that incestuous, that adulterate beast'). He is sickened at the thought of his betrayal by his 'seeming virtuous queen', and speaks bitterly of 'lust' and 'garbage'.

Actors often speculate about the past lives of their characters. Join in the speculation by writing a paragraph or two on these two questions:

- Had Gertrude been unfaithful while her husband was alive?
- Had Hamlet earlier suspected that Claudius had killed his father (when he says 'O my prophetic soul! My uncle?')?

Language in the play
Portray the vivid images (in small groups)

The script opposite is full of strikingly imaginative images. Here are just four:

Lines 29–31 'I with wings as swift / As meditation or the thoughts of love / May sweep to my revenge.'
Lines 39–40 'The serpent that did sting thy father's life / Now wears his crown.'
Line 42 'that incestuous, adulterate beast'
Lines 53–7 'But virtue as it never will be moved, / Though lewdness court it in a shape of heaven, / So lust, though to a radiant angel linked, / Will sate itself in a celestial bed, / And prey on garbage.'

a Choose one of these images (or another of your choice from the script opposite). Talk together about each element in the image – for example, in lines 29–31 how can you relate 'wings as swift / As meditation' and 'thoughts of love' to 'revenge'?

b Decide on a way of presenting your understanding of the image to the rest of the class. Ideas include: a mime, a drawing, a reading of the line(s) with sound effects.

c Consider what effect the images here have on the themes and characterisation of the play.

as in the best it is even if done for good reason

meditation thought, contemplation

apt ready to act

fat weed huge banks of weeds

Lethe a river in Hades, the world of the dead; drinking the river's water caused forgetfulness

'Tis given out it is generally the assumption; it is a rumour

whole ear of Denmark both the ear of the king, but also that of the people (in the sense of what they hear)

forgèd process false account

Rankly foully

incestuous having a sexual relationship with someone of one's own family

decline fall

lewdness court lust tempts

sate greedily satisfy, satiate

GHOST	Murder most foul, as in the best it is,
	But this most foul, strange, and unnatural.
HAMLET	Haste me to know't, that I with wings as swift
	As meditation or the thoughts of love
	May sweep to my revenge.
GHOST	I find thee apt,
	And duller shouldst thou be than the fat weed
	That rots itself in ease on Lethe wharf,
	Wouldst thou not stir in this. Now Hamlet, hear.
	'Tis given out that, sleeping in my orchard,
	A serpent stung me. So the whole ear of Denmark
	Is by a forgèd process of my death
	Rankly abused; but know, thou noble youth,
	The serpent that did sting thy father's life
	Now wears his crown.
HAMLET	O my prophetic soul!
	My uncle?
GHOST	Ay, that incestuous, that adulterate beast,
	With witchcraft of his wits, with traitorous gifts –
	O wicked wit and gifts that have the power
	So to seduce – won to his shameful lust
	The will of my most seeming virtuous queen.
	O Hamlet, what a falling off was there,
	From me whose love was of that dignity
	That it went hand in hand even with the vow
	I made to her in marriage, and to decline
	Upon a wretch whose natural gifts were poor
	To those of mine.
	But virtue as it never will be moved,
	Though lewdness court it in a shape of heaven,
	So lust, though to a radiant angel linked,
	Will sate itself in a celestial bed,
	And prey on garbage.
	But soft, methinks I scent the morning air;

30

35

40

45

50

55

1 Act out the Ghost's story (in fours)

Take parts as narrator, Hamlet's father, Claudius and Gertrude. The narrator reads lines 59–80, pausing often. The others act what is described. This type of 'dumb-show', or mimed version of a play, will prepare you for the play-within-a-play in Act 3.

▼ Compare this ghost to the one shown on page 10. Which do you prefer, and why?

secure unguarded, carefree

stole crept

cursèd hebenon poison

vial small bottle

porches cavities

leperous distilment evil mixture causing leprosy

Holds such an enmity fights

quicksilver mercury

courses runs

posset curdle (clotting the blood)

tetter skin disease

lazar-like like leprosy

dispatched removed

blossoms full bloom, height

Unhouseled taken out of my body, without sacrament

disappointed not prepared for death

unaneled removed from the years of my life, not blessed

reckoning weighing up of my good and bad traits

account i.e. with God

luxury lust

contrive work against

matin morning

gins ... fire begins to lose its glow

couple include (with heaven and earth: Hamlet suspects the Ghost may be an evil spirit)

globe head

Brief let me be. Sleeping within my orchard,
My custom always of the afternoon, 60
Upon my secure hour thy uncle stole,
With juice of cursèd hebenon in a vial,
And in the porches of my ears did pour
The leperous distilment, whose effect
Holds such an enmity with blood of man 65
That swift as quicksilver it courses through
The natural gates and alleys of the body,
And with a sudden vigour it doth posset
And curd, like eager droppings into milk,
The thin and wholesome blood. So did it mine, 70
And a most instant tetter barked about,
Most lazar-like, with vile and loathsome crust,
All my smooth body.
Thus was I, sleeping, by a brother's hand,
Of life, of crown, of queen, at once dispatched; 75
Cut off even in the blossoms of my sin,
Unhouseled, disappointed, unaneled;
No reckoning made, but sent to my account
With all my imperfections on my head –
Oh horrible, oh horrible, most horrible! 80
If thou hast nature in thee bear it not;
Let not the royal bed of Denmark be
A couch for luxury and damnèd incest.
But howsomever thou pursues this act
Taint not thy mind, nor let thy soul contrive 85
Against thy mother aught. Leave her to heaven
And to those thorns that in her bosom lodge
To prick and sting her. Fare thee well at once.
The glow-worm shows the matin to be near,
And gins to pale his uneffectual fire. 90
Adieu, adieu, adieu. Remember me. *Exit*

HAMLET   O all you host of heaven! O earth! what else?
And shall I couple hell? Oh fie! Hold, hold, my heart,
And you my sinews grow not instant old
But bear me stiffly up. Remember thee? 95
Ay thou poor ghost, whiles memory holds a seat
In this distracted globe. Remember thee?

Hamlet determines to remember only the Ghost's commandment to revenge. He writes in his notebook. When Horatio and Marcellus find him, he avoids telling them what he knows.

Characters

Claudius as a 'smiling damnèd villain!'

Shakespeare's imagination was haunted by the image of the smiling villain. He used it to express the theme of deceptive appearances:

'There's daggers in men's smiles' (*Macbeth*)

'I can smile, and murder whiles I smile' (*King Henry VI, Part 3*)

'Some that smile have in their hearts, I fear, millions of mischief' (*Julius Caesar*)

'I did but smile till now' (false Angelo in *Measure for Measure*)

'one may smile, and smile, and be a villain' (line 108 opposite).

• Would playing Claudius as a 'smiler' add to or lessen dramatic impact? Write a paragraph giving your views and reasons.

Themes

Madness: real or false?

There is much debate as to whether Hamlet is really mad, or feigning madness in order to disguise his true intent to revenge his father's death. Although most of the evidence points towards his pretending to be mad, there are strong arguments that the encounter with his father's Ghost has seriously disturbed him.

a Look at the opening lines of Hamlet's interplay with Horatio and Marcellus in the script opposite and in the rest of this scene. What evidence can you find for the real onset of madness on the one hand, and feigned madness on the other?

b Research 'madness' in Elizabethan and Jacobean culture. In particular, look up Robert Burton's *Anatomy of Melancholy*.

c Begin a set of notes on madness in the play. You will able to use these notes both in a discussion of the themes of the play, and in relation to Hamlet's character.

d Look further into the pattern of behaviour by heroes in revenge plays of the period, such as Thomas Kyd's *The Spanish Tragedy*. How many of these contemporary heroes show signs of madness in their words and actions, and what do your conclusions suggest about Hamlet and revenge?

e Does the fact that Hamlet appears to be keeping a record ('table') add to the sense that he is truly mad?

table of my memory (a reference to the belief that the mind was a *tabula rasa* – a 'cleared table' or 'clean state')

fond foolish

saws conventional sayings, platitudes

forms general ideas

pressures past impressions

baser cruder

pernicious malevolent, destructive

tables notebook

word watchword

Illo, ho, ho the falconer's cry to his hawk

arrant absolute, complete

knave fool

50

Yea, from the table of my memory
I'll wipe away all trivial fond records,
All saws of books, all forms, all pressures past,   100
That youth and observation copied there,
And thy commandment all alone shall live
Within the book and volume of my brain,
Unmixed with baser matter: yes, by heaven!
O most pernicious woman!   105
O villain, villain, smiling damnèd villain!
My tables – meet it is I set it down
That one may smile, and smile, and be a villain;
At least I'm sure it may be so in Denmark. [*Writing*]
So uncle, there you are. Now to my word: 110
It is 'Adieu, adieu, remember me.'
I have sworn't.

HORATIO   (*Within*)   My lord, my lord!
MARCELLUS   (*Within*)   Lord Hamlet!

Enter HORATIO *and* MARCELLUS

HORATIO   Heavens secure him!
HAMLET   So be it.
MARCELLUS   Illo, ho, ho, my lord!   115
HAMLET   Hillo, ho, ho, boy! Come bird, come.
MARCELLUS   How is't, my noble lord?
HORATIO   What news my lord?
HAMLET   Oh, wonderful!
HORATIO   Good my lord, tell it.
HAMLET   No, you will reveal it.
HORATIO   Not I my lord, by heaven.
MARCELLUS   Nor I my lord.   120
HAMLET   How say you then, would heart of man once think it –
              But you'll be secret?
HORATIO
MARCELLUS }   Ay, by heaven, my lord.
HAMLET   There's ne'er a villain dwelling in all Denmark
              But he's an arrant knave.
HORATIO   There needs no ghost, my lord, come from the grave,   125
              To tell us this.

Hamlet's replies puzzle Horatio. Hamlet asks the two men to keep secret all they have seen. They promise to do so. He demands they swear an oath of silence on his sword. The Ghost echoes his words.

Stagecraft

'wild and whirling words' (in threes)

In performance, Hamlet usually delivers lines 126–32 very quickly indeed, shaking hands vigorously, then making to go off and pray. Horatio expresses puzzlement at the hectic pace and seeming meaninglessness of Hamlet's words.

a To gain a sense of the rapid changes in Hamlet's language, take parts as Hamlet, Marcellus and Horatio and read lines 115–52. As you read, move around the room, with Hamlet frequently changing direction. The other two try to keep up with him.

b Afterwards, talk together about how the physical movement gives additional meaning to Horatio's claim of 'wild and whirling words'. Also discuss what the activity reveals about the state of Hamlet's mind.

circumstance formality

desire pleasure

whirling crazy, out of control

Saint Patrick (who, in legend, released sinners from purgatory)
Touching concerning

O'ermaster't overcome it

poor small

truepenny honest fellow
in the cellarage underground (beneath the stage)

1 Does only Hamlet hear the Ghost?

In most productions only Hamlet hears the Ghost. But what would be the dramatic effect if Marcellus and Horatio also heard the Ghost's demand 'Swear' (line 149)?

a Imagine you are directing the play. Write a set of notes listing the dramatic gains and losses if all three characters hear the Ghost's 'Swear'.

b Decide how you would like to play this part of the scene, and instruct the three actors how best to exploit the dramatic gains of the decision you have made. You can write this up in your Director's Journal, and/or act out the lines in a group.

2 Swearing the oath of silence (in pairs)

• Imagine the hilt of Hamlet's sword is shaped like a cross (see p. 42). Work out how he would hold it so the other two men could swear their promise of silence upon it. Decide whether you think Horatio and Marcellus are willing or unwilling to swear the oath (see line 147).

• In what other ways might Hamlet use his sword to encourage Marcellus and Horatio to swear?

HAMLET	Why right, you are i'th'right,
	And so without more circumstance at all
	I hold it fit that we shake hands and part –
	You as your business and desire shall point you,
	For every man hath business and desire,	130
	Such as it is, and for my own poor part,
	Look you, I'll go pray.
HORATIO	These are but wild and whirling words, my lord.
HAMLET	I'm sorry they offend you, heartily,
	Yes faith, heartily.
HORATIO	There's no offence my lord.	135
HAMLET	Yes by Saint Patrick but there is Horatio,
	And much offence too. Touching this vision here,
	It is an honest ghost, that let me tell you.
	For your desire to know what is between us,
	O'ermaster't as you may. And now good friends,	140
	As you are friends, scholars, and soldiers,
	Give me one poor request.
HORATIO	What is't my lord? we will.
HAMLET	Never make known what you have seen tonight.
HORATIO	
MARCELLUS	} My lord we will not.
HAMLET	Nay but swear't.
HORATIO	In faith	145
	My lord not I.
MARCELLUS	Nor I my lord in faith.
HAMLET	Upon my sword.
MARCELLUS	We have sworn my lord already.
HAMLET	Indeed, upon my sword, indeed.
GHOST	Swear. *Ghost cries under the stage*
HAMLET	Ha, ha, boy, sayst thou so? art thou there truepenny?	150
	Come on, you hear this fellow in the cellarage,
	Consent to swear.
HORATIO	Propose the oath my lord.
HAMLET	Never to speak of this that you have seen,
	Swear by my sword.
GHOST	Swear.	155

Hamlet demands that Horatio and Marcellus swear they will not reveal what has happened. They must also promise not to put on a show of knowing the true nature of any future strange behaviour by Hamlet.

Stagecraft
Stage directions for Hamlet

Hamlet shifts position to swear the oath as the Ghost's voice is again heard from beneath the stage. Often in the theatre this 'swearing' episode results in audience laughter.

Hamlet then orders his friends not to look knowing if they see him behaving oddly (lines 173–9). His instructions contain detailed stage directions about how he could behave as he speaks. There are more stage directions in Hamlet's final speech as he expresses friendship, again orders the two men to keep silent, and ends with 'let's go together'.

Imagine you are about to play Hamlet. Write detailed notes about how you will behave as you speak all the lines in the script opposite. Add reasons to justify that behaviour. Ensure you cover these points:

- Should I attempt to make the audience laugh as I order the others to move around the stage to 'swear'?
- What actions should accompany my instructions in lines 173–9 and 188?
- How might I show friendship in my final line?

Hic et ubique? here and everywhere?

old mole (the Ghost appears to working beneath the stage, 'under the ground')
worthy pioneer brave miner

meet appropriate
put an antic disposition on pretend to be mad

doubtful phrase broad hint

list wished
giving out hinting
aught anything

commend offer and give

still always
cursèd spite damned malice, evil fortune

▲ In this production, the Ghost wore a fencing mask and carried a thin epée.

HAMLET	*Hic et ubique?* then we'll shift our ground.
	Come hither gentlemen,
	And lay your hands again upon my sword.
	Never to speak of this that you have heard,
	Swear by my sword. 160
GHOST	Swear.
HAMLET	Well said old mole, canst work i'th'earth so fast?
	A worthy pioneer. Once more remove, good friends.
HORATIO	O day and night, but this is wondrous strange.
HAMLET	And therefore as a stranger give it welcome. 165
	There are more things in heaven and earth, Horatio,
	Than are dreamt of in your philosophy.
	But come –
	Here as before, never so help you mercy,
	How strange or odd some'er I bear myself, 170
	As I perchance hereafter shall think meet
	To put an antic disposition on –
	That you at such times seeing me never shall,
	With arms encumbered thus, or this head-shake,
	Or by pronouncing of some doubtful phrase, 175
	As 'Well, well, we know,' or 'We could and if we would,'
	Or 'If we list to speak,' or 'There be and if they might,'
	Or such ambiguous giving out, to note
	That you know aught of me: this not to do,
	So grace and mercy at your most need help you, 180
	Swear.
GHOST	Swear.
HAMLET	Rest, rest, perturbèd spirit. So gentlemen,
	With all my love I do commend me to you,
	And what so poor a man as Hamlet is 185
	May do t'express his love and friending to you,
	God willing shall not lack. Let us go in together,
	And still your fingers on your lips I pray. –
	The time is out of joint: O cursèd spite,
	That ever I was born to set it right. – 190
	Nay come, let's go together.

Exeunt

Looking back at Act 1
Activities for groups or individuals

1 'Who's there?' – Does appearance match reality?

The opening line of the play is the first of many anxious questions that establish the tone of uncertainty that runs throughout. It symbolises the search for personal identity, and for the reality that lies behind outward appearance.

a Write down one example from each of the five scenes in Act 1 where you feel that appearance does not match reality. In each case, write a commentary exploring what aspects of appearance and reality are being addressed.

b Examine the notion of duplicity (deceitfulness) in Act 1. How does this idea contribute to the questioning of identity?

2 Disordered society, disturbed individuals

Recurring dramatic motifs of the disordered state of society and of individuals run through Act 1: 'Something is rotten in the state of Denmark' (Scene 4, line 90); 'The time is out of joint' (Scene 5, line 189).

• Look in more depth at *The Elizabethan World Picture* by E.M.W Tillyard (see p. 8). Divide into groups. Each group takes a chapter of the book and works on a presentation about how the Elizabethan and Jacobean ideology in that chapter are relevant to Hamlet.

3 Political matters – family matters

Hamlet begins as if it will be a play centrally concerned with politics and affairs of state (descriptions of feverish preparations for war; Claudius's dispatch of ambassadors to old Fortinbras). But Hamlet, Laertes, Polonius and the Ghost appear to be obsessed with family matters, particularly the sexuality of Gertrude and Ophelia.

• Create two columns: head one column 'Political matters' and the other 'Family matters'. Work through Act 1, noting in the appropriate column the events and quotations relevant to the heading. Which column contains most entries? What are the connections between family and politics in the play so far?

4 Horatio's point of view

Horatio has come to Denmark from Wittenberg University. He appears in four of the five scenes in Act 1, and seems to know a great deal about state affairs. Yet, in Act 1 Scene 5, lines 166–7, Hamlet says in response to Horatio's amazement at the Ghost: 'There are more things in heaven and earth, Horatio, / Than are dreamt of in your philosophy.'

a Look back through Act 1 and trace the way in which Horatio responds to the Watch, to the Ghost and to Hamlet. What qualities and types of response does he show? As part of a character study, write down quotations that reveal Horatio's reactions and motivations.

b Horatio appears to be a 'foil' or counterpart to Hamlet. Compare the two characters. What qualities does Horatio have that contrast with Hamlet's?

5 Summarising the action

a Imagine that a daily court circular is issued, recording the activities of the royal family in this play. Write the court circular for one day in Act 1. You can find an example of a court circular, focused on the British royal family, in a copy of *The Times*.

b Write and present a two-minute version of Act 1. Be prepared to defend your inclusions, compressions and omissions.

Which of these images of Claudius, Gertrude and Hamlet best fits your conception of the characters – and why?

1 Polonius's approach

Polonius (right) tells Reynaldo that indirect ways of questioning will yield better information than direct approaches.

* How would you advise an actor to speak Polonius's lines in this scene in order to suggest his character and his role in the Danish court?

make inquire ask after

Danskers Danes
means resources
keep live
encompassment and drift roundabout ways of questioning

particular demands the specific and supposed purpose of your inquiries

Take you show, assume
distant indirect

Addicted given to vices
forgeries slanders, lies

wanton carefree, loose

drabbing whoring, using prostitutes

Act 2 Scene 1
A state room in the castle

Enter POLONIUS *and* REYNALDO

POLONIUS	Give him this money, and these notes, Reynaldo.
REYNALDO	I will my lord.
POLONIUS	You shall do marvellous wisely, good Reynaldo,
	Before you visit him, to make inquire
	Of his behaviour.
REYNALDO	My lord, I did intend it.

5

POLONIUS	Marry well said, very well said. Look you sir,
	Inquire me first what Danskers are in Paris,
	And how, and who, what means, and where they keep,
	What company, at what expense; and finding
	By this encompassment and drift of question
	That they do know my son, come you more nearer
	Than your particular demands will touch it.
	Take you as 'twere some distant knowledge of him,
	As thus, 'I know his father and his friends,
	And in part him' – do you mark this Reynaldo?
REYNALDO	Ay, very well, my lord.
POLONIUS	'And in part him, but' – you may say – 'not well,
	But if't be he I mean, he's very wild,
	Addicted so and so' – and there put on him
	What forgeries you please; marry, none so rank
	As may dishonour him, take heed of that,
	But sir, such wanton, wild, and usual slips
	As are companions noted and most known
	To youth and liberty.
REYNALDO	As gaming my lord?
POLONIUS	Ay, or drinking, fencing, swearing,
	Quarrelling, drabbing – you may go so far.
REYNALDO	My lord, that would dishonour him.

10

15

20

25

Polonius continues to advise Reynaldo to use indirect methods to find out whether Laertes is guilty of improper behaviour in Paris. But Polonius loses the thread of his argument.

1 Reynaldo – the fox? (in pairs)

This is Reynaldo's only appearance in the play. The actor playing him will wish to establish his character, even though he has such a small part. He might be guided by the knowledge that Reynaldo (Reynard) means 'the fox', an animal with a reputation for cunning. Take parts and read lines 1–72 in several ways to discover which works best:

- Reynaldo is an experienced secret agent
- Reynaldo thinks that Polonius is a rambling old fool
- Reynaldo is genuinely puzzled about what he's being asked to do, but wishes to be a loyal servant.

2 Losing the drift of his argument

Identify the line where Polonius begins to lose the thread of his argument. Advise the actor on how he should play this 'forgetful' episode to help establish the character of Polonius. For example, should he try to win audience sympathy for an old man's failing memory, or should he aim to get a laugh at Polonius's expense? In performance, the forgetfulness is often played for laughs.

Language in the play
Polonius's diction

Polonius's language (specifically, his individual diction or 'idiolect') is distinctive, as it is for many Shakespearean characters. He is a serious character in the play, but is also a figure of fun and ridicule – largely because of his language.

a Look over Polonius's speeches so far in this scene and identify the characteristics of his diction. Collect quotations to provide evidence of the different ways in which Polonius uses language to instruct Reynaldo. You might also look at his speeches to Laertes and Ophelia in Act 1 Scene 3. Why do you think Shakespeare makes Polonius appear so ridiculous?

b Write a short speech as Polonius, using the characteristic elements of his diction that you have identified. Read the speech aloud in a small group, in character as Polonius. Think about the tone, emphasis and gestures that you could use to bring the speech to life.

season it in the charge modify the accusation

incontinency rampant sexual misbehaviour

quaintly cleverly

taints stains

unreclaimèd blood untamed passion

Of general assault that attacks everyone

drift intention

fetch of warrant trick that is legitimate

sullies dirty marks

party the other person with whom Reynaldo is having a conversation in Paris

converse conversely, but also conversation

prenominate already mentioned

consequence final statement

addition custom

o'ertook in's rouse drunk

falling out at tennis having a disagreement during tennis, or being unable to finish a tennis game

Videlicet that is to say

POLONIUS   Faith no, as you may season it in the charge.
     You must not put another scandal on him,
     That he is open to incontinency,   30
     That's not my meaning. But breathe his faults so quaintly
     That they may seem the taints of liberty,
     The flash and outbreak of a fiery mind,
     A savageness in unreclaimèd blood,
     Of general assault.

REYNALDO   But my good lord –   35

POLONIUS   Wherefore should you do this?

REYNALDO   Ay my lord,
     I would know that.

POLONIUS   Marry sir, here's my drift,
     And I believe it is a fetch of warrant.
     You laying these slight sullies on my son,
     As 'twere a thing a little soiled i'th'working,   40
     Mark you,
     Your party in converse, him you would sound,
     Having ever seen in the prenominate crimes
     The youth you breathe of guilty, be assured
     He closes with you in this consequence,   45
     'Good sir', or so, or 'friend', or 'gentleman',
     According to the phrase and the addition
     Of man and country.

REYNALDO   Very good my lord.

POLONIUS And then sir does a this – a does – what was I about to say?
     By the mass I was about to say something. Where did I leave?   50

REYNALDO At 'closes in the consequence', at 'friend, or so', and
     'gentleman'.

POLONIUS   At 'closes in the consequence' – ay marry,
     He closes with you thus: 'I know the gentleman,
     I saw him yesterday, or th'other day,   55
     Or then, or then, with such or such, and as you say,
     There was a gaming, there o'ertook in's rouse,
     There falling out at tennis', or perchance,
     'I saw him enter such a house of sale' –
     Videlicet, a brothel – or so forth. See you now,   60
     Your bait of falsehood takes this carp of truth,

Polonius dispatches Reynaldo on his spying mission to Paris. Ophelia comes to report that she has been frightened by Hamlet's strange appearance. His clothing was dishevelled and his behaviour odd.

1 Act Hamlet's 'antic disposition' (in threes)

One film of the play added a scene showing Ophelia's encounter with Hamlet, and included lines 75–98 as a voice-over to Hamlet's behaviour.

- Act out your own version of this 'absent scene'. As one person slowly narrates the lines, the other two mime them.

2 Points of view on Hamlet's madness (in fours)

Lines 76–82 describe the first physical manifestation of Hamlet's madness.

- Take parts as Claudius, Gertrude, Polonius and Ophelia. In role, offer your explanation of Hamlet's appearance at this point in the play from your character's point of view. Begin by saying whether you think Hamlet is really mad or just putting on an act. Then go on to say why you think he is behaving as he is. Are there any points on which all four characters agree?

▶ As a director, how would you portray Hamlet and Ophelia as described by Ophelia opposite? Would you show their encounter, or leave it to the imagination of the audience?

of wisdom and of reach who are wise and perceptive

windlasses roundabout ways (like hunters circling their prey)

assays of bias indirect attempts (as, in a game of bowls, a bowl curves towards its target)

God buy ye God be with you (i.e. goodbye)

Observe … in yourself be like him yourself, observe his ways yourself

ply his music go his own way

closet private room

doublet close-fitting jacket

down-gyvèd fallen (like fetters around his ankles)

in purport in expression

perusal study

And thus do we of wisdom and of reach,
With windlasses and with assays of bias,
By indirections find directions out.
So, by my former lecture and advice,   65
Shall you my son. You have me, have you not?

REYNALDO   My lord, I have.
POLONIUS   God buy ye, fare ye well.
REYNALDO   Good my lord.
POLONIUS   Observe his inclination in yourself.
REYNALDO   I shall my lord.   70
POLONIUS   And let him ply his music.
REYNALDO   Well my lord.
POLONIUS   Farewell.

                                    Exit Reynaldo

                    Enter OPHELIA

                How now Ophelia, what's the matter?
OPHELIA   Oh my lord, my lord, I have been so affrighted.
POLONIUS   With what, i'th'name of God?
OPHELIA   My lord, as I was sewing in my closet,   75
Lord Hamlet with his doublet all unbraced,
No hat upon his head, his stockings fouled,
Ungartered, and down-gyvèd to his ankle,
Pale as his shirt, his knees knocking each other,
And with a look so piteous in purport   80
As if he had been loosèd out of hell
To speak of horrors – he comes before me.
POLONIUS   Mad for thy love?
OPHELIA   My lord I do not know,
But truly I do fear it.
POLONIUS   What said he?
OPHELIA   He took me by the wrist, and held me hard;   85
Then goes he to the length of all his arm,
And with his other hand thus o'er his brow
He falls to such perusal of my face
As a would draw it. Long stayed he so;

Ophelia says how strangely Hamlet behaved. Polonius guesses that Hamlet has been driven mad by Ophelia's rejection of his love. He decides to tell all to Claudius.

Stagecraft

'I am sorry' (in pairs)

a These three words from line 104 could have different meanings. Decide which of the following you prefer, based on your view of Polonius:

- Polonius is genuinely sorry for his daughter

- he feels sorry for Hamlet

- he doesn't care at all about Ophelia's or Hamlet's feelings

- he is worried about his own position as a state official who should know about such matters.

b Try a reading of the dialogue, from line 73 to the end of the scene, in which you make clear your view of how Polonius reacts to the fact that Hamlet has been visiting (in her private chambers – her 'closet') and writing to Ophelia. Does the mention of 'jealousy' at line 111 have any bearing on your portrayal?

Write about it

A letter from Hamlet

From what you know of the relationship between Hamlet and Ophelia so far, compose a letter from Hamlet to her. It should reveal some of the concerns, suspicions and melancholy that Hamlet has exhibited, but also touch on other aspects of their relationship. Be prepared to defend your letter by reference to the script. You might also compose one from Ophelia in return.

1 More references to madness

Look back at the 'Themes' box on madness on page 50. There is more talk of Hamlet's madness in the script opposite.

- Write a psychiatrist's preliminary report on the suggestion that Hamlet is mad. What evidence is there to support the notion, and what is the evidence against it? Include quotations from the play to support your evidence. How would you clinically describe this madness? In crafting your diagnosis, you could refer to the literature on love and madness that you found in the earlier activity, looking further into Robert Burton's *Anatomy of Melancholy* and also researching more widely.

bulk body

to the last up to the last second

bended ... on me looked in my direction

ecstasy madness

property quality, nature

fordoes destroys, confounds

undertakings deeds

repel send back

heed attention

quoted observed

trifle play

wrack dishonour, seduce, destroy

beshrew a curse on

proper to characteristic of

cast beyond ourselves seek wider advice

close secret

More grief ... love a complex statement, meaning 'not to tell about this occurrence might cause more grief than any expression of love – either of which course might lead to, or engender hate'

At last, a little shaking of mine arm,   90
And thrice his head thus waving up and down,
He raised a sigh so piteous and profound
As it did seem to shatter all his bulk,
And end his being. That done, he lets me go,
And with his head over his shoulder turned   95
He seemed to find his way without his eyes,
For out-a-doors he went without their helps
And to the last bended their light on me.

POLONIUS   Come, go with me, I will go seek the king.
This is the very ecstasy of love,   100
Whose violent property fordoes itself,
And leads the will to desperate undertakings
As oft as any passion under heaven
That does afflict our natures. I am sorry.
What, have you given him any hard words of late?   105

OPHELIA   No my good lord; but as you did command,
I did repel his letters, and denied
His access to me.

POLONIUS   That hath made him mad.
I am sorry that with better heed and judgement
I had not quoted him. I feared he did but trifle,   110
And meant to wrack thee, but beshrew my jealousy.
By heaven, it is as proper to our age
To cast beyond ourselves in our opinions
As it is common for the younger sort
To lack discretion. Come, go we to the king.   115
This must be known, which being kept close, might move
More grief to hide than hate to utter love.
Come.

Exeunt

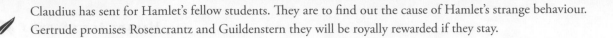

Claudius has sent for Hamlet's fellow students. They are to find out the cause of Hamlet's strange behaviour. Gertrude promises Rosencrantz and Guildenstern they will be royally rewarded if they stay.

Themes

A state of surveillance

The arrival of Rosencrantz and Guildenstern in the Danish court helps to build the sense not only that 'Denmark's a prison' (see line 234) but also that Hamlet will be under surveillance.

a Look back at Act 2 Scene 1 to find evidence of how Polonius might play a part in watching Hamlet. Use this evidence, and more from Scene 2, to build up a case that surveillance is part of the Danish state – and perhaps part of how Hamlet sees himself.

b In your Director's Journal, make notes on how you would use staging techniques to show the theme of surveillance in a production of *Hamlet*. Include details on the set design, props, costumes, lighting and actors' gestures.

▼ How do you envisage Rosencrantz and Guildenstern? In this 2010 National Theatre production they wore suits like Claudius and Polonius.

Moreover in addition to the fact
provoke bring about

Sith since
should could

entreat ask

vouchsafe your rest accept our hospitality
companies company, companionship
occasion favourable opportunities
glean harvest, gather, pick

adheres sticks, is close to
gentry gentlemanly behaviour, courtesy
expend spend
supply and profit help and benefit
fits befits

more into … entreaty i.e. you can command us rather than ask us

Act 2 Scene 2
The Great Hall of Elsinore Castle

Trumpet Call   Enter KING *and* QUEEN, ROSENCRANTZ *and*
GUILDENSTERN, *with others*

CLAUDIUS   Welcome dear Rosencrantz and Guildenstern!
Moreover that we much did long to see you,
The need we have to use you did provoke
Our hasty sending. Something have you heard
Of Hamlet's transformation – so call it,   5
Sith nor th'exterior nor the inward man
Resembles that it was. What it should be,
More than his father's death, that thus hath put him
So much from th'understanding of himself,
I cannot dream of. I entreat you both,   10
That being of so young days brought up with him,
And sith so neighboured to his youth and haviour,
That you vouchsafe your rest here in our court
Some little time, so by your companies
To draw him on to pleasures, and to gather   15
So much as from occasion you may glean,
Whether aught to us unknown afflicts him thus,
That opened lies within our remedy.

GERTRUDE   Good gentlemen, he hath much talked of you,
And sure I am, two men there is not living   20
To whom he more adheres. If it will please you
To show us so much gentry and good will
As to expend your time with us a while,
For the supply and profit of our hope,
Your visitation shall receive such thanks   25
As fits a king's remembrance.

ROSENCRANTZ   Both your majesties
Might by the sovereign power you have of us
Put your dread pleasures more into command
Than to entreaty.

Stagecraft

Rosencrantz or Guildenstern?! (in threes)

Many directors seize on Gertrude's line 34 as an opportunity to make the audience laugh and to make a point about the similarity between Rosencrantz and Guildenstern. These directors advise Gertrude to speak the line in one of two ways:

- She is unable to distinguish which man is which, and so speaks the line as an uncertain question, unsure whether she is addressing the right person.
- She corrects a mistake by Claudius, who has misidentified the two courtiers.

a How would you advise Gertrude to speak line 34? Would you want to get a laugh on the line by having the king or queen (or both) unable to differentiate between the two men? Take the parts of Gertrude, Rosencrantz and Guildenstern. Perform lines 19–39 in two ways: first comically, then seriously. Then try to combine the two approaches.

b Why do you think Shakespeare introduces the idea of their similarity or interchangeability? What other forms of 'doubling' have you noticed so far in the play?

Themes

Public and private (in pairs)

Gertrude and Claudius share a brief private moment together in lines 54–8. How would you stage the lines to emphasise the difference between their public life (as king and queen) and their domestic life (as mother and stepfather, and wife and husband)? Remember, the rest of the court on stage will be watching their every move, and hoping to overhear what they are saying.

a How significant is the distinction between private and public life in *Hamlet*? Why might this be an important theme of the play?

b Compare the notes you made on the theme of surveillance on page 66 to the emerging theme of public and private selves and responsibilities. Are the two themes related?

in the full bent completely (like a fully drawn archery bow)

practices behaviour (or deceits)

trail of policy affairs of state (or deceptions)

admittance welcome, entry
fruit final course of a meal
grace benign welcome

head and source cause
distemper illness
main major matter
sift him question Polonius (or Hamlet?) closely

brother fellow king

GUILDENSTERN   But we both obey,
                And here give up ourselves in the full bent   30
                To lay our service freely at your feet
                To be commanded.

CLAUDIUS   Thanks Rosencrantz, and gentle Guildenstern.

GERTRUDE   Thanks Guildenstern, and gentle Rosencrantz.
                And I beseech you instantly to visit   35
                My too much changèd son. Go some of you
                And bring these gentlemen where Hamlet is.

GUILDENSTERN   Heavens make our presence and our practices
                Pleasant and helpful to him.

GERTRUDE   Ay, amen.

                Exeunt Rosencrantz and Guildenstern [and some Attendants]

                Enter POLONIUS

POLONIUS   Th'ambassadors from Norway, my good lord,   40
                Are joyfully returned.

CLAUDIUS   Thou still hast been the father of good news.

POLONIUS   Have I my lord? Assure you, my good liege,
                I hold my duty, as I hold my soul,
                Both to my God and to my gracious king;   45
                And I do think, or else this brain of mine
                Hunts not the trail of policy so sure
                As it hath used to do, that I have found
                The very cause of Hamlet's lunacy.

CLAUDIUS   Oh speak of that, that do I long to hear.   50

POLONIUS   Give first admittance to th'ambassadors;
                My news shall be the fruit to that great feast.

CLAUDIUS   Thyself do grace to them and bring them in.

                                        [Exit Polonius]

                He tells me, my dear Gertrude, he hath found
                The head and source of all your son's distemper.   55

GERTRUDE   I doubt it is no other but the main:
                His father's death, and our o'erhasty marriage.

CLAUDIUS   Well, we shall sift him.

                Enter POLONIUS, VOLTEMAND and CORNELIUS

                        Welcome my good friends.
                Say Voltemand, what from our brother Norway?

Voltemand reports that the king of Norway has prevented Fortinbras from attacking Denmark, sending him instead to invade Poland. Polonius embarks on a long-winded explanation of Hamlet's madness.

1 Voltemand's report (in small groups)

Much political activity has taken place. To help your understanding of Voltemand's report, try one or more of the following activities.

a One person slowly reads aloud lines 60–85 (to 'Most welcome home.'). At every mention of a person, everyone in the group points to a group member as that person (allocate parts as you read). It sounds complicated, but you will very quickly pick it up and find it helps you understand who's who. The first 'point' is in line 61, 'our' (Voltemand and Cornelius); the next is on 'he' (king of Norway). If you do not have enough group members for everyone mentioned, just point to objects (e.g. a chair or table) to represent characters.

b One person reads aloud, pausing at each punctuation mark. The others act out each section of Voltemand's speech.

c What do you notice about Voltemand's language in this report? There are three sentences in the speech. Identify them, and discuss their structure.

d The king of Norway has sent a formal letter to Claudius. Among other things, it asks for safe passage through Denmark for Fortinbras's army as it marches to invade Poland. Write the document in full.

Characters

Polonius

Polonius has appeared in several scenes so far. He often speaks up at inappropriate moments or without due propriety.

a Look back at Polonius's speeches, so far and at those on the following page, and list his characteristics as evidenced by his words. In particular, look for contradictions in his character. What do his duplicity and obsequiousness suggest about the state of Denmark?

b Read lines 85–94 to yourself, thinking about how you would express them. Then work in pairs or threes to decide how you would share out the lines for maximum effect. Have a pair or group of three in the class perform the lines, justifying (and answering questions from others in the class) as to why they split up the speech in the way that they did.

---

desires good wishes
Upon our first when we raised the matter
levies troops

whereat at which news
impotence powerlessness
borne in hand deceived

in fine in conclusion

th'assay of arms battle

pass passage
dominions lands
allowance permission

it likes us well we approve

expostulate discuss, expound

flourishes decorations

VOLTEMAND   Most fair return of greetings and desires.   60
Upon our first, he sent out to suppress
His nephew's levies, which to him appeared
To be a preparation 'gainst the Polack;
But better looked into, he truly found
It was against your highness; whereat grieved   65
That so his sickness, age and impotence
Was falsely borne in hand, sends out arrests
On Fortinbras, which he in brief obeys,
Receives rebuke from Norway, and in fine
Makes vow before his uncle never more   70
To give th'assay of arms against your majesty.
Whereon old Norway, overcome with joy,
Gives him three thousand crowns in annual fee,
And his commission to employ those soldiers,
So levied as before, against the Polack;   75
With an entreaty, herein further shown,
That it might please you to give quiet pass
Through your dominions for this enterprise,
On such regards of safety and allowance
As therein are set down.
                 [*Gives a document*]

CLAUDIUS   It likes us well,   80
And at our more considered time we'll read,
Answer, and think upon this business.
Meantime, we thank you for your well-took labour.
Go to your rest; at night we'll feast together.
Most welcome home.
                     Exeunt Ambassadors

POLONIUS   This business is well ended.   85
My liege, and madam, to expostulate
What majesty should be, what duty is,
Why day is day, night night, and time is time,
Were nothing but to waste night, day, and time.
Therefore, since brevity is the soul of wit   90
And tediousness the limbs and outward flourishes,
I will be brief. Your noble son is mad.

Polonius rambles on, even though Gertrude urges him to come to the point. He reads aloud Hamlet's letter to Ophelia, and says his daughter has told him all about Hamlet's attempts to woo her.

▲ How do Polonius's words in this scene help to develop your understanding of his relationship with Ophelia?

More matter with less art more substance and less playing with language

figure figure of speech

Perpend consider carefully

mark note
gather and surmise draw your own conclusions

et cetera the full version of 'etc.', meaning 'and other things'

stay wait

ill not good
numbers verses
reckon my groans express (and count) my feelings
whilst this machine is to him as long as I live ('machine' = body)
solicitings pleadings, importunings
fell out occurred., were delivered

Write about it
Hamlet's letter

Polonius reads out part of the letter from Hamlet that Ophelia has given him, and mocks it in front of Claudius and Gertrude (lines 109–12 and lines 115–22).

a Do you believe Hamlet could have written in this florid and elaborate style? Is this a fabricated letter that Polonius has made up in order to degrade and frame Hamlet?

b Whether the letter is real or fake, try your hand at writing the middle part of it that Polonius indicates at line 112, with 'et cetera'. Start with the words given in lines 109–12, and finish with lines 115–22. You can insert as many lines as you like in between, but try to capture the same style.

Mad call I it, for to define true madness,
What is't but to be nothing else but mad?
But let that go.

GERTRUDE   More matter with less art.   95

POLONIUS Madam, I swear I use no art at all.
That he is mad, 'tis true; 'tis true 'tis pity,
And pity 'tis 'tis true – a foolish figure,
But farewell it, for I will use no art.
Mad let us grant him then, and now remains   100
That we find out the cause of this effect,
Or rather say, the cause of this defect,
For this effect defective comes by cause.
Thus it remains, and the remainder thus.
Perpend.   105
I have a daughter – have while she is mine –
Who in her duty and obedience, mark,
Hath given me this. Now gather and surmise.

                    Reads the letter

'To the celestial, and my soul's idol, the most beautified Ophelia,' –
That's an ill phrase, a vile phrase, 'beautified' is a vile phrase – but   110
you shall hear. Thus:
'In her excellent white bosom, these, *et cetera.*'

GERTRUDE   Came this from Hamlet to her?

POLONIUS   Good madam stay awhile, I will be faithful.
'Doubt thou the stars are fire,   115
Doubt that the sun doth move,
Doubt truth to be a liar,
But never doubt I love.
'O dear Ophelia, I am ill at these numbers, I have not art to reckon
my groans; but that I love thee best, O most best, believe it. Adieu.
'Thine evermore, most dear lady, whilst this machine is
to him, Hamlet.'
This in obedience hath my daughter shown me,
And, more above, hath his solicitings,
As they fell out, by time, by means, and place,   125
All given to mine ear.

CLAUDIUS   But how hath she
Received his love?

POLONIUS   What do you think of me?

CLAUDIUS   As of a man faithful and honourable.

Polonius reports that he ordered Ophelia to reject Hamlet's love, so causing the prince's madness. Polonius suggests a plan: he and Claudius will spy on an arranged meeting between Ophelia and Hamlet.

Stagecraft

Show what happened (in small groups)

a Shakespeare often builds stage directions into his language. In lines 141–9, Polonius describes at least eleven distinct actions. One person slowly narrates the lines while the others act out each event.

b 'Take this from this': what does Polonius do at line 154? Does he touch his head and shoulder ('chop off my head')? Or does he touch his official staff of office and his hand ('dismiss me')? Work out an appropriate action to accompany the line.

c With what movement would you accompany the final words of the short speech in lines 154–7: 'Within the centre'? What do you think is the significance of that phrase?

Themes

'I'll loose my daughter to him'

Themes in *Hamlet* and in other Shakespeare plays are often closely associated with – indeed suggested by – imagery. In this case, the image of release is associated with entrapment, the notion that 'Denmark's a prison' and the suppression of feelings and energies and ideas, perhaps resulting in forms of madness.

a 'Loose' sounds like the act of releasing a farmyard or wild animal. Reflect on what line 160 suggests about Polonius's view of Ophelia. Consider also how he refers to her in line 138.

b How does the theme of entrapment and release relate to other themes that have been mentioned so far: surveillance, identity and the personal/public and inner/outer self? As you build up your thoughts about emerging themes and the way they interrelate, highlight your notes with evidence of imagery in the quotations you are collecting.

c As you read on, identify and record further images of entrapment and release in the play.

fain gladly
on the wing in full flight

played the desk done nothing, lay still
given my heart a winking shut my eyes to the love affair
round directly

out of thy star far above you socially
prescripts orders
resort place of operation
tokens gifts
fruits essential points

watch sleeplessness
lightness delirium, light-headedness
declension decline or series of moves (downwards)

arras hanging tapestry (like a curtain covering a wall)

POLONIUS	I would fain prove so. But what might you think,
	When I had seen this hot love on the wing –
	As I perceived it, I must tell you that,
	Before my daughter told me – what might you,
	Or my dear majesty your queen here, think,
	If I had played the desk, or table-book,
	Or given my heart a winking, mute and dumb,
	Or looked upon this love with idle sight –
	What might you think? No, I went round to work,
	And my young mistress thus I did bespeak:
	'Lord Hamlet is a prince out of thy star.
	This must not be.' And then I prescripts gave her,
	That she should lock herself from his resort,
	Admit no messengers, receive no tokens.
	Which done, she took the fruits of my advice,
	And he, repulsed – a short tale to make –
	Fell into a sadness, then into a fast,
	Thence to a watch, thence into a weakness,
	Thence to a lightness, and by this declension
	Into the madness wherein now he raves,
	And all we mourn for.
CLAUDIUS	Do you think 'tis this?
GERTRUDE	It may be, very like.
POLONIUS	Hath there been such a time, I'ld fain know that,
	That I have positively said, 'tis so,
	When it proved otherwise?
CLAUDIUS	Not that I know.
POLONIUS	Take this from this, if this be otherwise.
	If circumstances lead me, I will find
	Where truth is hid, though it were hid indeed
	Within the centre.
CLAUDIUS	How may we try it further?
POLONIUS	You know sometimes he walks four hours together
	Here in the lobby.
GERTRUDE	So he does indeed.
POLONIUS	At such a time I'll loose my daughter to him.
	Be you and I behind an arras then.

Line numbers: 130, 135, 140, 145, 150, 155, 160

Claudius agrees to Polonius's plan to spy on Hamlet. Polonius tries to make sense of Hamlet's puzzling replies and questions.

Write about it

'*Enter* HAMLET *reading on a book*'

Each new production of the play takes decisions on the following questions. Write a paragraph in your Director's Journal in response to each, explaining the dramatic effect of your decisions.

- Does Hamlet see Polonius plotting with Claudius?
- How is Hamlet dressed, and how does he behave? (This is his first appearance since he was reported to be mad.)
- Is Hamlet aware of others on stage before Polonius greets him?
- Why, and to whom, does Polonius say 'Oh give me leave' (line 168)? To Claudius? Gertrude? The Attendants? Hamlet?

thereon because of his disappointment in love

assistant for a state important civil servant

carters horse-drawn carts – to Polonius, an image of rustic provinciality

board him presently greet him immediately

God-a-mercy thank you ('God have mercy on you', a conventional reply to a social inferior)

fishmonger a prostitute's pimp, a fisher for information, a person whose daughters would be both beautiful and prolific breeders of children (is this a bit of nonsense by Hamlet, or something Hamlet reads out of the book he is holding?)

carrion dead flesh

Conception becoming pregnant

harping on talking only of (like a harpist playing one string only)

1 Cross-talk comics? (in pairs)

Some critics argue that Hamlet treats Polonius as the 'straight man' in a comic duo. Take parts and read lines 169–212 in a variety of ways to discover if Hamlet and Polonius really do sound like a pair of comedians.

2 'kissing carrion'

Shakespeare sometimes uses a seemingly throwaway phrase that is packed with meaning. In this case (line 180), the literal meaning of the statement is clear: dead dogs provide good carrion (dead meat) for birds, like carrion crows. But the yoking together of 'kissing carrion' with his next statement – 'Have you a daughter?' – suggests that Hamlet (who knows that Polonius has a daughter!) is associating death with love, kissing and flesh.

Elizabethan and Jacobean revenge dramatists were obsessed with the connection between love and death, often assuming that sexuality and physicality were closely linked with decay, sin and putrefaction.

- What further evidence can you find for an obsession with the physicality of love and of existence in the character of Hamlet?

Mark the encounter: if he love her not,
And be not from his reason fallen thereon,
Let me be no assistant for a state,
But keep a farm and carters.

CLAUDIUS   We will try it.   165

Enter HAMLET *reading on a book*

GERTRUDE   But look where sadly the poor wretch comes reading.
POLONIUS   Away, I do beseech you both, away.
            I'll board him presently.

                    Exeunt Claudius and Gertrude [and Attendants]
            Oh give me leave.
            How does my good Lord Hamlet?
HAMLET   Well, God-a-mercy.   170
POLONIUS   Do you know me, my lord?
HAMLET   Excellent well, y'are a fishmonger.
POLONIUS   Not I my lord.
HAMLET   Then I would you were so honest a man.
POLONIUS   Honest my lord?   175
HAMLET   Ay sir. To be honest, as this world goes, is to be one man
            picked out of ten thousand.
POLONIUS   That's very true my lord.
HAMLET   For if the sun breed maggots in a dead dog, being a good
            kissing carrion – Have you a daughter?   180
POLONIUS   I have my lord.
HAMLET   Let her not walk i'th'sun. Conception is a blessing, but as your
            daughter may conceive – Friend, look to't.
POLONIUS   (*Aside*) How say you by that? Still harping on my daughter.
            Yet he knew me not at first, a said I was a fishmonger – a is far   185
            gone, far gone. And truly, in my youth I suffered much extremity
            for love, very near this. I'll speak to him again. – What do you read
            my lord?
HAMLET   Words, words, words.
POLONIUS   What is the matter, my lord?   190
HAMLET   Between who?
POLONIUS   I mean the matter that you read, my lord.

Hamlet insults Polonius who none the less persists in finding good sense in Hamlet's words. Polonius leaves, and Hamlet welcomes Rosencrantz and Guildenstern, exchanging sexual puns with them.

1 'the satirical rogue'

To ridicule Polonius, Hamlet quotes the author of the book he is reading. Two well-known writers mocked the handicaps of old age. Juvenal, a Roman satirist of the first century AD, ridiculed folly. Erasmus (1466–1536) was a Dutch Christian humanist who wrote *In Praise of Folly*.

- Research either Juvenal or Erasmus. Report on whether you think their writings would appeal to Hamlet, and why.

2 Young men joking together (in pairs)

Hamlet greets Rosencrantz and Guildenstern warmly. He joins in the wordplay and sexual innuendo. Fortune is **personified** as a female prostitute. So 'her privates we' might mean her genitals (private parts), but it could simply mean 'we are intimate with Fortune'. Similarly, 'favours' and 'secret parts' could also be **double entendres** (words or phrases that have double meanings, one of which is usually risqué), though their surface meanings are 'help' and 'private affairs' respectively.

- Shakespeare often indulges in such wordplay for fun. What are the dramatic purposes of its inclusion here, do you think?

Characters

The presentation of self in everyday life

One of the reasons that Hamlet is an attractive character to adolescent or young adults is that he appears to have a number of different selves. In the script opposite, he is putting on a humorous front to deal with Polonius, and then (differently) Rosencrantz and Guildenstern. Personal and public engagement is one of the major themes of the play – and perhaps it is most obviously seen in Hamlet himself.

a In role as Hamlet, tell an audience (e.g. a psychiatrist or a friend) your difficulties so far in the play. You might wish to refer to your relationship with Gertrude, Claudius, your dead father, Ophelia, Polonius, Rosencrantz and Guildenstern.

b Is there a 'true self' emerging in the soliloquies, or is Hamlet a reflection of his relationships with the other characters? Identify any lines in the play so far where you think he is speaking as his true self, then debate your view with the rest of the class.

Slanders defamatory and false reports

purging discharging, exuding

amber and plumtree gum resin, sap

hams thighs

out of the air from the outside to inside the room, i.e. would you come inside?

pregnant meaningful, apt

prosperously generously, naturally

suddenly immediately

withal with

indifferent ordinary

button topmost

strumpet prostitute

HAMLET   Slanders sir, for the satirical rogue says here that old men have
grey beards, that their faces are wrinkled, their eyes purging thick
amber and plumtree gum, and that they have a plentiful lack of wit,   195
together with most weak hams. All which sir, though I most
powerfully and potently believe, yet I hold it not honesty to have
it thus set down. For yourself sir shall grow old as I am, if like a
crab you could go backward.

POLONIUS   (*Aside*) Though this be madness, yet there is method   200
in't. – Will you walk out of the air, my lord?

HAMLET   Into my grave?

POLONIUS   Indeed that's out of the air. (*Aside*) How pregnant sometimes
his replies are! a happiness that often madness hits on, which reason
and sanity could not so prosperously be delivered of. I will leave   205
him, and suddenly contrive the means of meeting between him and
my daughter. – My honourable lord, I will most humbly take my
leave of you.

HAMLET   You cannot sir take from me anything that I will more
willingly part withal; except my life, except my life, except my life.   210

POLONIUS   Fare you well my lord.

HAMLET   These tedious old fools!

Enter GUILDENSTERN *and* ROSENCRANTZ

POLONIUS   You go to seek the Lord Hamlet, there he is.

ROSENCRANTZ   God save you sir.

[*Exit Polonius*]

GUILDENSTERN   My honoured lord!   215

ROSENCRANTZ   My most dear lord!

HAMLET   My excellent good friends! How dost thou Guildenstern? Ah,
Rosencrantz. Good lads, how do you both?

ROSENCRANTZ   As the indifferent children of the earth.

GUILDENSTERN   Happy in that we are not over-happy; on Fortune's   220
cap we are not the very button.

HAMLET   Nor the soles of her shoe?

ROSENCRANTZ   Neither, my lord.

HAMLET   Then you live about her waist, or in the middle of her favours?

GUILDENSTERN   Faith, her privates we.   225

HAMLET   In the secret parts of Fortune? Oh most true, she is a
strumpet. What news?

Hamlet, Rosencrantz and Guildenstern continue their banter, but Hamlet becomes more serious. He challenges the courtiers about why they have come to Elsinore. Have they come freely or been sent for?

Stagecraft

'Denmark's a prison' (in groups)

Some productions of *Hamlet* take up the line, 'Denmark's a prison', and build the design of the whole play around the image (and the theme of confinement). Stage sets have included heavy prison doors, chains and warders. Costume designs have included dark, prisoner-like clothes. Sound effects have been used to suggest the clanking, claustrophobic nature of prison life.

Work on a full design for *Hamlet*, either taking the **metaphor** (see p. 264) of the prison and confinement as your principal idea, or using another unifying image or theme. Split into four groups.

- Group 1 works on stage and set design, perhaps building a model of what the set would look like.
- Group 2 works on sound, identifying a range of sound effects that will accompany a reading or production of the play.
- Group 3 works on costume design, designing a set of clothes for any number of the characters in the play.
- Group 4 works on lighting.

1 True or false? (in small groups)

Hamlet says 'for there is nothing either good or bad but thinking makes it so' (lines 239–40).

- Do you believe that? Talk together about whether you agree with Hamlet's claim. Use practical examples from your own experience.

2 Verbal fencing (in threes)

On three or four occasions in lines 241–9, Rosencrantz and Guildenstern try to encourage Hamlet to talk about 'ambition'. Presumably they are following Claudius's instructions to discover what afflicts Hamlet. If they can get him to talk about his ambition, they will have something of real importance to report to the king.

- Take parts and experiment with ways of speaking the lines. Try to bring out how Rosencrantz and Guildenstern are attempting to get Hamlet to reveal his secret thoughts (for example, they might stress 'ambition'). Show how Hamlet warily fends them off. Keep the image of a sword-fencing match in your mind as you speak.

doomsday the Day of Judgement

Fortune goddess of chance

confines, wards cells in a prison

bounded confined

bodies people without ambition

outstretched heroes great men, or ambitious actors

fay faith

sort associate

am most dreadfully attended have useless servants (but also with the implication of being hampered with hangers-on like Rosencrantz and Guildenstern themselves)

in the beaten way of friendship as old friends

modesties restraint

craft enough to colour skill enough to hide embarrassed blushes

ROSENCRANTZ   None my lord, but that the world's grown honest.

HAMLET   Then is doomsday near – but your news is not true. Let me
question more in particular. What have you, my good friends,   230
deserved at the hands of Fortune, that she sends you to prison
hither?

GUILDENSTERN   Prison, my lord?

HAMLET   Denmark's a prison.

ROSENCRANTZ   Then is the world one.   235

HAMLET   A goodly one, in which there are many confines, wards, and
dungeons; Denmark being one o'th'worst.

ROSENCRANTZ   We think not so my lord.

HAMLET   Why then 'tis none to you, for there is nothing either good
or bad but thinking makes it so. To me it is a prison.   240

ROSENCRANTZ   Why then your ambition makes it one; 'tis too narrow
for your mind.

HAMLET   O God, I could be bounded in a nutshell, and count myself
a king of infinite space, were it not that I have bad dreams.

GUILDENSTERN   Which dreams indeed are ambition, for the very   245
substance of the ambitious is merely the shadow of a dream.

HAMLET   A dream itself is but a shadow.

ROSENCRANTZ   Truly, and I hold ambition of so airy and light a quality
that it is but a shadow's shadow.

HAMLET   Then are our beggars bodies, and our monarchs and out-   250
stretched heroes the beggars' shadows. Shall we to th'court? for by
my fay I cannot reason.

BOTH   We'll wait upon you.

HAMLET   No such matter. I will not sort you with the rest of my
servants; for to speak to you like an honest man, I am most   255
dreadfully attended. But in the beaten way of friendship, what make
you at Elsinore?

ROSENCRANTZ   To visit you my lord, no other occasion.

HAMLET   Beggar that I am, I am even poor in thanks, but I thank
you – and sure, dear friends, my thanks are too dear a halfpenny.   260
Were you not sent for? Is it your own inclining? Is it a free
visitation? Come, deal justly with me. Come, come. Nay, speak.

GUILDENSTERN   What should we say my lord?

HAMLET   Why, anything but to the purpose. You were sent for – and
there is a kind of confession in your looks which your modesties   265
have not craft enough to colour. I know the good king and queen
have sent for you.

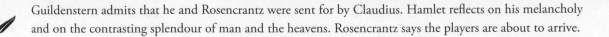

Guildenstern admits that he and Rosencrantz were sent for by Claudius. Hamlet reflects on his melancholy and on the contrasting splendour of man and the heavens. Rosencrantz says the players are about to arrive.

1 From friendship to suspicion (in threes)

Hamlet becomes increasingly suspicious of his two friends. Why have they come to Denmark? He decides to 'conjure' (seriously ask) them to tell, appealing to their 'consonancy' (youthful friendship).

- Take parts and read lines 215–77. Identify where you feel Hamlet's suspicions begin, and explain the reasons for your choices of line(s).

what more dear what greater reasons

a better proposer a more skilful speaker

Characters

Hamlet's melancholy

In lines 280–90, Hamlet reflects that he has 'lost all my mirth'. He speaks of the wonderful nature both of the world and of humankind, but says that nothing now gives him pleasure. Earth seems 'a sterile promontory'; the heavens 'a foul and pestilent congregation of vapours'; and humankind, though the 'paragon' (ideal of excellence) of animals, is merely 'dust', offering him no delight. It is possible that Shakespeare is referring ironically to the Globe Theatre: 'majestical roof' = the painted canopy over the stage; 'foul and pestilent . . . vapours' = the audience (see p. 272).

Every actor who plays Hamlet spends many hours deciding how to speak the lines. Is Hamlet's tone sincere, ironical, sarcastic, bitter, awe-struck – or does the mood vary from line to line?

a There is no single 'right' way to deliver these lines, so explore ways of speaking, then write notes on the version that you would recommend.

b Use these notes in your build-up of material on Hamlet's character (see p. 78). Note that these lines are in prose rather than Hamlet's usual verse. Does that make a difference?

c Research melancholy (sadness, depression) in some depth by looking not only at Robert Burton's *Anatomy of Melancholy*, but at early twentieth-century studies by Freud, such as his 1917 essay 'Mourning and Melancholy'. On page 78 you were asked to speak from Hamlet's point of view about his various selves. Here, turn the tables and write the psychiatrist's report on Hamlet's problems, and on the particular kind of depression from which he seems to be suffering.

anticipation insight, foresight
discovery exposure
moult no feather remain intact

fretted interwoven and supported

congregation gathering, but also with the religious sense of a community
express well made
apprehension understanding
paragon highest form
quintessence distillation

lenten frugal, thin
coted overtook

foil and target sword and shield
gratis without reward
tickle o'th'sere easily tickled to laughter (sere = gun trigger)

ROSENCRANTZ To what end my lord?

HAMLET That you must teach me. But let me conjure you, by the rights
of our fellowship, by the consonancy of our youth, by the obligation   270
of our ever-preserved love, and by what more dear a better proposer
can charge you withal, be even and direct with me, whether you
were sent for or no.

ROSENCRANTZ (*To Guildenstern*) What say you?

HAMLET (*Aside*) Nay then I have an eye of you. – If you love me, hold   275
not off.

GUILDENSTERN My lord, we were sent for.

HAMLET I will tell you why. So shall my anticipation prevent your
discovery, and your secrecy to the king and queen moult no feather.
I have of late, but wherefore I know not, lost all my mirth, forgone   280
all custom of exercises; and indeed it goes so heavily with my
disposition that this goodly frame, the earth, seems to me a sterile
promontory; this most excellent canopy the air, look you, this brave
o'erhanging firmament, this majestical roof fretted with golden
fire – why, it appeareth no other thing to me but a foul and pestilent   285
congregation of vapours. What a piece of work is a man! How noble
in reason, how infinite in faculties, in form and moving how express
and admirable, in action how like an angel, in apprehension how
like a god! The beauty of the world, the paragon of animals – and
yet to me, what is this quintessence of dust? Man delights not   290
me – no, nor woman neither, though by your smiling you seem to
say so.

ROSENCRANTZ My lord, there was no such stuff in my thoughts.

HAMLET Why did ye laugh then, when I said man delights not me?

ROSENCRANTZ To think, my lord, if you delight not in man, what   295
lenten entertainment the players shall receive from you. We coted
them on the way, and hither are they coming to offer you service.

HAMLET He that plays the king shall be welcome, his majesty shall have
tribute of me; the adventurous knight shall use his foil and target,
the lover shall not sigh gratis, the humorous man shall end his part   300
in peace, the clown shall make those laugh whose lungs are tickle
o'th'sere, and the lady shall say her mind freely – or the blank verse
shall halt for't. What players are they?

ROSENCRANTZ Even those you were wont to take such delight in, the
tragedians of the city.   305

HAMLET How chances it they travel? their residence, both in reputation
and profit, was better both ways.

1 The players

The arrival of the players is sudden, and enables Rosencrantz and Guildenstern to divert Hamlet from his musings on the world. Compare the players in this image with their appearance on pages 90 and 118.

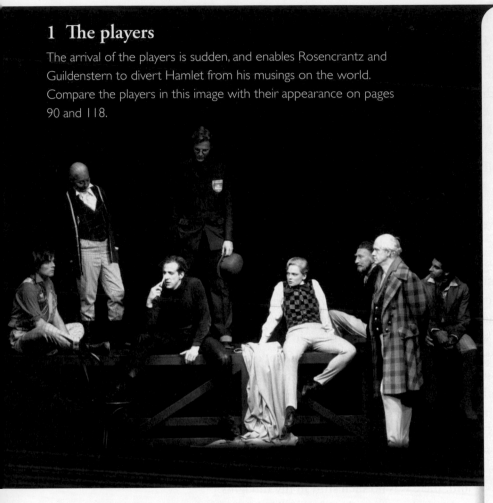

▲ The arrival of the players. Rosencrantz refers to the 'war of the theatres' in 1600, when the success of a company of boy actors threatened the adult acting companies in London. The boys specialised in bitter satire. Some noblemen were afraid to visit the theatre for fear of mockery ('many wearing rapiers are afraid of goose-quills').

2 Hamlet's questions

Note that almost the entire dialogue in the script opposite is driven by Hamlet's questions about the players. Identify the turning point where Hamlet uses the dialogue to make a point about Claudius and Denmark. Does he say anything before then to indicate that he was leading to this challenge to Rosencrantz?

inhibition ban on acting in their own theatre

late innovation recent political changes (see pp. 243–5)

estimation reputation

rusty out of practice

wonted pace usual standard

eyrie of children ... question nest of child actors, as noisy as unfledged hawks

escoted financed

quality profession (of acting)

no longer ... sing until their voices break (i.e. players' companies were only interested in children's pre-broken voices)

exclaim ... succession use their (broken) voices to argue themselves out of a part in the company

tar provoke

went to cuffs fought

Hercules and his load Hercules with the heavens on his back (the emblem of the Globe Theatre)

make mouths sneer

ducats gold coins

picture in little miniature picture

Th'appurtenance of what is appropriate to

comply with you show you a proper welcome

ROSENCRANTZ   I think their inhibition comes by the means of the late innovation.

HAMLET   Do they hold the same estimation they did when I was in the city? Are they so followed? 310

ROSENCRANTZ   No indeed are they not.

HAMLET   How comes it? Do they grow rusty?

ROSENCRANTZ   Nay, their endeavour keeps in the wonted pace, but there is sir an eyrie of children, little eyases, that cry out on the top of question and are most tyrannically clapped for't. These are now the fashion, and so be-rattle the common stages (so they call them) that many wearing rapiers are afraid of goose-quills, and dare scarce come thither. 315

HAMLET   What, are they children? Who maintains 'em? How are they escoted? Will they pursue the quality no longer than they can sing? Will they not say afterwards, if they should grow themselves to common players – as it is most like if their means are no better, their writers do them wrong to make them exclaim against their own succession? 320

325

ROSENCRANTZ   Faith, there has been much to do on both sides, and the nation holds it no sin to tar them to controversy. There was for a while no money bid for argument unless the poet and the player went to cuffs in the question.

HAMLET   Is't possible? 330

GUILDENSTERN   Oh there has been much throwing about of brains.

HAMLET   Do the boys carry it away?

ROSENCRANTZ   Ay that they do my lord, Hercules and his load too.

HAMLET   It is not very strange, for my uncle is king of Denmark, and those that would make mouths at him while my father lived give twenty, forty, fifty, a hundred ducats apiece for his picture in little. 'Sblood, there is something in this more than natural, if philosophy could find it out. 335

A flourish

GUILDENSTERN   There are the players.

HAMLET   Gentlemen, you are welcome to Elsinore. Your hands, come then. Th'appurtenance of welcome is fashion and ceremony. Let me comply with you in this garb, lest my extent to the players, which I tell you must show fairly outwards, should more appear like entertainment than yours. You are welcome – but my uncle-father and aunt-mother are deceived. 340

345

Polonius enters to tell Hamlet of the players' arrival. Hamlet mocks him. Polonius praises the actors in high-flown language. Hamlet taunts Polonius about his daughter.

1 Appearance versus reality – and hawks and handsaws

The talk about the players (lines 295–345) may seem to have little to do with the concerns of the play. But it is important because acting reflects the key theme of appearance versus reality (and Hamlet will shortly devise a scheme using the players to expose Claudius's guilt). Hamlet uses the change in acting fashions to make a barbed comment on Denmark: courtiers now buy Claudius's picture (lines 334–6). He ends with an enigmatic comment: 'I know a hawk from a handsaw' (line 348). A 'hawk' might be a bird of prey, or a plasterer's board for mortar. A 'handsaw' could be a 'hernshaw' (heron), or a carpenter's saw. Hamlet might be saying, 'I know the difference between one thing and another – I'm not mad.'

a Suggest what you think Hamlet's words might mean. For example, 'I can recognise a bird of prey [Guildenstern?] when I see one.' Trying out hand gestures to accompany the lines will help you explore the possible meanings.

b How does Hamlet's statement, 'I am but mad north-north-west. When the wind is southerly, I know a hawk from a handsaw' contribute to your understanding of his madness? You might like to add this quotation and your interpretation of it to the evidence you are collecting on Hamlet's state of mind and behaviour. Is it important to take the context of each quotation into account?

Stagecraft

A question of pace (in pairs)

The arrival of the players appears to excite Hamlet. Some productions play the lines with Polonius at a fast pace to emphasise Hamlet's state of mind and his very sane (or crazed?) command of wit.

• Try the dialogue between Hamlet and Polonius with both characters speaking at a fast pace; then try it again with one of the characters speaking slowly, and the other faster; finally, slow it down for both characters. What does this variation in pace tell you about the characters? Which of the versions worked best?

Well be with you (a greeting)

swaddling clouts baby clothes

You say right sir
(Hamlet pretends to be in mid-conversation with Rosencrantz)

Buzz, buzz! (usually interpreted as Hamlet mocking Polonius's gossip)

scene individable plays in a single act or scene
Seneca, Plautus tragic/comic Roman dramatists
law of writ drama
Jephtha a military leader and judge who sacrificed his daughter to God
'One fair daughter'
(Hamlet quotes rules from a song of the time)

wot knows

row verse
pious chanson religious song
abridgement
entertainment or interruption

GUILDENSTERN   In what my dear lord?

HAMLET   I am but mad north-north-west. When the wind is southerly, I know a hawk from a handsaw.

Enter POLONIUS

POLONIUS   Well be with you gentlemen.

HAMLET   Hark you Guildenstern, and you too – at each ear a hearer.   350
That great baby you see there is not yet out of his swaddling clouts.

ROSENCRANTZ   Happily he's the second time come to them, for they say an old man is twice a child.

HAMLET   I will prophesy: he comes to tell me of the players, mark it. – You say right sir, a Monday morning, 'twas then indeed.   355

POLONIUS   My lord, I have news to tell you.

HAMLET   My lord, I have news to tell you. When Roscius was an actor in Rome –

POLONIUS   The actors are come hither my lord.

HAMLET   Buzz, buzz!   360

POLONIUS   Upon my honour.

HAMLET   Then came each actor on his ass –

POLONIUS   The best actors in the world, either for tragedy, comedy, history, pastoral, pastoral-comical, historical-pastoral, tragical-historical, tragical-comical-historical-pastoral, scene individable or   365 poem unlimited. Seneca cannot be too heavy, nor Plautus too light. For the law of writ and the liberty, these are the only men.

HAMLET   O Jephtha judge of Israel, what a treasure hadst thou!

POLONIUS   What a treasure had he my lord?

HAMLET   Why –   370
   'One fair daughter and no more,
   The which he lovèd passing well.'

POLONIUS   Still on my daughter.

HAMLET   Am I not i'th'right, old Jephtha?

POLONIUS   If you call me Jephtha my lord, I have a daughter that I   375 love passing well.

HAMLET   Nay, that follows not.

POLONIUS   What follows then my lord?

HAMLET   Why –
   'As by lot God wot,'   380
And then you know –
   'It came to pass, as most like it was,' –
the first row of the pious chanson will show you more, for look where my abridgement comes.

Hamlet welcomes the players, some of whom he recognises. He asks the principal actor to declaim a speech about Pyrrhus. Hamlet begins with the speech which tells how Pyrrhus entered Troy in the wooden horse.

Write about it
A soliloquy

a List as many reasons as you can for Hamlet's enthusiasm over the arrival of the players.

b Work this list into a soliloquy or an aside in which Hamlet reveals his inner thoughts on the arrival of the players.

c It is at this time that Hamlet begins to formulate his plan for revenge on Claudius. Think about how you would include details of the plan in the soliloquy or aside, and where in the scene you would insert this speech.

Stagecraft
Hamlet's memory of the speech (in pairs)

Hamlet begins his recollection of the speech about Pyrrhus in stuttering style, as he tries to remember the words.

a Try reading the speech yourself. Be hesitant at the start, then move to a more assured flow as the speech (and memory) gains momentum. Do you think Hamlet is an accomplished actor, or an amateur having trouble with the lines?

b Reflect on the shift from prose to highly formal – and indeed, elaborate – verse at line 407. To achieve a sense of the difference, translate the previous ten lines of prose into Shakespearean verse, and rewrite the verse as prose. Read them out, and then discuss the difference with a partner. Finally, look again at the original script and discuss the qualities of each style.

1 The story of Pyrrhus

Pyrrhus, like Hamlet, was a son who vowed to avenge his dead father. Lines 404–6 refer to Virgil's *Aeneid*, in which Aeneas tells Queen Dido the story of Pyrrhus, whose father Achilles was killed at the siege of Troy. Pyrrhus was one of the Greek warriors in the wooden horse ('the ominous horse') that was used to defeat the Trojans. Hamlet begins the tale of how the 'rugged' (long-haired) Pyrrhus, like a savage tiger ('th'Hyrcanian beast'), clad in black armour ('sable arms'), but covered in blood ('total gules', 'o'er-sized with coagulate gore'), sought out Priam, king of Troy, to kill him in revenge for his own father.

• On a copy of the script opposite, highlight the words and phrases that Hamlet uses to enhance the drama and violence.

valanced bearded (literally 'skirted' with hair)

beard challenge

byrlady by Our Lady (the Virgin Mary)

chopine high-heeled shoe

uncurrent gold valueless cracked coins

fly ... see have a go at anything

caviary caviar

the general the general population, ordinary folk

cried in the top of mine exceeded mine in value and volume

sallets salads

indict prove guilty

sable dark

tricked decorated (a heraldic term, like 'sable', 'arms', 'gules')

impasted made into paste

coagulate gore clotted blood

carbuncles fire-red precious stones

Enter the PLAYERS

Y'are welcome masters, welcome all. I am glad to see thee well. 385
Welcome good friends. Oh, my old friend! why, thy face is valanced
since I saw thee last; com'st thou to beard me in Denmark? What,
my young lady and mistress – byrlady, your ladyship is nearer to
heaven than when I saw you last by the altitude of a chopine. Pray
God your voice like a piece of uncurrent gold be not cracked within 390
the ring. Masters, you are all welcome. We'll e'en to't like French
falconers, fly at anything we see: we'll have a speech straight. Come
give us a taste of your quality: come, a passionate speech.

I PLAYER   What speech, my good lord?

HAMLET   I heard thee speak me a speech once, but it was never acted, 395
or if it was, not above once, for the play I remember pleased not
the million: 'twas caviary to the general. But it was, as I received
it, and others whose judgements in such matters cried in the top
of mine, an excellent play, well digested in the scenes, set down with
as much modesty as cunning. I remember one said there were no 400
sallets in the lines to make the matter savoury, nor no matter in
the phrase that might indict the author of affectation, but called it
an honest method, as wholesome as sweet and by very much more
handsome than fine. One speech in't I chiefly loved, 'twas Aeneas'
tale to Dido, and thereabout of it especially where he speaks of 405
Priam's slaughter. If it live in your memory, begin at this line, let
me see, let me see –
    'The rugged Pyrrhus, like th'Hyrcanian beast' –
'Tis not so, it begins with Pyrrhus –
        'The rugged Pyrrhus, he whose sable arms, 410
        Black as his purpose, did the night resemble
        When he lay couchèd in the ominous horse,
        Hath now this dread and black complexion smeared
        With heraldy more dismal. Head to foot
        Now is he total gules, horridly tricked 415
        With blood of fathers, mothers, daughters, sons,
        Baked and impasted with the parching streets,
        That lend a tyrannous and a damnèd light
        To their lord's murder. Roasted in wrath and fire,
        And thus o'er-sizèd with coagulate gore, 420
        With eyes like carbuncles, the hellish Pyrrhus
        Old grandsire Priam seeks –'
So, proceed you.

The first player continues the speech from where Hamlet leaves off. He declaims how Pyrrhus finds Priam, pauses for a long moment, then slays him. The player is interrupted by Polonius, but Hamlet urges him on.

1 Bombast (in pairs)

Shakespeare may be 'sending up' an older stage tradition of acting and speaking. He gives the player a speech full of high-flown language.

- Work out a dramatic way of reading aloud the Player's lines 426–55 and Hamlet's lines 410–22. Try a bombastic, over-the-top, declamatory style, to match the highly coloured language. Add exaggerated gestures and formal movements to match the style. One of you plays Hamlet and the other directs.

2 'Did nothing': Pyrrhus and Hamlet both delay

Both Hamlet and Pyrrhus are sons who seek revenge for the killing of their fathers. The player's speech contains another parallel. Pyrrhus stood still and 'Did nothing' (line 440). His inability to act forecasts Hamlet's own inaction as he delays avenging his father's murder. Some productions heavily emphasise this moment, and Hamlet echoes 'Did nothing'.

- Explain the dramatic effect of that echo.

▼ Can you explain Hamlet's fascination and reverence for the players? (In this photograph, Hamlet is the character kneeling.)

discretion taste

Repugnant to command resisting orders

fell cruel

senseless Ilium unfeeling Troy

Stoops to his base crashes to the ground

Takes prisoner Pyrrhus' ear dazes Pyrrhus

milky white-haired

as a painted tyrant like a tyrant in a portrait

neutral to his will and matter unable to think or act

rack clouds

orb Earth

Cyclops one-eyed giants who worked as blacksmiths

Mars god of war

proof eterne eternal protection

synod gathering

fellies part of the wheel rim

nave hub

mobled veiled

POLONIUS 'Fore God my lord, well spoken, with good accent and good
discretion.   425

I PLAYER   'Anon he finds him,
   Striking too short at Greeks; his antique sword,
   Rebellious to his arm, lies where it falls,
   Repugnant to command. Unequal matched,
   Pyrrhus at Priam drives, in rage strikes wide,   430
   But with the whiff and wind of his fell sword
   Th'unvervèd father falls. Then senseless Ilium,
   Seeming to feel this blow, with flaming top
   Stoops to his base, and with a hideous crash
   Takes prisoner Pyrrhus' ear; for lo, his sword,   435
   Which was declining on the milky head
   Of reverend Priam, seemed i'th'air to stick.
   So, as a painted tyrant, Pyrrhus stood,
   And like a neutral to his will and matter,
   Did nothing.   440
   But as we often see against some storm,
   A silence in the heavens, the rack stand still,
   The bold winds speechless, and the orb below
   As hush as death, anon the dreadful thunder
   Doth rend the region; so after Pyrrhus' pause,   445
   A rousèd vengeance sets him new a-work,
   And never did the Cyclops' hammers fall
   On Mars's armour, forged for proof eterne,
   With less remorse than Pyrrhus' bleeding sword
   Now falls on Priam.   450
   Out, out, thou strumpet Fortune! All you gods,
   In general synod take away her power,
   Break all the spokes and fellies from her wheel,
   And bowl the round nave down the hill of heaven
   As low as to the fiends.'   455

POLONIUS This is too long.

HAMLET It shall to th' barber's with your beard. Prithee say on.
He's for a jig or a tale of bawdry, or he sleeps. Say on, come to
Hecuba.

I PLAYER 'But who – ah woe! – had seen the mobled queen –'   460

HAMLET The mobled queen?

POLONIUS That's good, 'mobled queen' is good.

91

The player, with tears in his eyes, ends his tale of Hecuba. Hamlet orders Polonius to treat the actors hospitably. He asks the player to perform a play the next night, including a specially written speech.

Language in the play
The shift from high poetry to prose

The players speak in a formalised, high-flown diction and style; much of the rest of *Hamlet* is in freer **blank verse**, and there is a good deal of prose in the play (see p. 267).

- Using examples from the script opposite, prepare director's notes for an actor on how he or she should speak the different types of lines. Look particularly at transitions between verse and prose, as at line 476.

Write about it
Pyrrhus

a An outline of the story of Pyrrhus is provided on page 88. Using this as a start, read through Hamlet's speech again and write a 100–200 word summary of the speech in prose.

b Rewrite the speech in one of the following styles:

- a sonnet
- a question-and-answer format (e.g. an interrogation)
- the blurb of a novel
- a news item.

c Once you have experimented with, and attained a good understanding of, the speech and its story, make comparisons between Pyrrhus and Hamlet.

1 'according to their desert'

Polonius appears to have strict notions of propriety in terms of how the actors should be welcomed: they are of lower social class, and therefore will be treated accordingly. Hamlet is more generous.

a Look at Hamlet's reaction to Polonius in lines 485–8. What does this tell us about Hamlet's character, and how does it fit with what we know about him so far?

b Read line 497 in various ways: tongue-in-cheek, forcefully, as a genuine warning, or in some other tone. Decide which seems most appropriate to match what is in Hamlet's mind at this moment.

bisson rheum blinding tears

clout piece of cloth

diadem crown

o'er-teemèd worn out (Hecuba was said to have had a hundred children)

milch milky

passion in the gods sympathy from the gods

bestowed accommodated

the abstract and brief chronicles those able to present a summary and reflection of the state of the age

their desert what they deserve

bodkin stiletto-like needle

bounty generosity

for a need if necessary

I PLAYER 'Run barefoot up and down, threat'ning the flames

With bisson rheum, a clout upon that head

Where late the diadem stood, and, for a robe, 465

About her lank and all o'er-teemèd loins

A blanket, in th'alarm of fear caught up –

Who this had seen, with tongue in venom steeped

'Gainst Fortune's state would treason have pronounced.

But if the gods themselves did see her then, 470

When she saw Pyrrhus make malicious sport

In mincing with his sword her husband's limbs,

The instant burst of clamour that she made,

Unless things mortal move them not at all,

Would have made milch the burning eyes of heaven,

And passion in the gods. 475

POLONIUS Look where he has not turned his colour, and has tears in's eyes. Prithee no more.

HAMLET 'Tis well, I'll have thee speak out the rest of this soon. – Good my lord, will you see the players well bestowed? Do you hear, let 480 them be well used, for they are the abstract and brief chronicles of the time. After your death you were better have a bad epitaph than their ill report while you live.

POLONIUS My lord, I will use them according to their desert.

HAMLET God's bodkin man, much better. Use every man after his 485 desert, and who shall scape whipping? Use them after your own honour and dignity; the less they deserve, the more merit is in your bounty. Take them in.

POLONIUS Come sirs. *Exit Polonius*

HAMLET Follow him friends, we'll hear a play tomorrow. – Dost thou 490 hear me old friend, can you play *The Murder of Gonzago*?

I PLAYER Ay my lord.

HAMLET We'll ha't tomorrow night. You could for a need study a speech of some dozen or sixteen lines, which I would set down and insert in't, could you not? 495

I PLAYER Ay my lord.

HAMLET Very well. Follow that lord, and look you mock him not.

Exeunt Players

My good friends, I'll leave you till night. You are welcome to Elsinore.

ROSENCRANTZ Good my lord. 500

Exeunt Rosencrantz and Guildenstern

Hamlet wonders at the player's ability to weep for a fictional character. He berates himself for doing nothing, even though he has real reasons for revenge. He curses Claudius, and cries for vengeance.

1 Self-reproach: 'And all for nothing?' (in pairs)

'What's Hecuba to him, or he to Hecuba … ?' demands Hamlet as he sees the player weeping for the sufferings of Hecuba. Faced with an actor who can cry at the imagined torments of a fictional character in a play, Hamlet reproaches himself for his own lack of action. The actor can weep 'for nothing', but Hamlet, with a murdered father, is incapable of taking revenge ('unpregnant of my cause'). Like a day-dreamer ('John-a-dreams'), he does nothing.

a Do you think that Hamlet is being too hard on himself? Consider in turn each of the things he calls himself and decide if they are true ('rogue', 'peasant slave', 'dull and muddy-mettled rascal', 'John-a-dreams', 'coward', 'pigeon-livered'). Why does he level these accusations at himself?

b Consider each of the seven things Hamlet calls Claudius in lines 532–3 and discuss how justified you think each description is.

c Shakespeare often inserts lists into his plays (a literary device called **copiousness**). The accumulation of items helps to increase the intensity of the mood being created. Pick out the following lists: the player's reactions (lines 506–9); what the player would do if he played Hamlet (lines 514–18); what Hamlet imagines a bully would do to him (lines 524–7); what Hamlet calls Claudius (lines 532–3). Write a new list to insert into the soliloquy opposite (for example, a list concerning his mother, or his false friends).

Themes

Procrastination and revenge

Hamlet is, for most of the play, delaying his revenge of his father's death. There are good reasons for this, as he wishes to be sure that what the Ghost has told him and his intuition about Claudius are correct. He can be fairly said to procrastinate (delay) but not to prevaricate (to straddle an issue, to act in collusion, to waver).

a Follow up your research on revenge plays (see page 50) and discuss to what extent *Hamlet* is the same as, and different from, a typical revenge tragedy.

b Now think about Hamlet as a revenge tragedy hero or protagonist (see 'Hamlet: a tragic hero?', p. 248). What are his heroic qualities? How do these interfere with his drive to revenge?

conceit imagination
visage wanned face paled
in's aspect in his look
function self and embodiment as an actor

cleave split

Confound confuse

muddy-mettled cowardly and sluggish
peak mope
unpregnant of my cause not having brought the motivation of my revenge to fruition
pate skull, top of the head

i'th'throat deep down

'swounds God's wounds (an oath)
gall courage

kites scavenging birds
offal guts
kindless without kin or kindness

HAMLET   Ay so, God bye to you. Now I am alone.

O what a rogue and peasant slave am I!

Is it not monstrous that this player here,

But in a fiction, in a dream of passion,

Could force his soul so to his own conceit   505

That from her working all his visage wanned,

Tears in his eyes, distraction in's aspect,

A broken voice, and his whole function suiting

With forms to his conceit? And all for nothing?

For Hecuba!   510

What's Hecuba to him, or he to Hecuba,

That he should weep for her? What would he do,

Had he the motive and the cue for passion

That I have? He would drown the stage with tears,

And cleave the general ear with horrid speech,   515

Make mad the guilty and appal the free,

Confound the ignorant, and amaze indeed

The very faculties of eyes and ears. Yet I,

A dull and muddy-mettled rascal, peak

Like John-a-dreams, unpregnant of my cause,   520

And can say nothing – no, not for a king,

Upon whose property and most dear life

A damned defeat was made. Am I a coward?

Who calls me villain, breaks my pate across,

Plucks off my beard and blows it in my face,   525

Tweaks me by th'nose, gives me the lie i'th'throat

As deep as to the lungs? Who does me this?

Ha, 'swounds, I should take it, for it cannot be

But I am pigeon-livered, and lack gall

To make oppression bitter, or ere this   530

I should ha' fatted all the region kites

With this slave's offal. Bloody, bawdy villain!

Remorseless, treacherous, lecherous, kindless villain!

Oh, vengeance!

Hamlet rebukes himself for his emotional outburst. He resolves to stage a play showing a murder similar to his father's. If the watching Claudius reveals his guilt, it will prove that the Ghost has spoken truly.

1 Changing moods (in threes or fours)

Hamlet goes through several changes of mood in lines 501–58. His soliloquy contains the following sections:

- **Line 501** dismissing Rosencrantz and Guildenstern
- **Line 502** self-criticism
- **Lines 503–12** wondering at the player's tears for Hecuba
- **Lines 512–18** imagining the player's reactions to real grievances
- **Lines 518–32** deepening self-disgust
- **Lines 532–4** rage against Claudius
- **Lines 535–40** self-reproach for his emotional outburst
- **Lines 541–51** working out a plan to test the Ghost's word
- **Lines 551–6** fear that the Ghost may be a devil, telling lies to tempt him to eternal damnation by killing Claudius
- **Lines 557–8** elation at the thought that he will prove Claudius's guilt.

a Make notes on each section, advising Hamlet on how to communicate his changes of mood through tone, pace, rhythm, volume, movement and gesture. Then speak your own version of the soliloquy. You may wish to use more than one voice to do so.

b Print out this soliloquy and cut it into the sections listed above. Without looking back at this text, see if you can put together the speech in the same order. Compare notes with other groups, and justify your sequence. Then look back at the book to discuss why Shakespeare puts it in the order in which it appears in the script.

2 'The play's the thing' (in pairs)

a Is theatre as powerful as Hamlet claims? Talk together about whether you think a criminal, watching a play with a similar theme to his or her own crime, will feel guilty and remorseful or will cry out and admit their guilt.

b Try to think of instances you have experienced or have read about when a play literally moves an audience to act, inciting demonstrations, violence or other actions. Use the library and the Internet to research some examples.

c Hamlet is planning a play within the play. Other instances of this device are in Thomas Kyd's *The Spanish Tragedy* and Shakespeare's *A Midsummer Night's Dream* and *The Taming of the Shrew*. A more recent example is Brecht's *Caucasian Chalk Circle*. Find the play-within-a-play in each of these examples.

the dear murderèd a murdered father

drab, scullion low-ranking servants (or prostitutes)

presently immediately
malefactions evil deeds

organ voice

tent probe
quick centre, most tender part
a do blench he flinches

potent powerful
grounds evidence
relative relevant, conclusive
conscience i.e. and therefore guilt

Why, what an ass am I! This is most brave,   535
That I, the son of the dear murderèd,
Prompted to my revenge by heaven and hell,
Must like a whore unpack my heart with words,
And fall a-cursing like a very drab,
A scullion!   540
Fie upon't, foh! About, my brains. Hum, I have heard
That guilty creatures sitting at a play
Have by the very cunning of the scene
Been struck so to the soul, that presently
They have proclaimed their malefactions;   545
For murder, though it have no tongue, will speak
With most miraculous organ. I'll have these players
Play something like the murder of my father
Before mine uncle. I'll observe his looks,
I'll tent him to the quick. If a do blench,   550
I know my course. The spirit that I have seen
May be a devil – and the devil hath power
T'assume a pleasing shape. Yea, and perhaps,
Out of my weakness and my melancholy,
As he is very potent with such spirits,   555
Abuses me to damn me. I'll have grounds
More relative than this. The play's the thing
Wherein I'll catch the conscience of the king.   *Exit*

Looking back at Act 2
Activities for groups or individuals

1 Players within a play

One of the activities on page 96 suggests that you look at plays within a play. Here, consider what players arriving on stage means for *Hamlet* as a whole. In watching a movie or theatre production of *Hamlet*, or reading it, we are engaged in a 'suspension of disbelief' and enter the fictional world of Elsinore. To then be presented with players is to be challenged yet further: is fictionality relative, with figures we take as fictional becoming 'real' as another dimension of fictionality is introduced? The notion of 'metatheatre' or 'theatre about theatre' is one way of looking at this issue; another is that of *mise en abyme* or 'standing between two mirrors'.

a Is the players' presence further emphasis on the theme of appearance and reality? If so, why is that theme so prevalent in Shakespeare's plays and *Hamlet* in particular?

b Looking at Activity 2 on this page, see if you can identify a unifying theme for the play as a whole. Is it appearance and reality or is there a further general theme in the play that unites all the others, such as the nature of existence and identity?

c Write a short essay on what you take to be the central themes in *Hamlet*. Be prepared to adapt your views as you explore further in the following acts.

2 The development of themes in Act 2

Several interconnected themes have been developed in Act 2: spying and surveillance; the notion of confinement and escape; distinctions between appearance and reality; personal and public engagement, and the formation of identity; the nature of madness; duplicity and delay; and the nature of love, including physicality.

a Add to the diagram of themes that you began on page 12. Try to include all the various themes that have been developed through Act 2. Provide quotations to illustrate each of the themes and the connections between them.

b Present a poster to the rest of the class showing how you see the emerging and related themes in the play.

3 Nine episodes

A great deal happens in Scene 2. You will find that new events begin at the following lines: 1, 40, 85, 166, 213, 295, 339, 490 and 501.

a Use these lines to identify the separate events in the scene, and write a single sentence or create a storyboard about each.

b Choose one line from each section that you think best expresses the dramatic action. Then use your chosen lines to work out a very short enactment of the whole scene.

4 Character development

Take one of the characters in the play and follow his or her progress through Acts 1 and 2. Almost all the main characters in *Hamlet* develop throughout the play. Can you identify the different sides of the character you have chosen, and provide evidence in the form of quotations to back up your ideas?

Can you identify the characters in these images from Act 2? Rank these character representations in order of preference and justify your choice to the rest of the class.

99

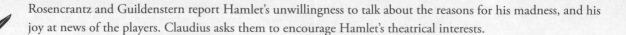
1 Rosencrantz and Guildenstern's report

Rosencrantz and Guildenstern report on their meeting with Hamlet. But how truthfully do they describe that conversation?

- Turn back to Act 2 Scene 2 and refresh your memory by quickly reading lines 215–348. Then read aloud what Rosencrantz and Guildenstern say in the script opposite and decide if they give Claudius a true and full account of their meeting.

▼ Rosencrantz with Hamlet in a National Theatre production from 2010.

Characters
Claudius

Claudius begins this third act with a thorough investigation of Hamlet's behaviour. He seems keen to find out the cause of Hamlet's madness, and is delighted that Hamlet is engaged by the arrival of the players.

- It appears that Claudius has been checking up on Hamlet's behaviour. Write an entry in Claudius's private diary to reflect his understanding of Hamlet's state.

drift of circumstance indirect talk
confusion seeming madness
Grating disturbing, roughening

distracted mad

forward ready, willing
sounded questioned

disposition inclination
Niggard sparse (Hamlet was unwilling to talk)
assay urge

o'er-raught overtook

about around
order a commission

a further edge
more encouragement

Act 3 Scene 1
The Great Hall of Elsinore Castle

Enter KING, QUEEN, POLONIUS, OPHELIA, ROSENCRANTZ,
GUILDENSTERN, LORDS

CLAUDIUS And can you by no drift of circumstance
Get from him why he puts on this confusion,
Grating so harshly all his days of quiet
With turbulent and dangerous lunacy?

ROSENCRANTZ He does confess he feels himself distracted, 5
But from what cause a will by no means speak.

GUILDENSTERN Nor do we find him forward to be sounded,
But with a crafty madness keeps aloof
When we would bring him on to some confession
Of his true state.

GERTRUDE   Did he receive you well? 10

ROSENCRANTZ Most like a gentleman.

GUILDENSTERN But with much forcing of his disposition.

ROSENCRANTZ Niggard of question, but of our demands
Most free in his reply.

GERTRUDE   Did you assay him
To any pastime? 15

ROSENCRANTZ Madam, it so fell out that certain players
We o'er-raught on the way; of these we told him,
And there did seem in him a kind of joy
To hear of it. They are about the court,
And as I think, they have already order 20
This night to play before him.

POLONIUS   'Tis most true,
And he beseeched me to entreat your majesties
To hear and see the matter.

CLAUDIUS With all my heart, and it doth much content me
To hear him so inclined. 25
Good gentlemen, give him a further edge,
And drive his purpose on to these delights.

ROSENCRANTZ We shall my lord.

Exeunt Rosencrantz and Guildenstern

Claudius and Polonius prepare to spy on Hamlet to discover if his love for Ophelia has really driven him mad. Claudius's guilty conscience surfaces and reminds him of the murder of King Hamlet.

Stagecraft

Do Polonius and/or Ophelia overhear? (in pairs or threes)

Every production must decide whether Ophelia and/or Polonius overhear Claudius's lines 28–37.

a Imagine that Ophelia does overhear. One person slowly reads Claudius's lines, pausing frequently. In each pause, the other person, as Ophelia, speaks her thoughts. Change roles and repeat. Then discuss whether you would have Ophelia overhear if you were directing the play. Consider the dramatic implications of each alternative.

b Now add Polonius into the mix. Does he hear, and how does it affect him? Would he acknowledge to Ophelia that he had heard?

c Starting from 'Madam, I wish it may', enact lines 42–55, showing how you would position yourselves as Claudius, Ophelia and Polonius. Compare your interpretation with that of other groups.

1 Catching the conscience of the king

Line 50 reveals that the Ghost's story is true – Claudius is guilty of murder. Claudius's conscience pricks him as he hears Polonius say that a pious appearance often covers evil.

a Design a mask that represents the disguises described in lines 47–9 or lines 51–3. As you read on, think about where masks might be appropriate in other parts of the play. How would masks help or hinder the interpretation in each case?

b Look through the rest of the play for other examples of asides. Divide the instances you find across the class, and work out individually or in pairs how you would present the aside to the audience. Would it be spoken directly to the audience; speaking to oneself, as if reflecting; to another character; or in some other way?

closely secretly

Affront meet, encounter
Lawful espials official and justified spies
bestow hide

is behaved behaves

wonted way usual behaviour, sanity
To both your honours to the credit of you both

Gracious your grace
this book probably a prayer book, which by its nature and paleness may reflect back on Ophelia's state
colour explain
devotion's visage the show of praying
sugar o'er conceal, sweetly cover

smart sharp
plastering art make-up

painted deceitful

102

CLAUDIUS   Sweet Gertrude, leave us too,
For we have closely sent for Hamlet hither,
That he, as 'twere by accident, may here   30
Affront Ophelia. Her father and myself,
Lawful espials,
Will so bestow ourselves, that seeing unseen,
We may of their encounter frankly judge,
And gather by him, as he is behaved,   35
If't be th'affliction of his love or no
That thus he suffers for.

GERTRUDE   I shall obey you.
And for your part Ophelia, I do wish
That your good beauties be the happy cause
Of Hamlet's wildness. So shall I hope your virtues   40
Will bring him to his wonted way again,
To both your honours.

OPHELIA   Madam, I wish it may.
                              [*Exit Gertrude with Lords*]

POLONIUS   Ophelia walk you here. – Gracious, so please you,
We will bestow ourselves. – Read on this book,
That show of such an exercise may colour   45
Your loneliness. – We are oft to blame in this:
'Tis too much proved, that with devotion's visage,
And pious action, we do sugar o'er
The devil himself.

CLAUDIUS   (*Aside*)   Oh, 'tis too true.
How smart a lash that speech doth give my conscience!   50
The harlot's cheek, beautied with plastering art,
Is not more ugly to the thing that helps it
Than is my deed to my most painted word.
O heavy burden!

POLONIUS   I hear him coming. Let's withdraw, my lord.   55
                              Exeunt Claudius and Polonius

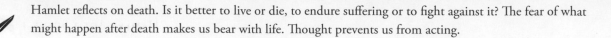

Hamlet reflects on death. Is it better to live or die, to endure suffering or to fight against it? The fear of what might happen after death makes us bear with life. Thought prevents us from acting.

1 Advising Hamlet (in pairs)

a Imagine you are a director working with the actor playing Hamlet on his speech opposite. Divide the speech into sections. You might agree or disagree with the following:

- **Line 56** Hamlet wonders whether to commit suicide.
- **Lines 57–60** He wonders whether to endure or fight.
- **Lines 60–4** He looks forward to the sleep of death.
- **Lines 64–8** He is troubled with thoughts of what happens after death.
- **Lines 68–82** He believes that what stops people committing suicide, in spite of all oppressions in this life, is the fear of terrors that await the dead.
- **Lines 83–8** He decides that thinking stops us from acting.

b Choose one or more of the following activities on the soliloquy:

- **An exercise in persuasion** Aim to build up the soliloquy as a developing argument, each speaking in turn one of the sections.
- **Speak it aloud in different ways** Examples could be: as if Hamlet has only suicide in mind; as if Hamlet has only killing Claudius in mind; as a philosophy lecture to a group of students.
- **A dramatic reading for radio** Use sound effects, music, and short phrases from elsewhere in the play to enhance the soliloquy.

c Afterwards, write director's notes on how best to speak the soliloquy on stage. You might also like to watch/listen to two or three different film or radio versions to inform your ideas.

Language in the play
'To be, or not to be': the metaphorical dimension

This is a speech often quoted or cited. Its language is rich, driven by the thought processes explored in the activities above. It says much about some of the themes (existence and death, identity and injustice, the relationship between thought and action); and Hamlet's character (the depth of his conscious reflection on his position, his dilemma).

- Focus on the metaphors that are used in this speech. Map them in thematic clusters, and draw links to show how they relate to each other and to the ideas expressed in the speech. The metaphors could also be sketched in order to understand them visually.

slings missiles, either hand-thrown or via cannons

arms weapons

is heir to inherits, experiences

consummation ending

rub obstacle

shuffled off … coil died (shaken off the physicality of human life)

pause pause for thought, or ending

respect aspect

the whips and scorns the hurts

contumely humiliating insults

disprized unvalued

office people in authority

patient merit of th'unworthy merit often goes unrecognised by unworthy people

quietus release

bare bodkin mere dagger

fardels burdens

bourn boundary

native hue of resolution natural determination to act

sicklied o'er unhealthily covered, hampered

of great pitch and moment of considerable scale and importance

Soft you quiet

orisons prayers

Enter HAMLET

HAMLET To be, or not to be, that is the question –
Whether 'tis nobler in the mind to suffer
The slings and arrows of outrageous fortune,
Or to take arms against a sea of troubles,
And by opposing end them. To die, to sleep –   60
No more; and by a sleep to say we end
The heart-ache and the thousand natural shocks
That flesh is heir to – 'tis a consummation
Devoutly to be wished. To die, to sleep –
To sleep, perchance to dream. Ay, there's the rub, 65
For in that sleep of death what dreams may come,
When we have shuffled off this mortal coil,
Must give us pause. There's the respect
That makes calamity of so long life,
For who would bear the whips and scorns of time, 70
Th'oppressor's wrong, the proud man's contumely,
The pangs of disprized love, the law's delay,
The insolence of office, and the spurns
That patient merit of th'unworthy takes,
When he himself might his quietus make   75
With a bare bodkin? Who would fardels bear,
To grunt and sweat under a weary life,
But that the dread of something after death,
The undiscovered country from whose bourn
No traveller returns, puzzles the will,   80
And makes us rather bear those ills we have
Than fly to others that we know not of?
Thus conscience does make cowards of us all,
And thus the native hue of resolution
Is sicklied o'er with the pale cast of thought, 85
And enterprises of great pitch and moment
With this regard their currents turn awry
And lose the name of action. Soft you now,
The fair Ophelia. – Nymph, in thy orisons
Be all my sins remembered.

OPHELIA   Good my lord, 90
How does your honour for this many a day?

Ophelia attempts to return Hamlet's gifts. Hamlet taunts her, saying that he once loved her, then denying it. He orders her to a nunnery and self-loathingly accuses himself of vices. Ophelia lies about her father.

1 Different stresses = different meanings (in pairs)

Try five different ways of speaking line 96 ('I never gave you aught.'). Each time, heavily stress a different word. Talk together about how each version results in different possible interpretations.

2 Three decisions – no 'right' answers!

a Draw up a list of possible reasons that might explain Hamlet's bitter treatment of Ophelia. Put them in order of 'most likely' to 'least likely'. What is your evidence?

b Does Hamlet urge Ophelia to go to a convent because there she will be safe from (or renounce) the temptations and corruption of the world? Or is Hamlet being sarcastic, and by 'nunnery' means 'brothel'? Which interpretation seems more likely to you, and why? Does Hamlet think she is lying when she says 'At home, my lord'? How might such a belief colour his future actions?

c Beauty will corrupt virtue more easily than virtue can make beautiful people virtuous or pure, asserts Hamlet (lines 111–14). Is he thinking mainly of Ophelia or of Gertrude at this moment? Is his pessimism characteristic? Give evidence for your decisions.

Themes

Sin and virtue; surveillance and power; and appearance and reality (in groups)

These three themes are manifest in the dialogue between Hamlet and Ophelia in the script opposite.

a In small groups, take one of these themes and identify lines where it is expressed. How does your theme and its expression here relate to the same theme elsewhere in the play? Present your case to the whole class.

b To bring the three themes together, draw a mind map of the themes and how (and where in the text) they interrelate.

c Identify any further themes in the dialogue between Hamlet and Ophelia, here and up to the end of this scene, and include them in the map.

remembrances gifts, love-tokens

wax grow

honest pure, a virgin

discourse to dealings with
commerce engagement

inoculate our old stock
graft on to our nature
relish of it still be tainted with
vice, i.e. we cannot graft virtue on
to a nature than is sinful
indifferent moderately
at my beck waiting to be
committed

HAMLET	I humbly thank you, well, well, well.
OPHELIA	My lord, I have remembrances of yours
	That I have longèd long to re-deliver.
	I pray you now receive them.
HAMLET	No, not I,
	I never gave you aught.
OPHELIA	My honoured lord, you know right well you did,
	And with them words of so sweet breath composed
	As made the things more rich. Their perfume lost,
	Take these again, for to the noble mind
	Rich gifts wax poor when givers prove unkind.
	There my lord.
HAMLET	Ha, ha, are you honest?
OPHELIA	My lord?
HAMLET	Are you fair?
OPHELIA	What means your lordship?
HAMLET	That if you be honest and fair, your honesty should admit no discourse to your beauty.
OPHELIA	Could beauty, my lord, have better commerce than with honesty?
HAMLET	Ay truly, for the power of beauty will sooner transform honesty from what it is to a bawd, than the force of honesty can translate beauty into his likeness. This was sometime a paradox, but now the time gives it proof. I did love you once.
OPHELIA	Indeed my lord you made me believe so.
HAMLET	You should not have believed me, for virtue cannot so inoculate our old stock but we shall relish of it. I loved you not.
OPHELIA	I was the more deceived.
HAMLET	Get thee to a nunnery – why wouldst thou be a breeder of sinners? I am myself indifferent honest, but yet I could accuse me of such things, that it were better my mother had not borne me. I am very proud, revengeful, ambitious, with more offences at my beck than I have thoughts to put them in, imagination to give them shape, or time to act them in. What should such fellows as I do crawling between earth and heaven? We are arrant knaves all, believe none of us. Go thy ways to a nunnery. Where's your father?
OPHELIA	At home my lord.
HAMLET	Let the doors be shut upon him, that he may play the fool nowhere but in's own house. Farewell.

Line numbers: 95, 100, 105, 110, 115, 120, 125

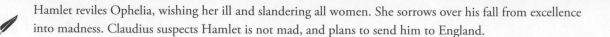

Hamlet reviles Ophelia, wishing her ill and slandering all women. She sorrows over his fall from excellence into madness. Claudius suspects Hamlet is not mad, and plans to send him to England.

1 Experiencing a tongue-lashing (in large groups)

This activity helps bring out the devastating power of Hamlet's verbal assault on Ophelia.

- One person volunteers to take the part of Ophelia. The others surround her as Hamlet. The 'Hamlets' select short extracts from lines 103–43 (e.g. 'are you honest?' 'Get thee to a nunnery', 'marry a fool'). The Hamlets hurl their insults at Ophelia, who tries to get away from them, saying 'What means your lordship?' It can be a very cruel experience for Ophelia – so don't force anyone to take on the role.

Characters

Ophelia and Hamlet

a **How should Ophelia be played?** There is debate about how to play Ophelia: as a meek, passive victim of Hamlet's anger, or as a stronger character. Try lines 144–55 in both ways.

b **Hamlet: Renaissance man – or idealised prince?** In lines 145–8, Ophelia paints a picture of the ideal prince. Hamlet exemplified the ideal qualities of the courtier, soldier and scholar. He was the hope and crowning glory of Denmark. He was the very mirror and model of behaviour and taste, looked up to as an ideal example by everyone.

- To what extent is Hamlet aware of his shortcomings as a person and as a prince? Do you think his inaction is a result of his sense of himself as a perfectionist and 'man of contemplation'? Write a paragraph or two about the complexities of his character as demonstrated here. You might like to compare him to Fortinbras and/or Laertes.

dowry wedding gift
chaste virginal
calumny malicious lies

paintings make-up
jig dance
amble walk seductively
lisp speak seductively
nickname God's creatures make affectionate nicknames for animals and people
make ... ignorance pretend your immorality comes from innocence
mo more
expectancy in line for the throne
glass mirror

blown blossoming-ripe

on brood brooding
hatch birth, outcome
disclose result
for to in order to
I have ... determination I have decided
tribute Danegeld (protection money paid by England to Denmark)

OPHELIA Oh help him you sweet heavens!   130

HAMLET If thou dost marry, I'll give thee this plague for thy dowry: be thou as chaste as ice, as pure as snow, thou shalt not escape calumny. Get thee to a nunnery, go. Farewell. Or if thou wilt needs marry, marry a fool, for wise men know well enough what monsters you make of them. To a nunnery go, and quickly too. Farewell.   135

OPHELIA O heavenly powers, restore him!

HAMLET I have heard of your paintings too, well enough. God hath given you one face and you make yourselves another. You jig, you amble, and you lisp, you nickname God's creatures, and make your wantonness your ignorance. Go to, I'll no more on't, it hath made   140
me mad. I say we will have no mo marriages. Those that are married already, all but one shall live, the rest shall keep as they are. To a nunnery, go.   *Exit*

OPHELIA Oh what a noble mind is here o'erthrown!
The courtier's, soldier's, scholar's, eye, tongue, sword,   145
Th'expectancy and rose of the fair state,
The glass of fashion and the mould of form,
Th'observed of all observers, quite, quite down,
And I of ladies most deject and wretched,
That sucked the honey of his music vows,   150
Now see that noble and most sovereign reason,
Like sweet bells jangled, out of time and harsh;
That unmatched form and feature of blown youth
Blasted with ecstasy. Oh woe is me
T'have seen what I have seen, see what I see.   155

Enter KING *and* POLONIUS

CLAUDIUS Love? His affections do not that way tend;
Nor what he spake, though it lacked form a little,
Was not like madness. There's something in his soul
O'er which his melancholy sits on brood,
And I do doubt the hatch and the disclose   160
Will be some danger; which for to prevent,
I have in quick determination
Thus set it down: he shall with speed to England
For the demand of our neglected tribute.

Polonius agrees with Claudius's plan to send Hamlet to England. He proposes to spy on Gertrude's meeting with Hamlet. In Scene 2, Hamlet instructs the players on acting style.

1 A loving father? (in small groups)

'How now Ophelia? / You need not tell us what Lord Hamlet said, / We heard it all.' These are the last words spoken by Polonius to his daughter in the play.

- Just how does he speak them? Remember that she has been on the receiving end of a brutal tongue-lashing from Hamlet. Is Polonius sympathetic, officious, uncaring or something else? Experiment with styles to see if you can agree on how he should speak the lines to match his character and the occasion.

2 'must not unwatched go'

Once again the theme of surveillance is given verbal expression in Claudius's final line in the scene.

- Suggest how Ophelia and Polonius react to it, and how they leave the stage.

Write about it
A framed scene (in fives)

Act 3 Scene 1 starts and ends with Claudius, who is engineering the surveillance of Hamlet. In the middle of the scene is Hamlet's soliloquy, 'To be or not to be'.

a Act out a symposium, chaired by a director, TV host or chairperson, who comments on all four characters and reacts to comments from each of the characters. Such enactment will enable an interrogation of the actions and motives of each character.

b Write about this scene from the point of view of one or more of the four main characters in it: Claudius, Hamlet, Polonius and Ophelia. The aim of the writing activity is to try a different genre from the essay: to speak in different voices, both from the point of view of the character, and perhaps also from the view of an actor playing the part. Make close reference to the text to support your views, as you would in a conventional essay.

c When you have explored the action and motivation from the 'inside', through the characters' voices, step back and consider again: why is the scene framed by Claudius?

Haply perhaps
variable objects notable sights
something-settled unsettled

From fashion of at odds with

commencement start

fit appropriate

round strict, forthright, straight

trippingly lightly
as lief rather
saw the air wave your arms about
temperance steadiness, balance, moderation
robustious violent, loud-mouthed
periwig-pated wig-wearing
groundlings poorest theatregoers, who stood in the open yard in front of the stage
are capable of understand
Termagant an imaginary god
Herod seen as the ranting tyrant of biblical stories

Haply the seas, and countries different, 165
With variable objects, shall expel
This something-settled matter in his heart,
Whereon his brains still beating puts him thus
From fashion of himself. What think you on't?

POLONIUS It shall do well. But yet do I believe 170
The origin and commencement of his grief
Sprung from neglected love. How now Ophelia?
You need not tell us what Lord Hamlet said,
We heard it all. My lord, do as you please,
But if you hold it fit, after the play, 175
Let his queen mother all alone entreat him
To show his grief. Let her be round with him,
And I'll be placed, so please you, in the ear
Of all their conference. If she find him not,
To England send him; or confine him where 180
Your wisdom best shall think.

CLAUDIUS   It shall be so.
Madness in great ones must not unwatched go.

Exeunt

Act 3 Scene 2
The Great Hall of Elsinore Castle

Enter HAMLET *and two or three of the* PLAYERS

HAMLET Speak the speech I pray you as I pronounced it to you,
trippingly on the tongue; but if you mouth it as many of our players
do, I had as lief the town-crier spoke my lines. Nor do not saw the
air too much with your hand thus, but use all gently; for in the
very torrent, tempest, and, as I may say, whirlwind of your passion, 5
you must acquire and beget a temperance that may give it
smoothness. Oh, it offends me to the soul to hear a robustious
periwig-pated fellow tear a passion to totters, to very rags, to split
the ears of the groundlings, who for the most part are capable of
nothing but inexplicable dumb-shows and noise. I would have such 10
a fellow whipped for o'erdoing Termagant – it out-Herods Herod.
Pray you avoid it.

Hamlet urges moderation in acting. He defines theatre as the mirror of nature and society. He criticises bad actors and overambitious clowns. Preparations for the play begin.

Themes

'some necessary question of the play'

Every play has a set of 'necessary questions' (lines 34–5): central themes or issues. In the 'Themes' boxes in this book, you will have identified a number of themes already. Another 'necessary question' of this play is revenge. But there is an irony in Hamlet's advice, because his delay in taking his revenge can be seen as his own continued refusal to consider that 'necessary question'.

a What are the 'necessary questions' in *Hamlet*? Make a list of what you consider these to be. Compare your list with those of other students and those discussed on pages 242–53. Remember that themes may not always be characterised by single words such as 'revenge' or 'death', but can be more complex; for example, 'the relationship between physicality and the soul'.

- If revenge is a theme, it is also a way of constructing the plot and positioning the characters in relation to the plot/theme.
- One further theme that is emerging in this central part of the play is via the device of the 'play-within-a-play'. Shakespeare uses the device in a number of plays, as we have seen, but he is also fascinated by the 'idea of the play'. Part of the idea seems to be to make the audience conscious of the artifice of the action.

b Update your themes mind map from Act 3 Scene 1 in the light of the themes of revenge and its relation to natural and formal justice; and the notion of 'the idea of the play'. How do these themes relate to those identified so far?

c Hold a forum in class in six groups, each of which argues that their theme is the dominant one in the play to date. Use these themes as a starting point:

- revenge and justice
- appearance and reality
- the notion of the play; or 'the play's the thing'
- physicality and the soul, and their relation to identity and existence
- death, sin, love and lust
- honour, duty and the individual in relation to the state.

warrant will do so

modesty moderation
from the purpose so far from the purpose

scorn be critical of
the very age ... pressure give a true representation of the times
come tardy off imperfectly done
censure judgement

profanely blasphemously
gait walk

journeymen unskilled workmen

indifferently to some extent

barren empty-headed

presently immediately

just well balanced
As e'er ... coped withal as I've ever met

1 PLAYER	I warrant your honour.
HAMLET	Be not too tame neither, but let your own discretion be your tutor. Suit the action to the word, the word to the action, with this special observance, that you o'erstep not the modesty of nature. For anything so o'erdone is from the purpose of playing, whose end both at the first and now, was and is, to hold as 'twere the mirror up to nature; to show virtue her own feature, scorn her own image, and the very age and body of the time his form and pressure. Now this overdone, or come tardy off, though it makes the unskilful laugh, cannot but make the judicious grieve, the censure of the which one must in your allowance o'erweigh a whole theatre of others. Oh, there be players that I have seen play, and heard others praise and that highly, not to speak it profanely, that neither having th'accent of Christians, nor the gait of Christian, pagan, nor man, have so strutted and bellowed that I have thought some of nature's journeymen had made men, and not made them well, they imitated humanity so abominably.
1 PLAYER	I hope we have reformed that indifferently with us, sir.
HAMLET	Oh reform it altogether. And let those that play your clowns speak no more than is set down for them, for there be of them that will themselves laugh, to set on some quantity of barren spectators to laugh too, though in the meantime some necessary question of the play be then to be considered. That's villainous, and shows a most pitiful ambition in the fool that uses it. Go make you ready.

Exeunt Players

Enter POLONIUS, ROSENCRANTZ *and* GUILDENSTERN

	How now my lord, will the king hear this piece of work?
POLONIUS	And the queen too, and that presently.
HAMLET	Bid the players make haste.

Exit Polonius

	Will you two help to hasten them?
ROSENCRANTZ	Ay my lord.

Exeunt Rosencrantz and Guildenstern

HAMLET	What ho, Horatio!

Enter HORATIO

HORATIO	Here sweet lord, at your service.
HAMLET	Horatio, thou art e'en as just a man As e'er my conversation coped withal.

Hamlet praises Horatio's well-balanced character and criticises obsequious flatterers. He urges Horatio to watch Claudius closely for any guilty reaction during the play.

Language in the play
Vivid images: flattery and fortune (in pairs)

Lines 50–2 describe the sweet-tongued courtier ('candied tongue') who flatters vain people in high positions ('lick absurd pomp'), and bows and scrapes readily ('crook the pregnant … knee') for profit ('thrift'). Lines 57–8 and 60–1 turn Fortune into a woman, buffeting and rewarding human beings, or treating them like a musical instrument ('pipe') on which she can play any tune she pleases ('sound what stop she please').

- Identify other images in Hamlet's speech opposite, and write down the quotations that contain them.
- Discuss the meaning of the images.
- How do these images, and those of sickly sweetness and fortune mentioned above, relate to the themes of the play you have explored so far?

1 Hamlet's speech (in pairs)

Hamlet's speech is not a soliloquy, but simply a speech as part of a conversational exchange with Horatio. Nevertheless, it has the weight of an extended reflection on human nature and fortune. It also includes a set of instructions about the observing of Claudius at the forthcoming play.

a The speech appears to fall into two halves. Can you identify where? Why do you think this is?

b Prepare a performance of the speech by deciding:

- how you will vary the pace throughout
- whether Horatio reacts to the questions posed in the first half (and how)
- which lines have a more public import, and which are intended for Horatio's ears only.

advancement favour
revenue wealth

fawning inappropriate pleading for money

election choice
Sh'ath sealed she has chosen

commeddled mingled

prithee pray you

afoot in action, presented

very comment keenest watching

occulted hidden

unkennel reveal

Vulcan's stithy god of fire's smithy (workshop)

rivet fix

censure of his seeming judgement of his looks

a steal aught he hides anything

pay the theft pay for my own lack of attention

idle unoccupied (or mad)

HORATIO	Oh my dear lord.
HAMLET	Nay, do not think I flatter,

For what advancement may I hope from thee,
That no revenue hast but thy good spirits
To feed and clothe thee? Why should the poor be flattered?
No, let the candied tongue lick absurd pomp   50
And crook the pregnant hinges of the knee
Where thrift may follow fawning. Dost thou hear?
Since my dear soul was mistress of her choice,
And could of men distinguish her election,
Sh'ath sealed thee for herself, for thou hast been   55
As one in suffering all that suffers nothing,
A man that Fortune's buffets and rewards
Hast tane with equal thanks. And blest are those
Whose blood and judgement are so well commeddled
That they are not a pipe for Fortune's finger   60
To sound what stop she please. Give me that man
That is not passion's slave, and I will wear him
In my heart's core, ay in my heart of heart,
As I do thee. Something too much of this.
There is a play tonight before the king: 65
One scene of it comes near the circumstance
Which I have told thee of my father's death.
I prithee when thou seest that act afoot,
Even with the very comment of thy soul
Observe my uncle. If his occulted guilt   70
Do not itself unkennel in one speech,
It is a damnèd ghost that we have seen,
And my imaginations are as foul
As Vulcan's stithy. Give him heedful note,
For I mine eyes will rivet to his face,   75
And after we will both our judgements join
In censure of his seeming.

HORATIO	Well my lord.

If a steal aught the whilst this play is playing
And scape detecting, I will pay the theft.

Sound a flourish

HAMLET	They are coming to the play. I must be idle. 80

Get you a place.

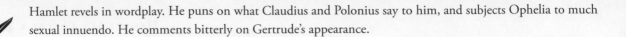

Hamlet revels in wordplay. He puns on what Claudius and Polonius say to him, and subjects Ophelia to much sexual innuendo. He comments bitterly on Gertrude's appearance.

1 Hamlet's wordplay: insulting and obsessive?

(in fives)

Hamlet has just promised to be 'idle' – perhaps to appear mad. His words now are deliberately disconcerting as he seizes on meanings that neither Claudius nor Polonius nor Ophelia intends. Claudius's line 82 means 'How are you?' but Hamlet interprets 'fares' as meaning 'feeds', so he replies as if Claudius had asked him what he has eaten.

Hamlet mocks Claudius about his earlier promise (that Hamlet should succeed him), suggesting that it is just empty air. He also mocks Polonius, punning on 'Brutus' and 'Capitol' with 'brute' and 'capital'. For Shakespeare's company, this was also a theatrical in-joke, because Shakespeare wrote *Julius Caesar* shortly before *Hamlet*, and the same pair of actors probably played Brutus/Caesar and Hamlet/Polonius.

a Take parts as Hamlet, Claudius, Polonius, Gertrude and Ophelia. Read the script opposite several times. Stress Hamlet's puns. Then, in role, say how you think each character regards Hamlet at this moment.

b There is a theatrical tradition that when Shakespeare's dialogue is set out as opposite (each speech in a single line) the lines are spoken rapidly, with no pauses between speeches. Experiment with that style of delivery, then speak again using pauses. Which style seems more effective dramatically?

c Notice that Hamlet ends by returning to his obsession: his mother's sexuality and marriage to Claudius. Explore ways of speaking lines 111–20 to express Hamlet's intense feelings.

d The dialogue is rapid here, reflecting perhaps Hamlet's excitement as the play is about to begin. Variations in pace are characteristic of productions of *Hamlet*, especially by Hamlet himself. Look through Act 3 Scene 2 and then, on a copy for your Director's Journal, mark it up for variations in pace. Why are some sections better played faster than others?

e Do you think Hamlet's lines to Ophelia are private or are they meant to be heard by the others present? What difference does that make to our understanding of their relationship and Hamlet's motive here? Is the exchange merely light sexual banter between two people who have a history of physical intimacy, or is it intended to humiliate Ophelia by publicly addressing her as if she was a whore?

fares does, eats

cousin (used for any close relative)

chameleon lizard that changes colour (and was thought to eat only air)

capons fattened chickens

Capitol seat of government in ancient Rome

calf fool

metal a pun on 'mettle' (= spirit)

country matters sexual intercourse

your only jig-maker I'm the only comedian here

Danish march (trumpets and kettle-drums). Enter KING, QUEEN, POLONIUS, OPHELIA, ROSENCRANTZ, GUILDENSTERN *and other* LORDS *attendant, with his* GUARD *carrying torches*

CLAUDIUS   How fares our cousin Hamlet?

HAMLET   Excellent i'faith, of the chameleon's dish: I eat the air, promise-crammed. You cannot feed capons so.

CLAUDIUS   I have nothing with this answer Hamlet, these words are not mine.   85

HAMLET   No, nor mine now. – My lord, you played once i'th'university, you say.

POLONIUS   That did I my lord, and was accounted a good actor.

HAMLET   And what did you enact?   90

POLONIUS   I did enact Julius Caesar. I was killed i'th'Capitol. Brutus killed me.

HAMLET   It was a brute part of him to kill so capital a calf there. – Be the players ready?

ROSENCRANTZ   Ay my lord, they stay upon your patience.   95

GERTRUDE   Come hither my dear Hamlet, sit by me.

HAMLET   No good mother, here's metal more attractive.

POLONIUS   Oh ho, do you mark that?

HAMLET   Lady, shall I lie in your lap?

OPHELIA   No my lord.   100

HAMLET   I mean, my head upon your lap?

OPHELIA   Ay my lord.

HAMLET   Do you think I meant country matters?

OPHELIA   I think nothing my lord.

HAMLET   That's a fair thought to lie between maids' legs.   105

OPHELIA   What is, my lord?

HAMLET   Nothing.

OPHELIA   You are merry my lord.

HAMLET   Who, I?

OPHELIA   Ay my lord.   110

HAMLET   O God, your only jig-maker. What should a man do but be merry? for look you how cheerfully my mother looks, and my father died within's two hours.

OPHELIA   Nay, 'tis twice two months my lord.

Hamlet comments bitterly on his mother's hasty second marriage. The dumb-show presents a mirror-image of the murder of Hamlet's father. Hamlet again vents his cynicism on Ophelia.

▲ Hamlet and the court watch the dumb-show. How would you arrange the onstage audience if you were directing this scene?

1 The dumb-show (in groups of four or five)

In Elizabethan drama, a dumb-show (mime) often preceded the play, summarising the action ('imports the argument'). In *Hamlet*, this mimed performance prefigures the play-within-a-play to come. The dumb-show presents a sleeping king being murdered by a man who steals both his crown and queen. It is a mirror-image of what Claudius did to his brother.

a Following the stage directions carefully, enact the mime, making it clear that the action is intended to mirror the death of Hamlet's father at the hands of Claudius.

b Discuss how you think Claudius will behave as he sees his own villainy being acted out in front of him. Might he ignore it altogether (as he talks lovingly to Gertrude)? Or does he gradually realise what it means, reacting in one of a variety of ways (with fear, suspicion, anger or in some other way)? Or do you think he might watch it imperturbably, utterly calm? Take turns in acting out different reactions from Claudius, and decide which you find the most convincing given the situation and what you know of Claudius's character.

sables expensive mourning clothes

a must build ... on he must build churches or be forgotten

hobby-horse prostitute, or character in a morris dance

Hoboys oboes

makes show of protestation shows her love

declines lays

passionate action frenzied expression of passion

mutes silent actors

condole as in 'condolences'

harsh resistant

miching mallecho sneaky villainy

imports signifies

the argument the story and its implications

naught improper, rude

clemency kindness

posy of a ring a motto engraved on a ring

HAMLET   So long? Nay then let the devil wear black, for I'll have a suit   115
of sables. O heavens! die two months ago, and not forgotten yet?
Then there's hope a great man's memory may outlive his life half
a year, but byrlady a must build churches then, or else shall a suffer
not thinking on, with the hobby-horse, whose epitaph is, 'For O,
for O, the hobby-horse is forgot.'   120

Hoboys play. The dumb-show enters

Enter a KING *and a* QUEEN, *very lovingly, the Queen embracing him. She kneels
and makes show of protestation unto him. He takes her up, and declines his head
upon her neck. He lies him down upon a bank of flowers. She, seeing him asleep,
leaves him. Anon comes in another man, takes off his crown, kisses it, pours poison
in the sleeper's ears, and leaves him. The Queen returns, finds the King dead, and
makes passionate action. The poisoner, with some two or three mutes, comes in again,
seeming to condole with her. The dead body is carried away. The poisoner woos the
Queen with gifts. She seems harsh awhile, but in the end accepts his love. Exeunt*

OPHELIA   What means this my lord?
HAMLET   Marry this is miching mallecho, it means mischief.
OPHELIA   Belike this show imports the argument of the play?

Enter PROLOGUE

HAMLET   We shall know by this fellow; the players cannot keep counsel,
they'll tell all.   125
OPHELIA   Will a tell us what this show meant?
HAMLET   Ay, or any show that you'll show him. Be not you ashamed
to show, he'll not shame to tell you what it means.
OPHELIA   You are naught, you are naught. I'll mark the play.

PROLOGUE   For us and for our tragedy,   130
Here stooping to your clemency,
We beg your hearing patiently.

HAMLET   Is this a prologue, or the posy of a ring?
OPHELIA   'Tis brief my lord.
HAMLET   As woman's love.   135

The Player King speaks of thirty years of loving and holy marriage. The Player Queen expresses worries about his health, but vows not to marry again. He replies that vows are often broken.

Stagecraft

The 'masque' (in pairs)

The play-within-a-play takes the form of a 'masque', a popular type of entertainment in aristocratic circles in the Elizabethan period. Such masques were often short plays in highly ornate verse, concerning mythological or legendary figures or, in the case of the play in *Hamlet*, containing references to classical Greek and Roman mythology. They were not dynamic in form, like Shakespeare's own plays, but relatively static. Their energy, therefore, comes from the language and often from costume and setting.

* Research Elizabethan masques, and use the research either to write up a study of masques as background to your emerging writing on *Hamlet*, or to inform your own performance of the masque presented here.

Characters

Gertrude's reactions

Much of the attention in Act 3 so far has been on Claudius, but here the players' performance sheds as much light on her as it does on her new husband.

* One person reads the Player Queen's speeches, pausing after each unit of meaning (usually about two or three lines). In each pause, the others, in role, suggest what Gertrude thinks as she hears and sees herself portrayed on stage with her first husband.

1 A difference in style? (in small groups)

Place ten to fifteen lines from the players' speeches (e.g. lines 142–53) alongside roughly the same number of lines of Hamlet's (e.g. Act 2 Scene 2, lines 511–23). Compare the movement of the lines, the flow across line endings, the feeling(s) expressed and the length of the sentences. Discuss the differences you discover.

Phoebus' cart the sun
Neptune's salt wash the sea
Tellus' orbèd ground Earth
borrowed sheen reflected light
Hymen god of marriage
Unite commutual ... bands join in marriage

distrust you worry about you

quantity balance, due measure

operant powers ... do faculties (eyesight, and so on) are failing

wormwood bitter

instances motives
base ... thrift thoughts of money

Enter the PLAYER KING *and* QUEEN

PLAYER KING Full thirty times hath Phoebus' cart gone round
Neptune's salt wash and Tellus' orbèd ground,
And thirty dozen moons with borrowed sheen
About the world have times twelve thirties been,
Since love our hearts, and Hymen did our hands,   140
Unite commutual in most sacred bands.

PLAYER QUEEN   So many journeys may the sun and moon
Make us again count o'er ere love be done.
But woe is me, you are so sick of late,
So far from cheer and from your former state,   145
That I distrust you. Yet though I distrust,
Discomfort you my lord it nothing must.
For women's fear and love hold quantity,
In neither aught, or in extremity.
Now what my love is, proof hath made you know;   150
And as my love is sized, my fear is so.
[Where love is great, the littlest doubts are fear;
Where little fears grow great, great love grows there.]

PLAYER KING Faith, I must leave thee love, and shortly too:
My operant powers their functions leave to do;   155
And thou shalt live in this fair world behind,
Honoured, beloved; and haply one as kind
For husband shalt thou —

PLAYER QUEEN   Oh confound the rest!
Such love must needs be treason in my breast.
In second husband let me be accurst: 160
None wed the second but who killed the first.

HAMLET   That's wormwood, wormwood.

PLAYER QUEEN   The instances that second marriage move
Are base respects of thrift, but none of love.
A second time I kill my husband dead   165
When second husband kisses me in bed.

PLAYER KING I do believe you think what now you speak,
But what we do determine oft we break.

The Player King argues that strong intentions don't last, because time makes us forget. Changing social conditions change the emotions. But the Player Queen swears she will never remarry.

1 Editing *Hamlet*

Editors as well as directors sometimes cut parts of the play in order to fit their own conception of the unity of action and theme.

a Putting yourself in the role of an editor, and a contemporary of Shakespeare helping him to produce the first printed edition of the play, edit either this speech, this scene, Act 3 or the play as a whole. Working either in electronic format or on paper, cut lines and parts of the play that do not fit in to your conception of it. Make sure the cuts you make do not unduly interrupt the flow of the play.

b Justify your cuts to others, and discuss their feedback on your edited version.

c Perform your version, comparing it to the 'full' version as presented here. Observers of your shortened version might like to review your work, again making comparisons with the full script.

▶ This *Hamlet* prompt book from the seventeenth century has been marked up with notes on staging as well as changes to the script. The page shown here includes line 49 to line 148 of Act 3 Scene 2.

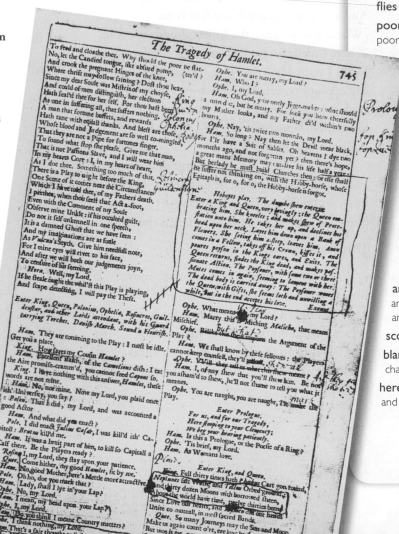

validity strength, sticking power

enactures actions

slender accident by chance
is not for aye does not last eternally

flies deserts him
poor advanced poor man promoted

not needs is rich
in want is poor
seasons him turns him into

devices still plans always

anchor's cheer hermit's food and condition (poverty and loneliness)
scope future
blanks the face of joy changes a happy face to a sad one
here and hence in this world and the next

Purpose is but the slave to memory,
Of violent birth but poor validity,   170
Which now like fruit unripe sticks on the tree,
But fall unshaken when they mellow be.
Most necessary 'tis that we forget
To pay ourselves what to ourselves is debt.
What to ourselves in passion we propose,   175
The passion ending, doth the purpose lose.
The violence of either grief or joy
Their own enactures with themselves destroy.
Where joy most revels, grief doth most lament;
Grief joys, joy grieves, on slender accident.   180
This world is not for aye, nor 'tis not strange
That even our loves should with our fortunes change,
For 'tis a question left us yet to prove,
Whether love lead fortune, or else fortune love.
The great man down, you mark his favourite flies;   185
The poor advanced makes friends of enemies,
And hitherto doth love on fortune tend;
For who not needs shall never lack a friend,
And who in want a hollow friend doth try
Directly seasons him his enemy.   190
But orderly to end where I begun,
Our wills and fates do so contrary run
That our devices still are overthrown;
Our thoughts are ours, their ends none of our own.
So think thou wilt no second husband wed,   195
But die thy thoughts when thy first lord is dead.

PLAYER QUEEN   Nor earth to me give food, nor heaven light,
Sport and repose lock from me day and night,
[To desperation turn my trust and hope,
An anchor's cheer in prison be my scope,]   200
Each opposite that blanks the face of joy
Meet what I would have well, and it destroy;
Both here and hence pursue me lasting strife,
If once a widow, ever I be wife.

HAMLET   If she should break it now!   205

The Player King sleeps. Hamlet hints that he knows Claudius is a murderer. He again subjects Ophelia to bitter sexual innuendo, and curses Lucianus, urging him to speak. Lucianus poisons the Player King.

Stagecraft

Gertrude and Lucianus (in pairs)

a Gertrude's judgement on the Player Queen has become a famous saying ('The lady doth protest too much methinks': she is over the top [too rash] with her promises of everlasting love.) Talk together about what lies behind Gertrude's comment. She probably suspects that Hamlet intends her to recognise herself in the Player Queen. So how might she speak line 211?

b Hamlet almost reveals his knowledge of Claudius's guilt when he seizes on the king's 'offence' and turns it into poison, traps and murder. But just how does Hamlet speak lines 214–20? Savagely? Off-handedly? Laughingly? Advise the actor.

c Lucianus speaks the language of melodrama. Judging by Hamlet's admonition ('Pox, leave thy damnable faces and begin'), he overacts too. Invent movement, expressions and gestures for lines 231–6.

fain … beguile I would gladly while away

Tropically metaphorically (a 'trope' is a figure of speech)
anon in due course
free souls clear consciences
galled jade saddle-sore horse
withers neck joints
unwrung not hurt

puppets some sexual reference is intended here, possibly to both male and female genitalia
dallying making love

Pox a curse on you
croaking … revenge (Hamlet misquotes an old play)

Confederate season good opportunity, perfect time
rank disgusting
Hecat queen of witches

usurp overthrow, destroy

1 Hamlet's seeming obsession with sex

Hamlet's sexual self seems highly charged, and highly distorted in his engagement with Ophelia in this act as a whole. He chastises her for sexual proclivity ('Get thee to a nunnery'). He seems to want to refer to sexual closeness with her. He frequently makes sexual puns.

a Imagine you are Hamlet's psychiatrist. You can either enact a consultancy with him, where you ask about his seeming obsession with sex and he talks in role, or go straight for a psychiatrist's report on his behaviour. How do you think Hamlet's obsessiveness is related to other aspects of his character?

b How would you play the role of Ophelia in lines 222–30? Coolly and at a polite distance from Hamlet's suggestiveness, or responding to him in kind, with sexual innuendo?

PLAYER KING   'Tis deeply sworn. Sweet, leave me here awhile;
My spirits grow dull, and fain I would beguile
The tedious day with sleep.

Sleeps

PLAYER QUEEN   Sleep rock thy brain,
And never come mischance between us twain.   *Exit*

HAMLET   Madam, how like you this play?   210

GERTRUDE   The lady doth protest too much methinks.

HAMLET   Oh but she'll keep her word.

CLAUDIUS   Have you heard the argument? Is there no offence in't?

HAMLET   No, no, they do but jest, poison in jest, no offence i'th'world.

CLAUDIUS   What do you call the play?   215

HAMLET   The Mousetrap. Marry how? Tropically. This play is the image of a murder done in Vienna. Gonzago is the duke's name, his wife Baptista. You shall see anon. 'Tis a knavish piece of work, but what o' that? Your majesty, and we that have free souls, it touches us not. Let the galled jade winch, our withers are unwrung.   220

Enter LUCIANUS

This is one Lucianus, nephew to the king.

OPHELIA   You are as good as a chorus my lord.

HAMLET   I could interpret between you and your love if I could see the puppets dallying.

OPHELIA   You are keen my lord, you are keen.   225

HAMLET   It would cost you a groaning to take off mine edge.

OPHELIA   Still better and worse.

HAMLET   So you mistake your husbands. Begin, murderer. Pox, leave thy damnable faces and begin. Come, the croaking raven doth bellow for revenge.   230

LUCIANUS   Thoughts black, hands apt, drugs fit, and time agreeing,
Confederate season, else no creature seeing.
Thou mixture rank, of midnight weeds collected,
With Hecat's ban thrice blasted, thrice infected,
Thy natural magic and dire property   235
On wholesome life usurp immediately.

Pours the poison in his ears

Claudius abruptly leaves the play, calling for light. Hamlet is delighted that his plot succeeded. He believes the Ghost has told the truth and that Claudius has revealed his guilt.

1 Claudius's reaction

Just how does Claudius react to Hamlet's words? Some productions show him terrified and agitated, and his confusion is reflected in his courtiers' behaviour. In other productions, his exit is calm and dignified. Write in your Director's Journal, with reasons, how you would stage lines 237–45.

2 A turning point?

The effect of the play on Claudius is often seen as a turning point for Hamlet. Which one line in the script opposite would you identify as the turning point, if any? When you have read to the end of the play, come back to this point and gauge for yourself whether or not you were right. If so, what is the significance of the turning point?

Themes

The fictional and the real (in small groups)

Claudius leaves the play with the telling statement, 'Give me some light. Away!' The fiction presented before him seems to have shocked him into a significant exit from the scene.

a Talk together about any plays, movies or texts that you may have come across that threw you into a reflection on your own life and experience, as if a 'mirror had been held up to nature'?

b Discuss the frames-within-frames that have been presented in the showing of the play: *Hamlet* itself is a fiction, and its lead character is also part of the fiction. Within the fiction, a dumb-show and 'The Mousetrap' have been presented. These have affected Claudius, and, in turn, ourselves as the audience. These frames-within-frames remind the audience of the power of plays and performance, linking to the 'necessary question' discussed on page 112. Update any notes you made then in the light of Claudius's sudden exit.

c How does the theme of fiction and reality link to themes you have already identified, like the relationship of sin to purity of conscience; of death to life; of the public and private; and of appearance and reality?

for's estate for his lands and title

is extant still exists

false fire blank ammunition (make-believe)

ungallèd unbloodied

a forest ... shoes elaborate actorly costume that Hamlet imagines he will be decked out in ('razed' is 'cut')

turn Turk get worse

cry pack

Damon close friend (from the legendary friendship of Damon and Pythias)

dismantled dead

Jove king of the ancient Roman gods

pajock villain

perdy by God (par dieu)

vouchsafe grant

HAMLET	A poisons him i'th'garden for's estate. His name's Gonzago. The story is extant, and written in very choice Italian. You shall see anon how the murderer gets the love of Gonzago's wife.
OPHELIA	The king rises.
HAMLET	What, frighted with false fire?
GERTRUDE	How fares my lord?
POLONIUS	Give o'er the play.
CLAUDIUS	Give me some light. Away!
LORDS	Lights, lights, lights!

240

245

Exeunt all but Hamlet and Horatio

HAMLET	Why, let the strucken deer go weep,
	The hart ungallèd play,
	For some must watch while some must sleep,
	Thus runs the world away.
	Would not this, sir, and a forest of feathers, if the rest of my fortunes turn Turk with me, with two provincial roses on my razed shoes, get me a fellowship in a cry of players, sir?
HORATIO	Half a share.
HAMLET	A whole one I.
	For thou dost know, O Damon dear,
	This realm dismantled was
	Of Jove himself, and now reigns here
	A very, very – pajock.
HORATIO	You might have rhymed.
HAMLET	O good Horatio, I'll take the ghost's word for a thousand pound. Didst perceive?
HORATIO	Very well my lord.
HAMLET	Upon the talk of the poisoning?
HORATIO	I did very well note him.

250

255

260

Enter ROSENCRANTZ *and* GUILDENSTERN

HAMLET	Ah ha! – Come, some music! Come, the recorders!
	For if the king like not the comedy,
	Why then – belike he likes it not, perdy.
	Come, some music!
GUILDENSTERN	Good my lord, vouchsafe me a word with you.
HAMLET	Sir, a whole history.
GUILDENSTERN	The king, sir –
HAMLET	Ay sir, what of him?

265

270

Hamlet disconcerts Guildenstern by deliberately misunderstanding him. He mocks Rosencrantz too, but agrees to visit Gertrude. Hamlet denies any hope of becoming king.

1 Shaking off old friends (in threes)

Hamlet begins to distance himself from Rosencrantz and Guildenstern as his purpose becomes clearer and he becomes more sure of Claudius's guilt.

- Take parts as Hamlet, Rosencrantz and Guildenstern, and read lines 269–336. Change roles so that everyone has a chance to read Hamlet. Emphasise the words with which Hamlet mocks the two courtiers. Notice particularly that lines 301–2 are the only time in the play that Hamlet uses the royal 'we'. Afterwards, talk together about the ways in which Hamlet clearly shows that their friendship is at an end.

2 Thoughts of kingship

a In line 308, Hamlet says that he lacks 'advancement' (has no ambition – or hope – to rule Denmark). But Rosencrantz assures Hamlet that he will succeed Claudius as king. Hamlet responds (line 311) with a proverb: 'But while the grass grows, the starving horse dies.' Think of one or two reasons why Hamlet makes this reply.

b There are few references in the play to Hamlet's rightful role as prince and successor to the throne of Denmark. Collect those that have been made up to this point (see in Act 1 Scene 2 and Act 1 Scene 5). Add to your list as you read on. When you reach the end of the play, write about the significance of these references.

c When we first meet Hamlet, he seems ill at ease in the Danish court, and more at ease with his friend Horatio and the members of the Watch. His relationship with Ophelia is a complex mix of the personal and public (his position as a prince). As we will see in Act 3 Scene 4, Hamlet's relationship with his mother, the queen, is also a potent mix of the personal and public. Continue to add to your map of the themes in the play, finding quotations to support your claims; or use the present scene as an opportunity to write a few paragraphs on the emerging theme of the personal and the public in *Hamlet*.

distempered disturbed

signify tell, explain
purgation cure, cleansing

discourse talk
frame order

breed kind
wholesome full and proper

admiration astonishment

no sequel no consequence
Impart tell me
closet bedroom or private room

pickers and stealers hands (from the *Book of Common Prayer*: 'keep my hands from picking and stealing')
distemper unease, illness

GUILDENSTERN   Is in his retirement marvellous distempered.

HAMLET   With drink sir?

GUILDENSTERN   No my lord, rather with choler.   275

HAMLET   Your wisdom should show itself more richer to signify this
to his doctor, for, for me to put him to his purgation would perhaps
plunge him into far more choler.

GUILDENSTERN   Good my lord, put your discourse into some frame,
and start not so wildly from my affair.   280

HAMLET   I am tame sir, pronounce.

GUILDENSTERN   The queen your mother, in most great affliction of
spirit, hath sent me to you.

HAMLET   You are welcome.

GUILDENSTERN   Nay good my lord, this courtesy is not of the right   285
breed. If it shall please you to make me a wholesome answer, I will
do your mother's commandment. If not, your pardon and my return
shall be the end of my business.

HAMLET   Sir, I cannot.

ROSENCRANTZ   What, my lord?   290

HAMLET   Make you a wholesome answer; my wit's diseased. But, sir,
such answer as I can make, you shall command, or rather, as you
say, my mother. Therefore no more, but to the matter. My mother,
you say.

ROSENCRANTZ   Then thus she says. Your behaviour hath struck her   295
into amazement and admiration.

HAMLET   O wonderful son that can so stonish a mother! But is there
no sequel at the heels of this mother's admiration? Impart.

ROSENCRANTZ   She desires to speak with you in her closet ere you go
to bed.   300

HAMLET   We shall obey, were she ten times our mother. Have you any
further trade with us?

ROSENCRANTZ   My lord, you once did love me.

HAMLET   And do still, by these pickers and stealers.

ROSENCRANTZ   Good my lord, what is your cause of distemper? You   305
do surely bar the door upon your own liberty if you deny your griefs
to your friend.

HAMLET   Sir, I lack advancement.

ROSENCRANTZ   How can that be, when you have the voice of the king
himself for your succession in Denmark?   310

HAMLET   Ay sir, but while the grass grows – the proverb is something
musty.

Hamlet bitterly accuses Guildenstern of treating him as a mere musical instrument, to be made to say anything at someone else's wish. He demonstrates that process on Polonius.

Stagecraft

Playing on Polonius (in pairs)

To show Rosencrantz and Guildenstern how they are treating him, Hamlet does the same to Polonius. He plays upon Polonius like a recorder, making him say anything that he, Hamlet, chooses. So Polonius is made to say he sees the imaginary shapes Hamlet suggests are in the clouds.

Some directors and critics challenge this view of Polonius as a silly old man humouring someone he thinks is a lunatic. They argue that Polonius replies in a dignified and tolerant manner, showing that he knows that Hamlet is trying to make fun of him. And certain critics have tried to show that 'camel', 'weasel' and 'whale' are symbols for certain themes of the play.

- One of you plays Polonius while the other takes the role of director and advises the actor on how he should behave in lines 337–47. Swap roles after the actor has read through the lines a few times.

withdraw be private
recover the wind of me direct me (like hunters keeping upwind of their prey)
toil net
unmannerly impolite

ventages, stops finger holes
discourse play

mystery innermost secrets
compass range
organ the recorder
'Sblood God's blood (an oath)
fret irritate, or add a fret on a lute

th'mass the Roman Catholic Mass

bent utmost limit (like a stretched bow)

Hamlet teases and taunts Polonius. In the production pictured here, he physically intimidates him. Do you think that this side of Hamlet's character is evident in the script?

Enter the PLAYERS *with recorders*

Oh, the recorders. Let me see one. To withdraw with you – Why
do you go about to recover the wind of me, as if you would drive
me into a toil? 315

GUILDENSTERN O my lord, if my duty be too bold, my love is too
unmannerly.

HAMLET I do not well understand that. Will you play upon this pipe?

GUILDENSTERN My lord, I cannot.

HAMLET I pray you. 320

GUILDENSTERN Believe me I cannot.

HAMLET I do beseech you.

GUILDENSTERN I know no touch of it my lord.

HAMLET 'Tis as easy as lying. Govern these ventages with your fingers
and thumb, give it breath with your mouth, and it will discourse 325
most eloquent music. Look you, these are the stops.

GUILDENSTERN But these cannot I command to any utterance of
harmony. I have not the skill.

HAMLET Why look you now how unworthy a thing you make of me.
You would play upon me, you would seem to know my stops, you 330
would pluck out the heart of my mystery, you would sound me from
my lowest note to the top of my compass – and there is much music,
excellent voice, in this little organ, yet cannot you make it speak.
'Sblood, do you think I am easier to be played on than a pipe? Call
me what instrument you will, though you can fret me, you cannot 335
play upon me.

Enter POLONIUS

God bless you sir.

POLONIUS My lord, the queen would speak with you, and presently.

HAMLET Do you see yonder cloud that's almost in shape of a camel?

POLONIUS By th'mass, and 'tis like a camel indeed. 340

HAMLET Methinks it is like a weasel.

POLONIUS It is backed like a weasel.

HAMLET Or like a whale?

POLONIUS Very like a whale.

HAMLET Then I will come to my mother by and by. – They fool me 345
to the top of my bent. – I will come by and by.

Hamlet threatens bloody revenge. He decides to visit Gertrude to upbraid but not harm her. Claudius, fearing Hamlet's growing dangerousness, briefs Rosencrantz and Guildenstern to take Hamlet to England.

Language in the play
The language of revenge (in pairs)

In lines 349–53, Hamlet uses the language of the traditional revenger in Elizabethan drama (see pp. 245–6). For example, conventional revengers in Elizabethan and Jacobean tragedy – like Hieronimo in *The Spanish Tragedy* and Vindice in *The Revenger's Tragedy* – draw on dark, nightmarish imagery to bolster their causes.

a Talk together about whether you think the lines are out of character with Hamlet's personality, reducing him to a stereotype of traditional revenge tragedy.

b Write ten lines in continuation of lines 349–53. You could refer to Macbeth's speech in Act 3 Scene 2, lines 46–55 (in Cambridge editions), where he invokes darkness, not for revenge, but for murder.

c Look up either Hieronimo's, Vindice's or Macbeth's speeches, and look at them alongside this soliloquy of Hamlet's. Write a critical comparison of their language, concentrating on imagery.

d If you wish to take the idea of revenge tragedy comparisons further, undertake some research on the genre and write a research report on *Hamlet*, discussing the extent to which you think it is a revenge tragedy.

Stagecraft
Work out the scene change (in pairs or threes)

In the Globe Theatre of Shakespeare's time the scenes flowed quickly and smoothly, without long intervals for changing from one to the next. Most modern productions also achieve smooth transitions between scenes.

- Work out how you would stage the change from Scene 2 to Scene 3. Start with Hamlet's soliloquy, deciding how you would have the actor speak it and how you would manage the apparent change of tone at line 353. Might Claudius actually glimpse Hamlet at line 1 of Scene 3?

witching when witches emerge
When churchyards yawn when graves open
Contagion evil

quake shake
Soft careful
Nero Roman emperor who murdered his mother

How in my words somever however much in my speech
shent punished, shamed
seals action

commission letters of instruction

The terms of our estate my status as king

provide make preparations

POLONIUS I will say so.   *Exit*

HAMLET By and by is easily said. – Leave me, friends.

Exeunt all but Hamlet

'Tis now the very witching time of night,
When churchyards yawn, and hell itself breathes out   350
Contagion to this world. Now could I drink hot blood,
And do such bitter business as the day
Would quake to look on. Soft, now to my mother.
O heart, lose not thy nature; let not ever
The soul of Nero enter this firm bosom.   355
Let me be cruel, not unnatural:
I will speak daggers to her but use none.
My tongue and soul in this be hypocrites,
How in my words somever she be shent,
To give them seals never my soul consent.   *Exit*   360

Act 3 Scene 3
The king's private chapel

Enter CLAUDIUS, ROSENCRANTZ *and* GUILDENSTERN

CLAUDIUS I like him not, nor stands it safe with us
To let his madness range. Therefore prepare you:
I your commission will forthwith dispatch,
And he to England shall along with you.
The terms of our estate may not endure   5
Hazard so near us as doth hourly grow
Out of his brows.

GUILDENSTERN   We will ourselves provide.
Most holy and religious fear it is
To keep those many many bodies safe
That live and feed upon your majesty.   10

Rosencrantz contrasts the private individual with a king. Everyone depends upon the ruler: when he dies, everyone suffers. Polonius reports that he will spy on Hamlet and Gertrude.

1 Flattering the king: Rosencrantz

Rosencrantz mouths the flattering belief that all tyrants love to hear: everything and everybody depends on the monarch ('That spirit'). In Tudor England, the ruling class made this the official ideology.

Rosencrantz uses two striking images. First, the king's death ('cess'), like a whirlpool ('gulf'), draws everything in to disaster. The second image is that of a huge ('massy') wheel, with the king at the centre and everybody else firmly attached ('mortised and adjoined'). When the wheel breaks, every tiny part ('annexment') suffers.

a Research the concept of 'the Chain of Being', a harmonious hierarchical society, depending on the king at the top (*The Elizabethan World Picture* by E.M.W. Tillyard is a good place to start). Shakespeare presents the belief clearly in *Troilus and Cressida*, Act 1 Scene 3, lines 77–123. But there, as here, a scheming character (Ulysses) speaks, so you need to be wary of taking this belief to be the truth.

b Advise an actor playing Claudius how to react to Rosencrantz's flattery, especially when he hears the words 'The cess of majesty'. Does Claudius show any signs of guilt at this point?

Characters

Polonius – servant and sycophant

Polonius is going to hide in order to spy on Hamlet and Gertrude. He has a number of motives of his own, as well as carrying out what appears to be an order from Claudius. Think about what you know of Polonius, then carry out the following activities:

a To what degree is Polonius a comic character, and to what degree a mere servant of a 'police state'? Find evidence to support both sides of his character.

b In terms of the relationship between the private and the public, what part does Polonius's suspicion of Hamlet's attitude towards Ophelia play in his actions?

c As well as being pompous, Polonius is a sycophant (a servile and self-serving flatterer). See if you can find other examples of this characteristic in Polonius's speech or actions.

single and peculiar life private individual

noyance harm

weal health

cess end, ceasing

boisterous tumultuous

a general groan the sorrow of everyone

fetters chains

process conversation

warrant bet, predict

tax him home criticise him strongly

'Tis meet it's fitting

partial biased

of vantage from an advantageous position

ROSENCRANTZ   The single and peculiar life is bound
              With all the strength and armour of the mind
              To keep itself from noyance; but much more
              That spirit upon whose weal depends and rests
              The lives of many. The cess of majesty   15
              Dies not alone, but like a gulf doth draw
              What's near it with it. It is a massy wheel
              Fixed on the summit of the highest mount,
              To whose huge spokes ten thousand lesser things
              Are mortised and adjoined, which when it falls,   20
              Each small annexment, petty consequence,
              Attends the boisterous ruin. Never alone
              Did the king sigh, but with a general groan.
CLAUDIUS   Arm you I pray you to this speedy voyage,
              For we will fetters put about this fear   25
              Which now goes too free-footed.
ROSENCRANTZ   We will haste us.
                    Exeunt Rosencrantz and Guildenstern

                  Enter POLONIUS

POLONIUS   My lord, he's going to his mother's closet.
              Behind the arras I'll convey myself
              To hear the process. I'll warrant she'll tax him home,
              And as you said, and wisely was it said,   30
              'Tis meet that some more audience than a mother,
              Since nature makes them partial, should o'erhear
              The speech of vantage. Fare you well my liege,
              I'll call upon you ere you go to bed
              And tell you what I know.
CLAUDIUS   Thanks, dear my lord.   35
                            Exit Polonius

Claudius hopes for divine mercy for his brother's murder. But he knows that pardon is impossible while he retains the fruits of his crime, even though villainy can triumph on Earth. He tries to pray.

1 The conscience of the king (in small groups)

Claudius agonises over his dilemma. He has committed murder, yet hopes for heavenly pardon. He knows that although he might escape judgement on Earth, there is no escape for him in heaven, except God's forgiveness through prayer and repentance. He is in too much turmoil to repent, but he calls on angels to help, and kneels to pray.

a Each person speaks a section of the soliloquy, then hands on to the next person. Read around the group in different ways:

- a line at a time
- a sentence at a time
- up to any punctuation mark
- saying only one powerful word from each line.

b Repeat the activity, making your reading sound like a developing argument that Claudius is having with himself. Experiment with whispers, fear, puzzlement and anger. Can you find moments of hope in the soliloquy? After your explorations, decide on the style you prefer and present your version to the class.

2 Heaven and hell: salvation and sin

Research the Christian iconography of heaven and hell as depicted in medieval and Renaissance times. Present your findings to show what bearing Christian morality (which prohibited revenge) has upon the play as a whole. Pages 249–50 will help you. What do they reveal about Hamlet's beliefs and ideology?

Characters
Claudius's confession

This is Claudius's most revealing speech in the play and his confession secures the truth of the matter: Claudius did murder his brother, Hamlet's father.

- Look back over Claudius's speeches in the play so far. To prepare for a character study, chart the various sides of his personality and collect quotations to support your depiction. You can present this in note form, or as a collective poster for display.

- What do lines 97–8 at the end of this scene suggest about Claudius?

rank stinking, rotten

primal eldest first and oldest (in the Bible the killing of Abel by Cain)

inclination desire

will determination

visage face

forestallèd prevented

May one … retain th'offence can one be forgiven and yet live with the evil deed?

corrupted currents wicked ways

Offence's gilded hand rich criminals

wicked prize profits from crimes

above in heaven

shuffling deceit

Even … evidence to tell our wickedest sins

limèd trapped (like a bird snared by lime)

assay attempt

Oh my offence is rank, it smells to heaven;
It hath the primal eldest curse upon't,
A brother's murder. Pray can I not,
Though inclination be as sharp as will.
My stronger guilt defeats my strong intent,   40
And like a man to double business bound,
I stand in pause where I shall first begin,
And both neglect. What if this cursèd hand
Were thicker than itself with brother's blood,
Is there not rain enough in the sweet heavens   45
To wash it white as snow? Whereto serves mercy
But to confront the visage of offence?
And what's in prayer but this two-fold force,
To be forestallèd ere we come to fall,
Or pardoned being down? Then I'll look up,   50
My fault is past. But oh, what form of prayer
Can serve my turn? 'Forgive me my foul murder'?
That cannot be, since I am still possessed
Of those effects for which I did the murder,
My crown, mine own ambition, and my queen.   55
May one be pardoned and retain th'offence?
In the corrupted currents of this world
Offence's gilded hand may shove by justice,
And oft 'tis seen the wicked prize itself
Buys out the law. But 'tis not so above;   60
There is no shuffling, there the action lies
In his true nature, and we ourselves compelled
Even to the teeth and forehead of our faults
To give in evidence. What then? What rests?
Try what repentance can. What can it not?   65
Yet what can it when one cannot repent?
Oh wretched state! Oh bosom black as death!
Oh limèd soul that struggling to be free
Art more engaged! Help, angels! – Make assay;
Bow stubborn knees, and heart with strings of steel   70
Be soft as sinews of the new-born babe.
All may be well.

        [He kneels]

1 Hamlet delays

Hamlet does not kill Claudius because the king is praying. Hamlet's own
father suffers after death because Claudius killed him at a moment when
he was unprepared for heaven ('grossly, full of bread' = full of sin, no
opportunity to fast), not having confessed his sins. Hamlet therefore decides
to wait for a moment when Claudius is committing a sin. Killing Claudius
then, when he has no thought of heaven in his mind, will surely send
Claudius to hell. Or is Hamlet merely finding another excuse for delay?

a Experiment with dramatic ways
of presenting Hamlet's lines.
You will find that intercutting Hamlet's
lines with Claudius's soliloquy in
lines 36–72 can lead to some
interesting readings.

b How does the image on
this page match your own
conception of the moment?

pat instantly, neatly

would be scanned
needs study (but also in the sense
of metrical scanning)

a he

hire and salary legal payment
(not punishment)

grossly with no
consideration, crudely

broad blown in full blossom

as flush full of life

audit account with God

in our … thought
it is generally believed

purging cleansing

fit and seasoned fully prepared

hent opportunity (literally 'grasp',
suggesting Hamlet puts the sword
back into its scabbard)

relish of salvation
hope of heaven

trip him literally, so that he dives
toward hell

physic medicine

Enter HAMLET

HAMLET   Now might I do it pat, now a is a-praying,
And now I'll do't – and so a goes to heaven,
And so am I revenged. That would be scanned.   75
A villain kills my father, and for that,
I his sole son do this same villain send
To heaven.
Why, this is hire and salary, not revenge.
A took my father grossly, full of bread,   80
With all his crimes broad blown, as flush as May,
And how his audit stands who knows save heaven?
But in our circumstance and course of thought
'Tis heavy with him. And am I then revenged
To take him in the purging of his soul,   85
When he is fit and seasoned for his passage?
No.
Up sword, and know thou a more horrid hent,
When he is drunk asleep, or in his rage,
Or in th'incestuous pleasure of his bed,   90
At game a-swearing, or about some act
That has no relish of salvation in't –
Then trip him that his heels may kick at heaven,
And that his soul may be as damned and black
As hell whereto it goes. My mother stays.   95
This physic but prolongs thy sickly days.   *Exit*

CLAUDIUS   My words fly up, my thoughts remain below.
Words without thoughts never to heaven go.   *Exit*

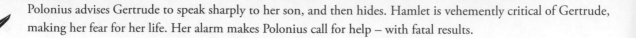

Stagecraft

Where is the scene set?

Act 3 Scene 4 is known as 'the closet scene' (a closet was a private room – see also Act 2 Scene 1). But for the last 100 years the stage convention has been to set this scene in Gertrude's bedroom. This heightens the impression of Hamlet having an Oedipus complex (a desire to sleep with his mother – see p. 255). Laurence Olivier's 1948 movie heavily emphasised this Oedipal interpretation, as did the 1990 film in which Mel Gibson played Hamlet.

a Imagine you are directing the play and you have a leading Shakespeare scholar as your consultant. They write to you: 'In Shakespeare's day, "closet" meant private room, and the Oedipus complex hadn't been thought of, so I advise you not to bring a bed on stage.' Do you take their advice? Why or why not? Write your reply.

b Compare the two film versions of *Hamlet* mentioned above. Which do you prefer? Why? Which gives the strongest interpretation of the Oedipal theme?

Characters

Hamlet's state of mind (in pairs)

What is Hamlet's state of mind as he enters his mother's private room? He has just come from an encounter with Claudius in which he refrained from taking revenge on the king for his father's death. Prior to that, he 'saw off' Rosencrantz and Guildenstern, and Polonius – at least verbally – in the wake of the play-within-a-play.

a Discuss with your partner what you think this rapid sequence of events does for Hamlet's state of mind. In the light of your response to the activity on the Oedipus complex above, what bearing might your interpretation have on your reading of Hamlet's state of mind at this point? Add your thoughts to your collection of notes on Hamlet.

b Write a diary entry for Gertrude in which she reflects on Hamlet's state of mind, his character, and how she sees his development up to this point.

lay home deal firmly with, talk severely

broad far-ranging

your grace ... and him like a firescreen you have shielded Hamlet from criticism

idle wayward

rood holy cross of Christ

I'll set ... speak I'll fetch others to correct you

Act 3 Scene 4
Gertrude's private room

Enter GERTRUDE *and* POLONIUS

POLONIUS	A will come straight. Look you lay home to him.
	Tell him his pranks have been too broad to bear with,
	And that your grace hath screened and stood between
	Much heat and him. I'll silence me e'en here.
	Pray you be round with him. 5
HAMLET	(*Within*) Mother, mother, mother!
GERTRUDE	I'll warrant you, fear me not. Withdraw, I hear him coming.
	[*Polonius hides himself behind the arras*]

Enter HAMLET

HAMLET	Now mother, what's the matter?
GERTRUDE	Hamlet, thou hast thy father much offended.
HAMLET	Mother, you have my father much offended. 10
GERTRUDE	Come, come, you answer with an idle tongue.
HAMLET	Go, go, you question with a wicked tongue.
GERTRUDE	Why, how now Hamlet?
HAMLET	What's the matter now?
GERTRUDE	Have you forgot me?
HAMLET	No by the rood, not so.
	You are the queen, your husband's brother's wife, 15
	And, would it were not so, you are my mother.
GERTRUDE	Nay, then I'll set those to you that can speak.
HAMLET	Come, come and sit you down, you shall not budge.
	You go not till I set you up a glass
	Where you may see the inmost part of you. 20
GERTRUDE	What wilt thou do? thou wilt not murder me?
	Help, help, ho!
POLONIUS	(*Behind*) What ho! Help, help, help!
HAMLET	(*Draws*) How now, a rat? Dead for a ducat, dead.
	Kills Polonius
POLONIUS	(*Behind*) Oh, I am slain!

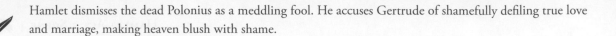

Hamlet dismisses the dead Polonius as a meddling fool. He accuses Gertrude of shamefully defiling true love and marriage, making heaven blush with shame.

1 Did Gertrude know?

'As kill a king?' echoes Gertrude (line 30). But does she know that Claudius murdered her first husband? On stage, a clue is often given in the way Gertrude behaves as she speaks these four words. Interestingly, there is no further discussion of whether she knows what Claudius did.

- Write notes advising an actor playing Gertrude on how to deliver the line.

2 Did Hamlet know? (in small groups)

Hamlet does not seem to know what he is doing, or, rather, he thinks that in thrusting his sword through the arras, he is killing Claudius (line 26). The death of Polonius means little to him. This is the first killing by Hamlet in the play, and appears to come via a moment of hot-headed rashness, or an impulsive sense that the surveillance he is under must stop.

a In your groups, discuss Hamlet's motivation for thrusting his sword through the arras, particularly in the light of his reluctance to avenge his father's death on Claudius in the previous scene.

b How would you stage Polonius's killing? Act out three different mime versions, and decide as a group which one you think works best.

thy better the king

damnèd custom wicked habits
brazed hardened (like brass)
proof and bulwark armoured strongly
sense feeling
grace and blush innocence

blister indicating harlotry through venereal disease
dicers' oaths gamblers' promises
body of contraction marriage contract
rhapsody confusion
glow blush
solidity and compound mass the world
tristful visage sad face
doom Day of Judgement
index list of sins

GERTRUDE	Oh me, what hast thou done?	25
HAMLET	Nay I know not, is it the king?	
GERTRUDE	Oh what a rash and bloody deed is this!	
HAMLET	A bloody deed? Almost as bad, good mother,	
	As kill a king and marry with his brother.	
GERTRUDE	As kill a king?	
HAMLET	Ay lady, 'twas my word.	30

[*Lifts up the arras and reveals the body of Polonius*]

	Thou wretched, rash, intruding fool, farewell.	
	I took thee for thy better. Take thy fortune.	
	Thou find'st to be too busy is some danger. –	
	Leave wringing of your hands. Peace! Sit you down	
	And let me wring your heart, for so I shall	35
	If it be made of penetrable stuff,	
	If damnèd custom have not brazed it so,	
	That it be proof and bulwark against sense.	
GERTRUDE	What have I done, that thou dar'st wag thy tongue	
	In noise so rude against me?	
HAMLET	Such an act	40
	That blurs the grace and blush of modesty,	
	Calls virtue hypocrite, takes off the rose	
	From the fair forehead of an innocent love	
	And sets a blister there, makes marriage vows	
	As false as dicers' oaths. Oh such a deed	45
	As from the body of contraction plucks	
	The very soul, and sweet religion makes	
	A rhapsody of words. Heaven's face doth glow;	
	Yea, this solidity and compound mass,	
	With tristful visage as against the doom,	50
	Is thought-sick at the act.	
GERTRUDE	Ay me, what act,	
	That roars so loud and thunders in the index?	

Hamlet compares his father with Claudius: the good man against the bad. He berates Gertrude for not seeing the difference, and deplores her inability to control her sexual desires.

Characters

Gertrude's point of view (in pairs)

What does Gertrude feel at being subjected to such a tongue-lashing?

* Write some lines for Gertrude and interject them at key points in Hamlet's verbal attack on her.
* Then perform the speech by Hamlet and the interjections by Gertrude, asking your audience to comment critically on how you have depicted Gertrude.

1 Editing again (in pairs)

Note the lines in square brackets in the script opposite. They suggest that something worse than madness has happened to Gertrude's common sense (and senses). Some argue that these lines were deleted by Shakespeare after the script was first published (see p. 268), perhaps because he thought that they were too complicated. This leaves directors with a decision to make.

a Try the speech in two ways: first, with the bracketed lines included, and then again without them. One of you argues for their inclusion; the other for their exclusion. You might like to bear in mind ideas of sense, language and dramatic impact as you argue your case and make your decision.

b Compare notes with the rest of the class – as a whole, do you think the inclusion of the bracketed lines is justified or not?

2 Gertrude's relationship with Claudius

On page 124, you were asked to consider Hamlet's obsession with sex. In the script opposite, Hamlet questions and challenges his mother on her attitudes towards sex.

a What does Hamlet's attack on Gertrude say about his own attitude and sense of moral propriety? How do you think his diatribe to Gertrude relates to the criticism he made of Ophelia?

b Put Hamlet on the psychiatrist's couch once again, to ask him questions about his attitude to his mother. Is his attack on Gertrude a fair one?

c Look at the language in Hamlet's speech opposite. There is something driven, clear and passionate about his words. Is it the 'real' Hamlet coming through, brought to his senses by the killing of Polonius and expressing his concerns directly with his mother? What does the language tell you about him?

counterfeit presentment portrait
brow forehead

station posture
Mercury winged messenger of the gods
New-lighted recently landed

mildewed ear rotten ear of corn

batten greedily feed

Sense sexual desire
motion emotions
apoplexed paralysed
err make a mistake
thralled enslaved
But it ... difference that it couldn't choose good from bad
cozened cheated
hoodman-blind blind man's buff
sans all without anything else
so mope be so stupid

mutine mutiny

panders succumbs to

HAMLET   Look here upon this picture, and on this,
The counterfeit presentment of two brothers.
See what a grace was seated on this brow;   55
Hyperion's curls, the front of Jove himself,
An eye like Mars, to threaten and command;
A station like the herald Mercury,
New-lighted on a heaven-kissing hill;
A combination and a form indeed,   60
Where every god did seem to set his seal
To give the world assurance of a man.
This was your husband. Look you now what follows.
Here is your husband, like a mildewed ear
Blasting his wholesome brother. Have you eyes?   65
Could you on this fair mountain leave to feed
And batten on this moor? Ha! have you eyes?
You cannot call it love, for at your age
The heyday in the blood is tame, it's humble,
And waits upon the judgement; and what judgement   70
Would step from this to this? [Sense sure you have,
Else could you not have motion, but sure that sense
Is apoplexed, for madness would not err,
Nor sense to ecstasy was ne'er so thralled,
But it reserved some quantity of choice   75
To serve in such a difference.] What devil was't
That thus hath cozened you at hoodman-blind?
[Eyes without feeling, feeling without sight,
Ears without hands or eyes, smelling sans all,
Or but a sickly part of one true sense   80
Could not so mope.]
O shame, where is thy blush? Rebellious hell,
If thou canst mutine in a matron's bones,
To flaming youth let virtue be as wax
And melt in her own fire. Proclaim no shame   85
When the compulsive ardour gives the charge,
Since frost itself as actively doth burn,
And reason panders will.

Hamlet expresses his disgust at Gertrude's sexuality. She pleads with him to stop. He reviles Claudius. The Ghost reminds Hamlet of his mission and urges him to comfort Gertrude. She is amazed by his words.

▲ The first published version of *Hamlet* had the stage direction '*Enter the Ghost in his nightgown*'. In the production pictured above, the Ghost was very dominating in his behaviour towards Hamlet, physically demanding his attention as he spoke the lines. Work out how you would stage the Ghost's entry, movement and manner of speech.

1 Why does the Ghost return? (in small groups)

Why does the Ghost return? It appears that Hamlet was getting through to Gertrude ('These words like daggers …').

- Each person in the group suggests several reasons for the Ghost's reappearance at this critical moment. Pool your ideas, arrange them in order of priority, and put them to the class as a whole.
- As a whole class, vote on the reason(s) that you find most convincing.

grainèd indelibly stained
leave their tinct lose their stain

enseamèd sewn up, embroidered; or enclosed

tithe tenth part
vice clown in medieval morality plays, dressed in multicoloured costume ('A king of shreds and patches')
cutpurse thief
rule reign, rule of law

tardy slow
chide reproach, tell off

whet sharpen
amazement bewilderment

Conceit imagination

bend your eye look
vacancy emptiness
th'incorporal bodiless

GERTRUDE	O Hamlet, speak no more.
	Thou turn'st my eyes into my very soul,
	And there I see such black and grainèd spots	90
	As will not leave their tinct.
HAMLET	Nay, but to live
	In the rank sweat of an enseamèd bed,
	Stewed in corruption, honeying and making love
	Over the nasty sty.
GERTRUDE	Oh speak to me no more.
	These words like daggers enter in my ears.	95
	No more sweet Hamlet.
HAMLET	A murderer and a villain,
	A slave that is not twentieth part the tithe
	Of your precedent lord, a vice of kings,
	A cutpurse of the empire and the rule,
	That from a shelf the precious diadem stole	100
	And put it in his pocket.
GERTRUDE	No more!

Enter GHOST

HAMLET	A king of shreds and patches –
	Save me and hover o'er me with your wings,
	You heavenly guards! – What would your gracious figure?
GERTRUDE	Alas he's mad!	105
HAMLET	Do you not come your tardy son to chide,
	That lapsed in time and passion lets go by
	Th'important acting of your dread command? Oh say!
GHOST	Do not forget. This visitation
	Is but to whet thy almost blunted purpose.	110
	But look, amazement on thy mother sits.
	Oh step between her and her fighting soul:
	Conceit in weakest bodies strongest works.
	Speak to her, Hamlet.
HAMLET	How is it with you lady?
GERTRUDE	Alas, how is't with you,	115
	That you do bend your eye on vacancy,
	And with th'incorporal air do hold discourse?
	Forth at your eyes your spirits wildly peep,

Gertrude, unable to see the Ghost, is bewildered by Hamlet's behaviour. Hamlet fears that his impulse to revenge might soften to pity. He says he is not mad, and urges Gertrude to repent.

1 'Do not look upon me' (in threes)

Hamlet says the combination of the Ghost's appearance and plea for justice would make even stones feel pity ('form and cause conjoined … capable'). Hamlet implores the Ghost to turn his gaze away because it weakens his impulse to revenge (lines 126–9).

a Enact lines 115–37, concentrating on facial expression and positioning/movement of the three characters in relation to each other.

b How does Hamlet speak lines 140–56? Does he plead with Gertrude, trying to appeal to her reason with rational argument? Or does he speak vehemently and accusingly, stressing intensely all the words to do with madness and corruption? Experiment with ways of speaking the lines to express Hamlet's emotional state at this point in the play, and adjust Gertrude's reaction accordingly.

Themes
Revenge

Look back at your work so far on the theme of revenge. What do the lines opposite add to the development of this theme and its related themes (sexuality, the mother–son relationship)? Add to your map of themes any key quotations you select from the lines opposite, with your own commentary and analysis.

Write about it
Why can't Gertrude see the Ghost?

It is clear that Gertrude does not see the Ghost. Write two or three paragraphs about whether you think Gertrude's inability to see the Ghost signifies her moral blindness, and what other possible explanations there might be. Support your writing with quotations.

in th'alarm woken by call to battle
bedded smoothed down
excrements outgrowths (hair)
distemper unease

conjoined joined together

stern effects intention to revenge
want true colour lose its real character

habit as he lived everyday clothes
portal door

coinage creation
ecstasy / Is very cunning in madness invents

temperately in balance, steadily

gambol leap, shy away
unction ointment
trespass transgression
film cover over

pursy sick

curb and woo flatter
leave permission

	And, as the sleeping soldiers in th'alarm,	
	Your bedded hair, like life in excrements,	120
	Start up and stand an end. O gentle son,	
	Upon the heat and flame of thy distemper	
	Sprinkle cool patience. Whereon do you look?	
HAMLET	On him, on him! Look you how pale he glares.	
	His form and cause conjoined, preaching to stones,	125
	Would make them capable. – Do not look upon me,	
	Lest with this piteous action you convert	
	My stern effects. Then what I have to do	
	Will want true colour: tears perchance for blood.	
GERTRUDE	To whom do you speak this?	130
HAMLET	Do you see nothing there?	
GERTRUDE	Nothing at all, yet all that is I see.	
HAMLET	Nor did you nothing hear?	
GERTRUDE	No, nothing but ourselves.	
HAMLET	Why, look you there – look how it steals away –	135
	My father in his habit as he lived –	
	Look where he goes, even now out at the portal.	

Exit Ghost

GERTRUDE	This is the very coinage of your brain.	
	This bodiless creation ecstasy	
	Is very cunning in.	
HAMLET	Ecstasy?	140
	My pulse as yours doth temperately keep time,	
	And makes as healthful music. It is not madness	
	That I have uttered. Bring me to the test,	
	And I the matter will reword, which madness	
	Would gambol from. Mother, for love of grace,	145
	Lay not that flattering unction to your soul,	
	That not your trespass but my madness speaks;	
	It will but skin and film the ulcerous place,	
	Whiles rank corruption, mining all within,	
	Infects unseen. Confess yourself to heaven,	150
	Repent what's past, avoid what is to come,	
	And do not spread the compost on the weeds	
	To make them ranker. Forgive me this my virtue,	
	For in the fatness of these pursy times	
	Virtue itself of vice must pardon beg,	155
	Yea, curb and woo for leave to do him good.	

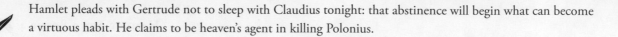

Hamlet pleads with Gertrude not to sleep with Claudius tonight: that abstinence will begin what can become a virtuous habit. He claims to be heaven's agent in killing Polonius.

Language in the play
What's the missing word?

No one knows what Shakespeare intended to write in line 170. The word is missing in all the earliest printed editions.

- Which word do you think would fit? Suggestions have been: curb, master, aid, shame, speed, quell, house, lodge and oust. You may come up with some other suggestions.

1 Is Hamlet God's agent? (in pairs)

Traditional revengers do not see themselves as agents for good, but for a type of rough justice in the world. In lines 174–6, Hamlet appears not to blame heaven for the death of Polonius, but rather to see himself as God's agent, as well as being punished for the act of murder.

a Discuss to what extent to which you see Hamlet as a force for good in the play.

b Look back at speeches by Hamlet in this act. How far does this speech reflect the 'true' Hamlet, if we can say there is such a thing? Referring to your developing notes on his character, provide for each of the speeches a few keywords that describe the nature of his character at that point.

c 'heaven hath pleased it so': this phrase suggests that Hamlet feels he is impelled by a force for good, but also that he is in the hands of Fortune, unable to exercise his own will. Do you agree?

d 'I must be cruel only to be kind': this apparent contradiction in terms is central to the notion of revenge and also to the purging of the sickness that Hamlet perceives in Denmark as well as in himself. Find quotations and instances in the play (e.g. Act 1 Scene 3; Act 3 Scene 1) to support this dichotomy of cruelty/kindness (and remember that 'kindness' shares a root with 'kinship').

2 Playing Gertrude

Gertrude has two lines in the script opposite, and speaks little in the face of Hamlet's tirades and persuasions.

- How genuine are Gertrude's responses? Make notes in your Director's Journal as to how an actor should play Gertrude in this scene.

cleft my heart in twain broken my heart in two

Assume a virtue pretend to be pure

custom habit

sense finer feelings, sensibility

Of habits devil the evil spirit of all habits

frock or livery clothing or uniform

Refrain don't go to bed with him

abstinence denial of love-making

stamp of nature natural inclination

wondrous potency amazing power

scourge and minister whip and officer who wields it

bestow dispose of

remains behind lies ahead

GERTRUDE	Oh Hamlet, thou hast cleft my heart in twain.
HAMLET	Oh throw away the worser part of it
	And live the purer with the other half.
	Good night – but go not to my uncle's bed; 160
	Assume a virtue if you have it not.
	[That monster custom, who all sense doth eat,
	Of habits devil, is angel yet in this,
	That to the use of actions fair and good
	He likewise gives a frock or livery 165
	That aptly is put on.] Refrain tonight,
	And that shall lend a kind of easiness
	To the next abstinence, [the next more easy,
	For use almost can change the stamp of nature,
	And either . . . the devil, or throw him out, 170
	With wondrous potency.] Once more good night,
	And when you are desirous to be blessed,
	I'll blessing beg of you. For this same lord,
	I do repent; but heaven hath pleased it so,
	To punish me with this, and this with me, 175
	That I must be their scourge and minister.
	I will bestow him, and will answer well
	The death I gave him. So again, good night.
	I must be cruel only to be kind;
	Thus bad begins, and worse remains behind. 180
	One word more good lady.
GERTRUDE	What shall I do?

Hamlet urges Gertrude not to reveal his pretended madness to Claudius. He threatens her. She promises to keep silent. Hamlet plans to kill Rosencrantz and Guildenstern, who are involved in a plot against him.

1 Irony or sarcasm? (in pairs)

Lines 183–92 are heavily ironic, even sarcastic. Hamlet seems to order Gertrude to reveal his secrets to Claudius. But line 182 makes his intention clear: she is not to do as he commands.

- Advise the actor playing Hamlet on how to speak lines 182–92. Your interpretation of these lines will have a bearing on whether you take Hamlet's 'mad in craft' at face value, or as a poor attempt by Hamlet to explain his actions and inaction.

2 To cut or not to cut?

Lines 203–11, which are in square brackets (see p. 268), suggest that Hamlet already has plans to kill Rosencrantz and Guildenstern. As Act 5 Scene 2 shows, that may not be true.

- Try Hamlet's final speech in two ways: with the bracketed lines and without them. Take it from line 201 to the end of the scene. Which version works best, and why? If you were directing the play, would you cut these lines?

Characters

How does Gertrude feel? (in pairs)

Gertrude has been on the receiving end of Hamlet's tirade. What she believes at the end of this scene may not be the same as that which she reports to Claudius at the start of Act 4.

a Before you move on to Act 4, discuss Gertrude's probable feelings and then write a diary entry describing her unspoken thoughts and reactions about Hamlet.

b What do Gertrude's words in this scene say about her knowledge of the situation as a whole?

bloat flabby, bloated
wanton lustfully
reechy filthy

ravel unravel, explain

craft pretence, cunning

paddock, gib toad, cat
dear concernings important matters

Unpeg the basket…down these lines suggest a simple story: an ape lets birds free from a basket on a rooftop, crawls in and breaks its neck

adders fanged poisonous snakes
mandate orders

hoist with his own petar blown up with his own bomb
delve dig

crafts plots

lug the guts drag the body

HAMLET	Not this by no means that I bid you do:
	Let the bloat king tempt you again to bed,
	Pinch wanton on your cheek, call you his mouse,
	And let him for a pair of reechy kisses,

Not this by no means that I bid you do:
Let the bloat king tempt you again to bed,
Pinch wanton on your cheek, call you his mouse,
And let him for a pair of reechy kisses,   185
Or paddling in your neck with his damned fingers,
Make you to ravel all this matter out,
That I essentially am not in madness,
But mad in craft. 'Twere good you let him know,
For who that's but a queen, fair, sober, wise,   190
Would from a paddock, from a bat, a gib,
Such dear concernings hide? Who would do so?
No, in despite of sense and secrecy,
Unpeg the basket on the house's top,
Let the birds fly, and like the famous ape,   195
To try conclusions, in the basket creep
And break your own neck down.

GERTRUDE   Be thou assured, if words be made of breath,
And breath of life, I have no life to breathe
What thou hast said to me.   200

HAMLET   I must to England, you know that?

GERTRUDE   Alack,
I had forgot. 'Tis so concluded on.

HAMLET   [There's letters sealed, and my two schoolfellows,
Whom I will trust as I will adders fanged,
They bear the mandate. They must sweep my way   205
And marshal me to knavery. Let it work,
For 'tis the sport to have the engineer
Hoist with his own petar, an't shall go hard
But I will delve one yard below their mines
And blow them at the moon. Oh 'tis most sweet   210
When in one line two crafts directly meet.]
This man shall set me packing.
I'll lug the guts into the neighbour room.
Mother, good night. Indeed, this counsellor
Is now most still, most secret, and most grave,   215
Who was in life a foolish prating knave.
Come sir, to draw toward an end with you.
Good night mother.

                    Exit Hamlet tugging in Polonius; [Gertrude remains]

Looking back at Act 3
Activities for groups or individuals

1 Hamlet: speech, action and response

Hamlet appears in each of the four scenes in Act 3. To further your understanding of his relationships with other characters, copy the table below onto a large sheet of paper and then fill it in.

Scene	Hamlet speaks to or about	A typical line or lines	Hamlet's mood and intention
1	Ophelia		
2	The players		
	Horatio		
	Claudius		
	Polonius		
	Gertrude		
	Ophelia		
	Rosencrantz and Guildenstern		
3	Claudius		
4	Gertrude		

2 Developing themes

Throughout the play so far, you have been encouraged to identify themes and map them in relation to each other.

a Review your work to date, and update it to take into account the major themes to have emerged in Act 3: the mother–son relationship; the relationship between appearance and reality as manifested in the play-within-a-play; the 'idea of the play'; Hamlet's madness; attitudes towards sex and their relation to death and honour; and any others that you might identify.

b Do you think that the emphasis of Act 3 has been primarily on the personal or the public?

3 Staging a shortened version of Act 3

Divide into four groups. Each group works out a shortened version of one scene in Act 3 – two or three minutes per scene (Scene 2 is the longest, so you might want to give it a little more time). Present the shortened scenes to the rest of the class in sequence. You can present the scenes in any one of four ways:

- as a mime
- as an edited version of the original Shakespearean language
- in modern English
- in the language or dialect of your choice.

When all four scenes have been shown, discuss as a whole class what has been lost, and what gained, in your compressed version of the act.

4 Hamlet as playwright

Hamlet asks the First Player (Act 2 Scene 2, lines 493–4) to 'study a speech of some dozen or sixteen lines' he would write specially for *The Murder of Gonzago*. No one knows for certain if those lines were actually spoken in Scene 2.

- Try to identify (giving reasons) which lines were those written by Hamlet. If you think none of the lines were his, write a dozen lines that you think he would have put in.

5 The plot thickens …

… but does it advance? Look back at the plot of the play so far, and write 100-word written summaries of each act. How does Act 3 move the story forward? If you haven't read the whole play, predict three possible ways in which the story might develop from this point onwards. Extend one of these into a longer written piece: an alternative ending to *Hamlet*, in play or prose form.

Find lines from Act 3 Scene 4 that could make suitable captions for these pictures of Hamlet and Gertrude. In pairs or small groups, discuss what you think the director of each production might have had in mind about the mother–son relationship. Which production comes closest to your own imagined version, and why?

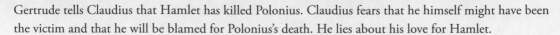

Gertrude tells Claudius that Hamlet has killed Polonius. Claudius fears that he himself might have been the victim and that he will be blamed for Polonius's death. He lies about his love for Hamlet.

Stagecraft

Director's decisions

At the end of Act 3 the stage direction 'Gertrude remains' is in square brackets because it does not appear in one of the early editions of the play (see p. 268).

a As director, advise Gertrude whether she should remain on stage until the arrival of Claudius, Rosencrantz and Guildenstern, or whether she should exit and re-enter with Claudius. Which is the more dramatically convincing?

b Decide if you would cut line 4 opposite, 'Bestow this place on us a little while' – why bring on Rosencrantz and Guildenstern only to dismiss them? You can discuss this and/or record your notes in your Director's Journal.

matter substance (i.e. 'there's something behind these sighs')

profound heaves deep sighs and shudders

translate explain

Bestow this place on us leave this place to us

contend dispute

lawless unruly

1 A chorus of disapproval (whole class)

This short scene is the only time that Claudius and Gertrude are alone together. Rather than take the roles of Rosencrantz and Guildenstern, who are complicit in the surveillance of Hamlet and unreliable in terms of speaking the truth, set up the following:

- Claudius and Gertrude speak the lines in the script opposite. As they rehearse for this reading, they can decide what state Gertrude is in and how she will speak her lines, and how self-interested Claudius is.

- The rest of the class, in groups, prepares accusations to put to Claudius and Gertrude at lines 5, 12 and 23. These challenges are prepared on the basis of the play so far, and might include: reflections of Claudius's and Gertrude's conscience; genuine accusations that they do not see or speak the truth; comments and questions on their own relationship as king and queen, and as lovers.

- To frame the performance, Claudius and Gertrude stand or sit at the centre of a circle. The rest of the class surrounds them and makes the challenges and comments.

- Afterwards, Claudius and Gertrude can speak in role describing how it felt to be challenged, and whether they wish to defend their speeches and actions. Is the rest of the class satisfied with the two characters' answers?

brainish apprehension frenzied state of mind

laid to us blamed on us

providence foresight

short confined

out of haunt out of the public eye

fit appropriate

divulging becoming generally open to the world

pith core, essence

draw apart cut up

ore ... pure pure metal shining among crude ones

Act 4 Scene 1
Gertrude's private room

Enter CLAUDIUS *with* ROSENCRANTZ *and* GUILDENSTERN

CLAUDIUS	There's matter in these sighs, these profound heaves.
	You must translate, 'tis fit we understand them.
	Where is your son?
GERTRUDE	[Bestow this place on us a little while.]

[Exeunt Rosencrantz and Guildenstern]

	Ah mine own lord, what have I seen tonight!	5
CLAUDIUS	What, Gertrude? How does Hamlet?	
GERTRUDE	Mad as the sea and wind, when both contend	
	Which is the mightier. In his lawless fit,	
	Behind the arras hearing something stir,	
	Whips out his rapier, cries 'A rat, a rat!',	10
	And in this brainish apprehension kills	
	The unseen good old man.	
CLAUDIUS	Oh heavy deed!	
	It had been so with us had we been there.	
	His liberty is full of threats to all,	
	To you yourself, to us, to everyone.	15
	Alas, how shall this bloody deed be answered?	
	It will be laid to us, whose providence	
	Should have kept short, restrained, and out of haunt,	
	This mad young man. But so much was our love,	
	We would not understand what was most fit,	20
	But like the owner of a foul disease,	
	To keep it from divulging, let it feed	
	Even on the pith of life. Where is he gone?	
GERTRUDE	To draw apart the body he hath killed,	
	O'er whom his very madness, like some ore	25
	Among a mineral of metals base,	
	Shows itself pure; a weeps for what is done.	

Claudius decides to send Hamlet away from Denmark. He orders Rosencrantz and Guildenstern to join with others to find Polonius's body and take it to the chapel. He hopes he can avoid slanderous accusations.

Write about it
Character and relationships

Neither Gertrude nor Claudius offers comforting words to the other in Scene 1. Lines 28–45 afford dramatic opportunities for actors to express character and relationships.

Write a paragraph on each of the following, saying how you would use each to give the audience insight into character and relationships:

- Claudius three times gives an order to Gertrude: 'come away', 'Come', 'come away'. How might she respond each time?
- Gertrude says nothing during Claudius's final speech. What is she doing throughout?
- Claudius makes a decision to exile Hamlet, but to whom might he speak lines 29–32?
- In lines 41–4, Claudius seems concerned that slanders and rumours must not damage his reputation. He proposes to brief his 'wisest friends' to prevent it happening. What does that suggest about his character?

countenance condone, accept

join you with … aid recruit more help

speak fair humour him

our wisest friends this suggests Claudius and Gertrude are supported by a coterie of close advisers

untimely wrongly, inappropriately

o'er the world's diameter to the ends of the world

level accurately

blank target

name reputation

woundless invulnerable

Compounded mixed, blended

kin related

1 Ambiguous lines (in pairs)

Lines 40–4 present an interesting problem for a director. The incomplete line 40 (thought to be lost) and the bracketed lines 41–4 (thought to be a deletion by Shakespeare) leave a decision for every director (see p. 268). The incomplete line is the lesser of the problems. The meaning is clear without any further text, from 'Come Gertrude' to 'And what's untimely done'. But what about the bracketed lines?

a Explore the meaning of the bracketed lines by reading them through and then drawing what you think is being described.

b Read the passage from 'Come Gertrude' to the end of the scene without the excised passage. Then read it again with the passage left in.

c Discuss with your partner, and then in the class a whole, what is lost and gained through the inclusion or exclusion of the lines.

d Record in your Director's Journal how you would direct the last twelve lines of the scene.

CLAUDIUS   Oh Gertrude, come away!
The sun no sooner shall the mountains touch
But we will ship him hence, and this vile deed   30
We must with all our majesty and skill
Both countenance and excuse. Ho, Guildenstern!

Enter Rosencrantz and Guildenstern

Friends both, go join you with some further aid.
Hamlet in madness hath Polonius slain,
And from his mother's closet hath he dragged him.   35
Go seek him out, speak fair, and bring the body
Into the chapel. I pray you haste in this.

Exeunt Rosencrantz and Guildenstern

Come Gertrude, we'll call up our wisest friends
And let them know both what we mean to do
And what's untimely done.   40
[Whose whisper o'er the world's diameter,
As level as the cannon to his blank,
Transports his poisoned shot, may miss our name
And hit the woundless air.] Oh come away,
My soul is full of discord and dismay.   45

Exeunt

Act 4 Scene 2

A corridor in the castle

Enter HAMLET

HAMLET   Safely stowed.

GENTLEMEN (*Within*) Hamlet! Lord Hamlet!

HAMLET   But soft, what noise? Who calls on Hamlet? Oh here they
come.

Enter ROSENCRANTZ *and* GUILDENSTERN

ROSENCRANTZ   What have you done my lord with the dead body?   5

HAMLET   Compounded it with dust whereto 'tis kin.

Hamlet's replies bewilder Rosencrantz and Guildenstern. He does not reveal where Polonius's body is hidden. Claudius feels he cannot punish Hamlet severely because the prince is popular in Denmark.

1 Act it out – Hamlet's evasiveness (in threes)

The very short Scene 2 offers excellent opportunities for acting. Hamlet has been presented in many different ways (washing a bloodstained shirt, waking from sleep and so on), and his mocking language invites the actor to all kinds of stage business.

Take parts and act the scene to maximise dramatic effect. It will help your performance if you think about the different strategies Hamlet uses in lines 9–27 to avoid telling Rosencrantz and Guildenstern where Polonius's body is hidden:

• He insults Rosencrantz with the 'sponge' and 'ape' comparisons.
• He brands Rosencrantz as too dull to recognise satire.
• He speaks an enigmatic riddle, 'The body is with the king …'.
• 'Hide fox, and all after!' In some productions, Hamlet runs away as he speaks line 27, chased by the two courtiers. But consider other possibilities and work out how the three characters leave the stage. Discuss how the hunting image might be applicable to the play as a whole.

be demanded of a sponge when questioned by a sponge-like character

replication reply

countenance favour, goodwill

authorities influence

like an ape in the corner of his jaw in the sense that an ape chews and retains food in its mouth before swallowing it

gleaned gathered, harvested

knavish sarcastic, satirical

Characters
Hamlet's mercurial nature

We have seen different aspects of Hamlet's character so far in the play: his impulsiveness, his procrastination, his melancholy, his gravity.

a What further aspect is reflected in the lines opposite, as Hamlet mocks Rosencrantz and Guildenstern and refuses to reveal where the body is? Remember that, according to the time in the play, he has just killed a man.

b Using your own new terms to describe his state of mind, build up a longer list to explore the different sides to Hamlet's character.

c Putting together all the aspects of his character, write a psychiatrist's or counsellor's report on Hamlet.

Hide fox a reference to hunting or a children's game.

the strong law strict restraints

distracted muddled, irrational

like … eyes love him for his looks rather than for sound reasons

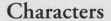

ROSENCRANTZ Tell us where 'tis, that we may take it thence and bear it to the chapel.

HAMLET Do not believe it.

ROSENCRANTZ Believe what?   10

HAMLET That I can keep your counsel and not mine own. Besides, to be demanded of a sponge, what replication should be made by the son of a king?

ROSENCRANTZ Take you me for a sponge my lord?

HAMLET Ay sir, that soaks up the king's countenance, his rewards, his   15
authorities. But such officers do the king best service in the end: he keeps them like an ape in the corner of his jaw, first mouthed to be last swallowed. When he needs what you have gleaned, it is but squeezing you, and, sponge, you shall be dry again.

ROSENCRANTZ I understand you not my lord.   20

HAMLET I am glad of it, a knavish speech sleeps in a foolish ear.

ROSENCRANTZ My lord, you must tell us where the body is, and go with us to the king.

HAMLET The body is with the king, but the king is not with the body. The king is a thing –   25

GUILDENSTERN A thing my lord?

HAMLET Of nothing. Bring me to him. Hide fox, and all after!

Exeunt

Act 4 Scene 3

A state room

Enter CLAUDIUS, *and two or three* ATTENDANTS

CLAUDIUS I have sent to seek him, and to find the body.
How dangerous is it that this man goes loose,
Yet must not we put the strong law on him;
He's loved of the distracted multitude,
Who like not in their judgement, but their eyes;   5

Claudius reflects that he must use desperate methods. Hamlet is brought in. He taunts Claudius with images of the corruption of dead bodies, then reveals where Polonius's body is hidden.

1 'through the guts of a beggar' (in pairs)

In taunting Claudius, Hamlet stresses corruption ('worms') and the levelling nature of death: a king may go 'a progress' (a royal journey) through the guts of a beggar. Hamlet also puns on the Diet ('convocation') of Worms (a town in Germany), where in 1521 the Protestant Martin Luther defended his anti-papal views. The worms are 'politic' because they infiltrate the body in the same way that Polonius had insinuated his way into state affairs and Hamlet's privacy.

- Take parts and speak lines 16–49. Hamlet should be mockingly ironic and Claudius should struggle to control his anger.

▼ Does this representation of Hamlet align with the reading of the lines suggested in Activity 1 above?

scourge punishment
weighed noted

Deliberate pause planned
appliance remedies

Without outside

variable service different dishes in a menu

i'th'other place hell
nose smell

A will stay till you come he won't move (in the theatre, Hamlet's ironic remark often makes the audience laugh)

162

And where 'tis so, th'offender's scourge is weighed,
But never the offence. To bear all smooth and even,
This sudden sending him away must seem
Deliberate pause. Diseases desperate grown
By desperate appliance are relieved,   10
Or not at all.

Enter ROSENCRANTZ

How now, what hath befallen?

ROSENCRANTZ   Where the dead body is bestowed, my lord,
We cannot get from him.

CLAUDIUS   But where is he?

ROSENCRANTZ   Without, my lord, guarded, to know your pleasure.

CLAUDIUS   Bring him before us.

ROSENCRANTZ   Ho! bring in my lord.   15

Enter HAMLET *and* GUILDENSTERN

CLAUDIUS   Now Hamlet, where's Polonius?

HAMLET   At supper.

CLAUDIUS   At supper? Where?

HAMLET   Not where he eats, but where a is eaten. A certain convocation
of politic worms are e'en at him. Your worm is your only emperor   20
for diet: we fat all creatures else to fat us, and we fat ourselves for
maggots. Your fat king and your lean beggar is but variable service,
two dishes, but to one table; that's the end.

CLAUDIUS   Alas, alas.

HAMLET   A man may fish with the worm that hath eat of a king, and   25
eat of the fish that hath fed of that worm.

CLAUDIUS   What dost thou mean by this?

HAMLET   Nothing but to show you how a king may go a progress
through the guts of a beggar.

CLAUDIUS   Where is Polonius?   30

HAMLET   In heaven, send thither to see. If your messenger find him not
there, seek him i'th'other place yourself. But if indeed you find him
not within this month, you shall nose him as you go up the stairs
into the lobby.

CLAUDIUS   Go seek him there.   35

HAMLET   A will stay till you come.

[*Exeunt Attendants*]

Claudius tells Hamlet a ship and attendants wait to take him to England. Hamlet bids Claudius an ironic farewell. Claudius reveals he has written letters ordering Hamlet's immediate execution in England.

1 Two crucial moments (in pairs)

a **Hamlet's suspicions** Who is the 'cherub'? At line 44, Claudius replies to Hamlet's positive acceptance of exile to England with: 'So is it if thou knew'st our purposes.' The words have sinister implications: Claudius is planning to have Hamlet killed. Hamlet responds: 'I see a cherub that sees them' (line 45). At whom (or what) does Hamlet look when he says 'cherub', and why does he use that word? Discuss reasons for your decisions, and say whether you think Hamlet suspects that Claudius intends to have him killed.

b **Hamlet's obsession** 'man and wife is one flesh'. Throughout the play, Hamlet has been obsessed by his mother's sexuality. His lines 48–9 reveal that fixation. But how does he speak the lines (with loathing, humour, calm logic, or with some other feeling or combination of feelings)? Advise the actor, giving reasons.

2 'Do it England'

The first performances of *Hamlet* would have been in London, so the resonance of the passage about England would have had a special significance for the English audience. England (or possibly the King of England) would have been seen at the time as an ally of Denmark, and a country that owes Claudius a favour.

a Divide the class into two groups: those who favour the death of Hamlet, and those who do not. Have Claudius stand in the middle of the two groups and deliver his lines. They consist of three sentences. At the end of each sentence, each group expresses its thoughts about what Claudius is saying. This can be done chorally, and/or with individual voices.

b Afterwards, sit together and reflect: how did Claudius feel about the response of the choral groups? And how did they, in turn feel about his resolution to kill Hamlet?

c As choruses again, change your allegiance to 'England' and 'Denmark', or two countries you know that are both closely allied but potentially competitive. How does this shift affect your understanding of what the London audience might have felt?

---

do tender have concern for

fiery impassioned, seemingly impulsive
bark ship
at help in the right direction
Th'associates tend a team is prepared
bent leaning towards, ready for

one flesh Hamlet is alluding to the Bible – see Genesis 2:24, Matthew 19:5 and Corinthians 6:16
at foot closely

else leans on is connected with

at aught as having any value

cicatrice scar
free awe England pays a bounty to Denmark
coldly set look at with indifference
congruing leading, agreeing

hectic terrible fever

haps fortunes

CLAUDIUS   Hamlet, this deed, for thine especial safety,
              Which we do tender, as we dearly grieve
              For that which thou hast done, must send thee hence
              With fiery quickness. Therefore prepare thyself.   40
              The bark is ready and the wind at help,
              Th'associates tend, and everything is bent
              For England.

HAMLET   For England?

CLAUDIUS   Ay Hamlet.

HAMLET   Good.

CLAUDIUS   So is it if thou knew'st our purposes.

HAMLET   I see a cherub that sees them. But come, for England! Farewell   45
           dear mother.

CLAUDIUS   Thy loving father, Hamlet.

HAMLET   My mother. Father and mother is man and wife, man and wife
           is one flesh, and so, my mother. Come, for England.   *Exit*

CLAUDIUS   Follow him at foot, tempt him with speed aboard.   50
              Delay it not, I'll have him hence tonight.
              Away, for everything is sealed and done
              That else leans on th'affair. Pray you make haste.
                        [*Exeunt Rosencrantz and Guildenstern*]
              And England, if my love thou hold'st at aught,
              As my great power thereof may give thee sense,   55
              Since yet thy cicatrice looks raw and red
              After the Danish sword, and thy free awe
              Pays homage to us – thou mayst not coldly set
              Our sovereign process, which imports at full,
              By letters congruing to that effect,   60
              The present death of Hamlet. Do it England,
              For like the hectic in my blood he rages,
              And thou must cure me. Till I know 'tis done,
              Howe'er my haps, my joys were ne'er begun.   *Exit*

Fortinbras sends a captain to ask Claudius for permission to pass through Danish territory. The captain tells Hamlet the army will fight for a tiny, unprofitable part of Poland. Hamlet reflects on a sick society.

Themes

Sickness and corruption

The use of the word 'rank', and the metaphor of 'th'impostume … / That inward breaks, and shows no cause without / Why the man dies' raises again the imagery and theme of sickness and corruption.

a Look back through the play and try to identify some of the images and themes of sickness and corruption (for example, see Act 1 Scene 5, lines 82–3). Hamlet's own melancholy is closely associated with the health and well-being of the state of Denmark: his sickness reflects that of the country, and vice-versa. The purging of this sickness is part of the action of the play, and reveals much about Hamlet as a character: his inward melancholy and imbalance, his sense that 'the time is out of joint'.

b Yet another theme that is evident here is the contrast between action and thought/reflection. How does it relate to the theme of sickness and corruption? Fortinbras represents to Hamlet the epitome of action – even over a seemingly pointless piece of land in Poland. Look at the two parts of this scene, and perform them to mark the change of mood and resolution in Hamlet.

▼ Fortinbras and his army in the Russian film director Kozintsev's imaginative re-creation of Scene 4. What is Fortinbras's function in the play as a whole?

conveyance passage
You know the rendezvous you know the terms of the agreement and a possible meeting
would aught wishes to negotiate
in his eye face to face
softly quietly, carefully

How purposed with what purpose

main entire country

addition exaggeration

ranker rate greater price
in fee outright
garrisoned defended, ready for battle
Will not debate … straw will not be enough to resolve this trivial matter
impostume abscess, inner sore

God buy you God be with you

Act 4 Scene 4

The sea coast near Elsinore

Enter FORTINBRAS *with his* army

FORTINBRAS	Go captain, from me greet the Danish king.
	Tell him that by his licence, Fortinbras
	Craves the conveyance of a promised march
	Over his kingdom. You know the rendezvous.
	If that his majesty would aught with us, 5
	We shall express our duty in his eye,
	And let him know so.
CAPTAIN	I will do't, my lord.
FORTINBRAS	Go softly on.

[Exit Fortinbras, with the army]

[Enter HAMLET, ROSENCRANTZ, *etc.*

HAMLET	Good sir, whose powers are these?
CAPTAIN	They are of Norway sir. 10
HAMLET	How purposed sir I pray you?
CAPTAIN	Against some part of Poland.
HAMLET	Who commands them sir?
CAPTAIN	The nephew to old Norway, Fortinbras.
HAMLET	Goes it against the main of Poland sir, 15
	Or for some frontier?
CAPTAIN	Truly to speak, and with no addition,
	We go to gain a little patch of ground
	That hath in it no profit but the name.
	To pay five ducats, five, I would not farm it, 20
	Nor will it yield to Norway or the Pole
	A ranker rate, should it be sold in fee.
HAMLET	Why then the Polack never will defend it.
CAPTAIN	Yes, it is already garrisoned.
HAMLET	Two thousand souls and twenty thousand ducats 25
	Will not debate the question of this straw.
	This is th'impostume of much wealth and peace,
	That inward breaks, and shows no cause without
	Why the man dies. I humbly thank you sir.
CAPTAIN	God buy you sir. *[Exit]*

167

Hamlet criticises his delay in revenging his father's death. Is it forgetfulness or too much thought that stops him? Prompted by his encounter with Fortinbras's army, he resolves to speed to his revenge.

1 Hamlet is spurred on to revenge (in pairs)

The soliloquy opposite marks a turning point for Hamlet: between inaction and reflection on the one hand (putting aside the impulsive killing of Polonius), and the carrying out of his revenge mission on the other. Sometimes the soliloquy is cut in performance because it does not appear in the First Folio (see p. 268). Although Hamlet finally decides on revenge, he deludes himself when in line 45 he says he has 'cause, and will, and strength, and means' to do it: he is a prisoner under guard being escorted to exile. Scene 6 will reveal that another chance encounter (this time with pirates) frees him to find the strength and means for revenge.

a First, divide the soliloquy into sections. You might feel that it splits into three parts or more, according to your interpretation of the meaning and the state of Hamlet's resolve.

b Read the soliloquy, taking turns to read each of the sections to each other. Does your interpretation fit the structure and meaning of the speech? Does it work well?

c Now perform some of these interpretations to the class as a whole. What differences did pairs see in terms of the sections and structure?

d Explore different ways of speaking the soliloquy: individually; echoing words and phrases you think especially important; speaking short sections in turn as a kind of anxious 'conversation'; or as if you are trying to persuade someone of the argument you are developing. You might also decide that some parts of the soliloquy are best performed chorally.

e After your explorations, write notes in your Director's Journal on how the soliloquy might be delivered on stage.

2 Hamlet's soliloquies

In preparation for work later in your study of the play, look back at the previous soliloquies by Hamlet.

a Draw up a table to indicate the key characteristics of each of these soliloquies, and to consider the extent to which each marks a turning point in the play so far. Column headings such as 'Quotation', 'Language/ theatrical device', 'Effect', and 'Significance' (in the play as a whole or in Hamlet's development) will help you organise your ideas.

---

inform against rebuke

spur sharpen

good and market profit

large discourse powerful intelligence and capability

fust go stale

Bestial oblivion animal lack of awareness of the past or future

craven scruple cowardly restraint

gross as earth as mundane and obvious as the ground before me

mass and charge numbers and cost

Makes … event mocks death

stained defiled

for a fantasy and trick of fame on the basis of a mere idea and a promise of honour

Whereon … the cause where there is not enough room to fight

continent large enough container

ROSENCRANTZ	Will't please you go my lord?	30
HAMLET	I'll be with you straight; go a little before.	

[*Exeunt all but Hamlet*]

How all occasions do inform against me,
And spur my dull revenge! What is a man
If his chief good and market of his time
Be but to sleep and feed? A beast, no more.   35
Sure he that made us with such large discourse,
Looking before and after, gave us not
That capability and god-like reason
To fust in us unused. Now whether it be
Bestial oblivion, or some craven scruple   40
Of thinking too precisely on th'event –
A thought which quartered hath but one part wisdom
And ever three parts coward – I do not know
Why yet I live to say this thing's to do,
Sith I have cause, and will, and strength, and means   45
To do't. Examples gross as earth exhort me.
Witness this army of such mass and charge,
Led by a delicate and tender prince,
Whose spirit with divine ambition puffed
Makes mouths at the invisible event,   50
Exposing what is mortal and unsure
To all that fortune, death and danger dare,
Even for an egg-shell. Rightly to be great
Is not to stir without great argument,
But greatly to find quarrel in a straw   55
When honour's at the stake. How stand I then,
That have a father killed, a mother stained,
Excitements of my reason and my blood,
And let all sleep, while to my shame I see
The imminent death of twenty thousand men,   60
That for a fantasy and trick of fame
Go to their graves like beds, fight for a plot
Whereon the numbers cannot try the cause,
Which is not tomb enough and continent
To hide the slain. Oh from this time forth,   65
My thoughts be bloody or be nothing worth.   *Exit*]

Gertrude refuses to see Ophelia, but is told that Ophelia is mad and needs pity. Gertrude agrees to admit Ophelia, but expresses guilt and misgivings about the future.

Themes

More sickness and corruption

See the previous reference to sickness and corruption on page 166. While it cannot be said that Ophelia is corrupt, she is certainly corrupted – and she appears to be sick. Link your exploration of the imagery and theme of sickness to Ophelia's state in this scene.

1 Does Gertrude share Claudius's secret? (in pairs)

Gertrude's lines 17–20 display a guilty conscience. She speaks of her 'sick soul', and says that guilty people give themselves away because they cannot hide their fear of being found out. Some critics argue that these lines show she shares, or suspects, Claudius's secret, and is complicit in her first husband's murder. What is your view?

a Look back at Gertrude's appearances (Act 1 Scene 2; Act 2 Scene 2; Act 3 Scenes 1, 2 and 4; Act 4 Scene 1). One person looks for evidence to support the view that Gertrude does not know that Claudius killed King Hamlet. The other person tries to find evidence that Gertrude *does* know about Claudius's crime.

b Present your conflicting arguments as powerfully as possible in one of the following forms: question-and-answer (spoken or written); an essay; a scene in a legal court (like a disciplinary hearing or public hearing).

Stagecraft

Ophelia enters – 'playing on a lute'?

In the First Quarto (see p. 268) the stage direction at line 20 is 'Enter Ophelia playing on a lute, and her hair down singing'. In Shakespeare's time it was customary for madness in women to be marked by a long wig of loose hair.

a How would you stage Ophelia's entrance? The images on pages 172 and 180 might help you decide.

b What signs of madness in women might be used in a modern production? Give reasons for your answer.

importunate persistent
distract mad
What would she have? what does she want?
hems clears her throat
Spurns … straws gets angry at little things

to collection to work out a meaning
yawn guess

conjectures suppositions, ideas
ill-breeding suspicious, trouble-makers'

toy trifle, petty thing
prologue precursor
amiss misfortune

Act 4 Scene 5
The Great Hall of Elsinore Castle

Enter HORATIO, GERTRUDE *and a* GENTLEMAN

GERTRUDE	I will not speak with her.
GENTLEMAN	She is importunate, indeed distract;
	Her mood will needs be pitied.
GERTRUDE	What would she have?
GENTLEMAN	She speaks much of her father, says she hears

There's tricks i'th'world, and hems, and beats her heart,   5
Spurns enviously at straws, speaks things in doubt
That carry but half sense. Her speech is nothing,
Yet the unshapèd use of it doth move
The hearers to collection. They yawn at it,
And botch the words up fit to their own thoughts,   10
Which, as her winks and nods and gestures yield them,
Indeed would make one think there might be thought,
Though nothing sure, yet much unhappily.

HORATIO   'Twere good she were spoken with, for she may strew
Dangerous conjectures in ill-breeding minds.   15

GERTRUDE   Let her come in.

[Exit Gentleman]

(*Aside*) To my sick soul, as sin's true nature is,
Each toy seems prologue to some great amiss.
So full of artless jealousy is guilt,
It spills itself in fearing to be spilt.   20

Enter OPHELIA *distracted*

OPHELIA   Where is the beauteous majesty of Denmark?

Ophelia's first song recalls the death of her father. She replies enigmatically to Claudius, declares that the future is uncertain, then sings a song about the loss of virginity.

▼ Ophelia's mental and emotional derangement has been acted in many ways: dreamily trance-like, frantically angry, sexually obsessed, distanced. This picture shows how Ophelia appeared in a 2003 Birmingham Repertory Theatre/Edinburgh International Festival co-production. How closely does she match your idea of Ophelia driven into madness?

cockle hat hat with a shell emblem, worn by pilgrims

shoon shoes

imports means

mark pay attention

shrowd death sheet, shroud

Larded decorated

good dild God reward

owl (symbol of death?)

baker's daughter (symbol of lust? Another suggestions is that the references are to a folktale in which a baker's daughter was skimpy with the dough when a beggar asked her for bread – she was transformed into an owl as a result)

Conceit wild thoughts

betime early

dupped undid

GERTRUDE	How now Ophelia?
OPHELIA	*She sings*

How should I your true love know
From another one?
By his cockle hat and staff   25
And his sandal shoon.

GERTRUDE	Alas sweet lady, what imports this song?
OPHELIA	Say you? Nay, pray you mark.

He is dead and gone lady,   *Song*
He is dead and gone;   30
At his head a grass-green turf,
At his heels a stone.

Oho!

GERTRUDE	Nay but Ophelia –
OPHELIA	Pray you mark. 35

White his shrowd as the mountain snow –   *Song*

Enter CLAUDIUS

GERTRUDE	Alas, look here my lord.
OPHELIA	

Larded all with sweet flowers,
Which bewept to the grave did not go
With true-love showers.   40

CLAUDIUS How do you, pretty lady?

OPHELIA Well good dild you. They say the owl was a baker's daughter. Lord, we know what we are, but know not what we may be. God be at your table.

CLAUDIUS Conceit upon her father.   45

OPHELIA Pray let's have no words of this, but when they ask you what it means, say you this –

Tomorrow is Saint Valentine's day,   *Song*
All in the morning betime,
And I a maid at your window,   50
To be your Valentine.
Then up he rose and donned his clothes
And dupped the chamber door;
Let in the maid that out a maid
Never departed more.   55

CLAUDIUS Pretty Ophelia!

1 Act out Ophelia's troubled state (in threes)

Ophelia's song tells of young men's sexual appetite, and how they refuse to marry women with whom they have slept. The song has been interpreted both as Ophelia's seduction by Hamlet, and as Gertrude's seduction by Claudius. Ophelia's songs, her sorrow for her father, her threat that 'My brother shall know of it' and her strange farewell – 'Good night ladies …' – both enthrall and disturb audiences in the theatre.

- To experience the emotional and dramatic power of Ophelia's first 'mad' appearance, take parts as Gertrude, Claudius and Ophelia, and act out lines 21–72.

Characters

Ophelia's attitude to sex

Shakespeare provides no evidence that Hamlet and Ophelia have had sex together, although both his and her obsession with sexual matters suggests a preoccupation with the subject. We have already identified that Hamlet associates sex with death, corruption, his mother's infidelity and licentiousness. But what about Ophelia?

a Look back at Ophelia's appearances before this moment, especially in Act 1 Scene 3 and Act 3 Scene 2, and gauge the degree to which she was 'innocent' of sex. Look at her speeches in the present scene, where 'madness' is associated with an obsessiveness about sex.

b Can you characterise the different approach to this theme of love, identity and sexuality between Hamlet and Ophelia? Ophelia is depicted as a victim for much of the play, and subject to the directions of her father, brother and lover. Is this a fair reflection of your view of her, or would you see her as stronger and more independent than this 'victim' theory allows?

c If you wish to make notes at this stage, you could do so in the form of character notes (building up toward a more considered view and piece of writing later) or in the form of a letter from a courtier who has observed Ophelia's behaviour.

Gis Jesus

By Cock by God, but with obvious double meaning
tumbled had sex with

single spies on their own

remove banishment
muddied agitated
greenly naively, foolishly
In hugger-mugger in secret

as much containing as serious

Feeds … clouds imagines all kinds of things
buzzers gossips
infect his ear poison his mind
necessity, of matter beggared they are obliged, lacking facts
our … arraign to accuse me
murdering piece small cannon
superfluous death multiple deaths

OPHELIA   Indeed la! Without an oath I'll make an end on't.

             By Gis and by Saint Charity,
                Alack and fie for shame,
             Young men will do't if they come to't –   60
                By Cock, they are to blame.
             Quoth she, 'Before you tumbled me,
                You promised me to wed.'

    He answers –

             So would I ha' done, by yonder sun,   65
                And thou hadst not come to my bed.

CLAUDIUS   How long hath she been thus?

OPHELIA   I hope all will be well. We must be patient, but I cannot choose but weep to think they would lay him i'th' cold ground. My brother shall know of it, and so I thank you for your good counsel.   70 Come, my coach. Good night ladies, good night sweet ladies, good night, good night.   *Exit*

CLAUDIUS   Follow her close, give her good watch I pray you.

                                   [Exit Horatio]

    Oh this is the poison of deep grief, it springs
    All from her father's death, [and now behold –]   75
    Oh Gertrude, Gertrude,
    When sorrows come, they come not single spies,
    But in battalions. First, her father slain;
    Next, your son gone, and he most violent author
    Of his own just remove; the people muddied,   80
    Thick and unwholesome in their thoughts and whispers
    For good Polonius' death – and we have done but greenly
    In hugger-mugger to inter him; poor Ophelia
    Divided from herself and her fair judgement,
    Without the which we are pictures, or mere beasts;   85
    Last, and as much containing as all these,
    Her brother is in secret come from France,
    Feeds on his wonder, keeps himself in clouds,
    And wants not buzzers to infect his ear
    With pestilent speeches of his father's death,   90
    Wherein necessity, of matter beggared,
    Will nothing stick our person to arraign
    In ear and ear. O my dear Gertrude, this,
    Like to a murdering piece, in many places
    Gives me superfluous death.   95

A Messenger tells Claudius that Laertes and an angry mob are coming, and that some of the rioters shout that Laertes should be king. Laertes bursts in and demands to know what happened to his father.

1 A political crisis (in pairs)

After so much attention to 'family matters' in the play, politics makes a full-blooded return. Laertes, leading a 'rabble' of citizens, has swept aside Claudius's bodyguards. The citizens wish to overthrow Claudius's regime and place Laertes on the throne. The Messenger gives a graphic account of the insurrection, comparing the violent approach of the citizens to the ocean's tide rushing over the shore.

a Take turns to speak the Messenger's lines 98–108. Bring out the urgency (and fear?) he feels as he sees the potential collapse of Claudius's regime.

b Talk together about how you would stage the episode between lines 110 and 116, in which the ordinary people of Denmark are briefly glimpsed and heard.

c Discuss what might have prompted the people to support Laertes for the kingship, and to overthrow Claudius.

Characters
Laertes's return

Laertes has returned from France on the news of his father's death. He has acted swiftly and with some degree of reason, though he seems impelled by motives of revenge. Laertes provides another model for Hamlet, after the prince's recent encounter with Fortinbras.

a Look particularly at lines 118–21, where Polonius's death has been converted in Laertes's mind to an act that has made him a 'bastard', as if he were not born of a true marriage between Polonius and Laertes's mother (whom we do not see in the play). Why is there reference to a 'harlot', and how might a director ask an actor to play these lines? For example, branding the harlot 'Even here' could be interpreted as a reference to Gertrude. Is Gertrude his mother, or is he making a more general point?

b Although it is unlikely you will write a full character study of Laertes himself, his similarities and differences in relation to Hamlet are worth recording as you move through the play. Indeed, Laertes and Fortinbras act as foils to Hamlet. In what ways do each of them, and their actions, shed light on Hamlet himself? Conversely, what does Hamlet's presence suggest about them?

Attend! attention!
Swissers Swiss guards

overpeering of his list
breaking its boundary
flats shore
impitious impetuous, without pity
head advance party
The rabble the people

ratifiers and props supporters

counter wrong-headed, improper

That drop ... calm my reason and inner calm
cuckold deceived husband
unsmirchèd
untouched, clean, pure

A noise within

GERTRUDE Alack, what noise is this?

CLAUDIUS Attend! Where are my Swissers? Let them guard the door.

Enter a MESSENGER

What is the matter?

MESSENGER   Save yourself my lord.
                    The ocean, overpeering of his list,
                    Eats not the flats with more impitious haste   100
                    Than young Laertes in a riotous head
                    O'erbears your officers. The rabble call him lord,
                    And, as the world were now but to begin,
                    Antiquity forgot, custom not known,
                    The ratifiers and props of every word,   105
                    They cry 'Choose we! Laertes shall be king.'
                    Caps, hands and tongues applaud it to the clouds,
                    'Laertes shall be king, Laertes king!'

GERTRUDE   How cheerfully on the false trail they cry!
                    Oh this is counter, you false Danish dogs!   110

A noise within

CLAUDIUS   The doors are broke.

Enter LAERTES *with others*

LAERTES   Where is this king? – Sirs, stand you all without.

ALL   No, let's come in.

LAERTES   I pray you give me leave.

ALL   We will, we will.   115

LAERTES   I thank you. Keep the door.

[Exeunt followers]

                              O thou vile king,
                    Give me my father.

GERTRUDE   Calmly, good Laertes.

LAERTES   That drop of blood that's calm proclaims me bastard,
                    Cries cuckold to my father, brands the harlot
                    Even here, between the chaste unsmirchèd brow   120
                    Of my true mother.

Claudius is unafraid to face the wrath of Laertes. Claudius claims to be protected by the divine aura of kingship. He urges Laertes to distinguish between friends and foes, and says he is innocent of Polonius's death.

1 Claudius the hypocrite (in threes)

Claudius is unperturbed by Laertes's anger. He asserts that God prevents a monarch coming to harm ('There's such divinity doth hedge a king'). Claudius sounds completely confident, but his words betray his utter hypocrisy: God did not protect old Hamlet from being murdered by his own brother.

* Take parts and speak all the lines in the script opposite. Bring out Claudius's devious self-assurance, Gertrude's protectiveness and Laertes's enraged desire for revenge.

Write about it
Claudius the manipulator

Claudius continues to scheme. He is engineering Hamlet's removal to England, and planning Hamlet's death there. But perhaps it is also occurring to him that Laertes might wish to kill Hamlet himself. Claudius's skill in manoeuvring others to his will is evident; yet, at the same time, do you think he is stupid and incompetent in trying to cover his own malevolent acts?

a Design a diagram or set of notes in which Claudius is at the centre, with the other characters around him. Indicate, in a few words, how hypocritical he is to all the characters linked to him.

b If hypocrisy is one of Claudius's defining characteristics, what are the other aspects of his character? Write a paragraph or two to capture the complexity of his character as revealed so far in the play. Include quotations.

2 Four revengers

Laertes swears to avenge his father's death. He becomes the fourth revenger in the play. The others are Hamlet (revenge for his father's death); Fortinbras (campaigns to win back his father's lost land); and Pyrrhus (slaughters Priam to avenge his own father's death).

In lines 130–6 Laertes uses the exaggerated language of the traditional hero of revenge tragedy.

a Speak the lines as bombastically as you can. Then identify lines earlier in the play where Hamlet's language is similar in tone to Laertes's.

b Which of the four has the greatest motive and justification for revenge?

---

hedge surround

Acts little of his will cannot do what it would like to

incensed angry

vows promises of loyalty

both … negligence I care not for heaven or hell

stay you hold you back

husband manage

soopstake sweepstake, as in gambling

pelican the pelican was thought to pierce its own breast with its bill, to allow young to feed on its blood

Repast feed

most sensibly in grief grieving deeply

level well aimed

CLAUDIUS	What is the cause, Laertes,
	That thy rebellion looks so giant-like? –
	Let him go, Gertrude, do not fear our person.
	There's such divinity doth hedge a king
	That treason can but peep to what it would, 125
	Acts little of his will. – Tell me Laertes,
	Why thou art thus incensed. – Let him go Gertrude. –
	Speak man.
LAERTES	Where is my father?
CLAUDIUS	Dead.
GERTRUDE	But not by him.
CLAUDIUS	Let him demand his fill.
LAERTES	How came he dead? I'll not be juggled with. 130
	To hell allegiance, vows to the blackest devil,
	Conscience and grace to the profoundest pit!
	I dare damnation. To this point I stand,
	That both the worlds I give to negligence,
	Let come what comes, only I'll be revenged 135
	Most throughly for my father.
CLAUDIUS	Who shall stay you?
LAERTES	My will, not all the world.
	And for my means, I'll husband them so well,
	They shall go far with little.
CLAUDIUS	Good Laertes,
	If you desire to know the certainty 140
	Of your dear father, is't writ in your revenge
	That, soopstake, you will draw both friend and foe,
	Winner and loser?
LAERTES	None but his enemies.
CLAUDIUS	Will you know them then?
LAERTES	To his good friends thus wide I'll ope my arms, 145
	And like the kind life-rendering pelican,
	Repast them with my blood.
CLAUDIUS	Why now you speak
	Like a good child and a true gentleman.
	That I am guiltless of your father's death,
	And am most sensibly in grief for it, 150
	It shall as level to your judgement pierce
	As day does to your eye.

Laertes is appalled by Ophelia's madness. It moves him even more strongly to revenge. Ophelia sings again of death. She distributes herbs and flowers.

sense and virtue power and effectiveness

paid with weight revenged beyond proportion and due balance

our scale turn the beam revenge tilts the scales our way

fine refined

instance part

bier funeral carriage

a-down with lower tone (also a refrain)

how the wheel becomes it how the wheel of Fortune turns

steward servant

nothing's nonsense is

matter sense

document lesson

thoughts melancholy

a made a good end he died well

favour good manners

1 Ophelia trapped

The photograph above is from a 2011 production of *Hamlet*. It shows Ophelia trapped in a net, mad and unable to relate to the social situation in which she finds herself. Although entrapment is not a major image or theme in the play, the notion of general confinement is – and it is not just Ophelia who is confined.

- Discuss how appropriate you think the depiction of Ophelia is in the photograph, and in what other ways you could imagine presenting her in this scene.

2 'There's rosemary' (in pairs)

There is a symbolic significance in the herbs and flowers that Ophelia mentions, which include: fennel (flattery), columbines (ingratitude and infidelity), rue (sorrow), daisy (springtime, love) and violets (sweetness).

a Which flowers does Ophelia give to whom, and why?

b What is the dramatic effect of giving these gifts?

A noise within: 'Let her come in'

LAERTES   How now, what noise is that?

Enter OPHELIA

O heat dry up my brains, tears seven times salt
Burn out the sense and virtue of mine eye!   155
By heaven, thy madness shall be paid with weight
Till our scale turn the beam. O rose of May,
Dear maid, kind sister, sweet Ophelia –
O heavens, is't possible a young maid's wits
Should be as mortal as an old man's life?   160
Nature is fine in love, and where 'tis fine,
It sends some precious instance of itself
After the thing it loves.

OPHELIA   They bore him bare-faced on the bier   *Song*
              Hey non nonny, nonny, hey nonny,   165
          And in his grave rained many a tear –
Fare you well my dove.

LAERTES   Hadst thou thy wits, and didst persuade revenge,
It could not move thus.

OPHELIA   You must sing a-down a-down, and you call him a-down-a.   170
Oh how the wheel becomes it. It is the false steward that stole his
master's daughter.

LAERTES   This nothing's more than matter.

OPHELIA   There's rosemary, that's for remembrance – pray you, love,
remember – and there is pansies, that's for thoughts.   175

LAERTES   A document in madness, thoughts and remembrance fitted.

OPHELIA   There's fennel for you, and columbines. There's rue for you,
and here's some for me; we may call it herb of grace a Sundays.
Oh you must wear your rue with a difference. There's a daisy. I
would give you some violets, but they withered all when my father   180
died. They say a made a good end.

[Sings]
For bonny sweet Robin is all my joy.

LAERTES   Thought and affliction, passion, hell itself,
She turns to favour and to prettiness.

Ophelia again sings about her father's death. Claudius sympathises with Laertes's grief, and makes an offer: if Claudius proves to blame, Laertes can be king. If not, Claudius will help Laertes find justice and revenge.

1 Songs in Shakespeare (in small groups)

Ophelia's songs are typical of many that appear in Shakespeare's plays. Most of them conform to a simple rhyming pattern, and they are often performed live on stage with lute or guitar accompaniment to suit the production style and the director's conception of the play.

a Research other songs in Shakespeare, and work out which types of characters sing these songs, and why.

b Find some recordings of songs in Shakespeare, and listen to them (there are four songs in this scene alone). Work in small groups to research and interpret the songs, then present them to the rest of the class.

2 The end of Ophelia

This is the last time we see Ophelia alive in the play. In Scene 7, we hear from Gertrude that she has drowned, either through suicide or accident.

- In the light of this information, how would you design Ophelia's exit from the stage at line 195?

3 Claudius seizes his opportunity (in pairs)

Claudius has been trying to control and direct Laertes's anger. Now, the entrance of Ophelia and her effect on Laertes give the king an opportunity to exploit the situation to his own advantage.

a Take parts and read lines 196–214 several times. Make Claudius as persuasive as you can, and consider Laertes's confused feelings as he watches his sister's bizarre behaviour. Express his anger about his father being buried without ceremony. Also, think about whether you should leave a long pause before Laertes says 'Let this be so' in line 207.

b Talk together about how Claudius manages to turn Laertes's passion for revenge to his own ends.

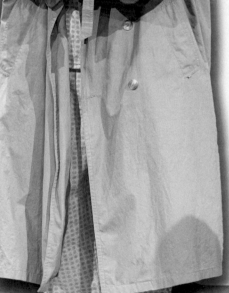

All flaxen was his poll his hair was white

commune with share

of whom of whichever

collateral indirect
touched guilty

lend grant
labour work

hatchment coat of arms
ostentation display of mourning

where th'offence … axe fall let the guilty be punished

OPHELIA   And will a not come again?   *Song*   185
                 And will a not come again?
                     No, no, he is dead,
                     Go to thy death-bed,
                 He never will come again.
                 His beard was as white as snow,   190
                 All flaxen was his poll,
                     He is gone, he is gone,
                     And we cast away moan,
                 God-a-mercy on his soul.
                 And of all Christian souls, I pray God. God buy you.   *Exit*   195

LAERTES   Do you see this, O God?

CLAUDIUS   Laertes, I must commune with your grief,
                 Or you deny me right. Go but apart,
                 Make choice of whom your wisest friends you will,
                 And they shall hear and judge 'twixt you and me.   200
                 If by direct or by collateral hand
                 They find us touched, we will our kingdom give,
                 Our crown, our life, and all that we call ours,
                 To you in satisfaction. But if not,
                 Be you content to lend your patience to us,   205
                 And we shall jointly labour with your soul
                 To give it due content.

LAERTES   Let this be so.
                 His means of death, his obscure funeral,
                 No trophy, sword, nor hatchment o'er his bones,
                 No noble rite, nor formal ostentation,   210
                 Cry to be heard, as 'twere from heaven to earth,
                 That I must call't in question.

CLAUDIUS   So you shall.
                 And where th'offence is, let the great axe fall.
                 I pray you go with me.
                                                                               Exeunt

Hamlet's letter reveals that he has been captured in a sea battle. By doing a deal with the pirates, he has returned to Denmark. He has sent letters to the king, and urgently wishes to meet Horatio.

1 Hamlet and the pirates (in groups of four or more)

One production solved the problem of why Horatio reads the letter aloud by having the sailor hold the letter up in front of him. Horatio gently turned the letter the right way up (showing that the sailors cannot read). He began to read it silently. The sailors then threatened him, obviously wanting to know how the letter affected them, having done a deal with Hamlet. So Horatio was forced to read it aloud.

a Act it out Occasionally, a production has acted out the letter's contents at the back of the stage, as Horatio reads the action. Follow that example. As one person speaks as Horatio, the others enact what is described in lines 13–18.

b Improvise Imagine the scene where Hamlet has boarded the pirate ship. The pirates would be puzzled to find out who Hamlet was, where he was going and why he needed to return to Denmark. Some of them may wish to kill him. Others see him as a valuable prisoner whom they can exchange for a large ransom. Improvise the scene where Hamlet persuades the pirates to spare him and to help him return to Denmark. Start with his being threatened by them. What deal might he strike with the pirates?

c Write a movie script Work in pairs. You are the joint directors of a movie of *Hamlet*. Movies have different opportunities from stage productions: settings can be changed instantly, a character's thoughts can be presented visually, 'realistic' settings can be used. Work out how you will film Scene 6. For example, Horatio's reading might be done as a voice-over, while the movie shows the action described. Your task is to rewrite Scene 6 as a movie script.

Language in the play
Letter style as opposed to blank verse

The difference between prose and verse style is always significant in Shakespeare.

* Translate the letter into blank verse; then take one section of the verse part of the play (for example, the beginning of the following scene) and translate it into prose.
* What difference does it make, and why do you think Shakespeare uses such variation?

and please him if it pleases God

overlooked read

of very warlike appointment heavily armed

put on a compelled valour were obliged to be brave and fight

thieves of mercy thieves with compassion

repair thou return, come

for the bore of the matter for the weight of their meaning

give you way allow you passage

Act 4 Scene 6

A room in the castle

Enter HORATIO *with an* ATTENDANT

HORATIO	What are they that would speak with me?
ATTENDANT	Seafaring men sir, they say they have letters for you.
HORATIO	Let them come in.

[*Exit Attendant*]

I do not know from what part of the world
I should be greeted, if not from Lord Hamlet.   5

Enter SAILORS

I SAILOR	God bless you sir.
HORATIO	Let him bless thee too.
I SAILOR	A shall sir, and please him. There's a letter for you sir, it came from th'ambassador that was bound for England, if your name be Horatio, as I am let to know it is. 10
HORATIO	(*Reads the letter*) 'Horatio, when thou shalt have overlooked this, give these fellows some means to the king; they have letters for him. Ere we were two days old at sea, a pirate of very warlike appointment gave us chase. Finding ourselves too slow of sail, we put on a compelled valour, and in the grapple I boarded them. On 15 the instant they got clear of our ship, so I alone became their prisoner. They have dealt with me like thieves of mercy, but they knew what they did: I am to do a good turn for them. Let the king have the letters I have sent, and repair thou to me with as much speed as thou wouldest fly death. I have words to speak in thine 20 ear will make thee dumb, yet are they much too light for the bore of the matter. These good fellows will bring thee where I am. Rosencrantz and Guildenstern hold their course for England. Of them I have much to tell thee. Farewell.

He that thou knowest thine,   25
Hamlet.'

Come, I will give you way for these your letters,
And do't the speedier that you may direct me
To him from whom you brought them.

Exeunt

Claudius claims that Hamlet not only killed Polonius, but was intent on killing him, too. He explains that he did not punish Hamlet for two reasons: love of Gertrude, and Hamlet's popularity with the people.

1 Why doesn't he mention Hamlet's madness?

The previous 'letter' scene has given Claudius time to tell Laertes how Polonius was killed. Now he gives two reasons why he took no action against Hamlet (lines 9–24). He does not mention Hamlet's madness.

*   Suggest a reason for Claudius's omission. Relate your answer to the image below.

▼ This image of Laertes from a 2008 production shows him as resolute, noble and flanked by guards. Imagine, as the Messenger reported in Act 4 Scene 5, lines 106–8, that 'Laertes shall be king'. What kind of king would he make? Does he have the right qualities?

my acquittance seal confirm my innocence

knowing understanding

feats deeds
capital deserving of death

mainly mightily, greatly

unsinewed weak

My virtue or my plague to my advantage and pleasure on the one hand; a difficult burden on the other
conjunctive closely joined
sphere orbit
but by her move without her
count account
general gender populace
spring lime-rich water
gyves chains (vices)
Too slightly timbered not strong enough
loud strong

Stood ... perfections was more perfect than all other women

Act 4 Scene 7

A state room in the castle

Enter CLAUDIUS *and* LAERTES

CLAUDIUS	Now must your conscience my acquittance seal,
	And you must put me in your heart for friend,
	Sith you have heard, and with a knowing ear,
	That he which hath your noble father slain
	Pursued my life.
LAERTES	It well appears. But tell me	5
	Why you proceeded not against these feats,
	So crimeful and so capital in nature,
	As by your safety, wisdom, all things else,
	You mainly were stirred up.
CLAUDIUS	Oh for two special reasons,
	Which may to you perhaps seem much unsinewed,	10
	But yet to me they're strong. The queen his mother
	Lives almost by his looks, and for myself,
	My virtue or my plague, be it either which,
	She's so conjunctive to my life and soul,
	That as the star moves not but in his sphere,	15
	I could not but by her. The other motive,
	Why to a public count I might not go,
	Is the great love the general gender bear him,
	Who, dipping all his faults in their affection,
	Work like the spring that turneth wood to stone,	20
	Convert his gyves to graces, so that my arrows,
	Too slightly timbered for so loud a wind,
	Would have reverted to my bow again,
	And not where I had aimed them.
LAERTES	And so have I a noble father lost,	25
	A sister driven into desperate terms,
	Whose worth, if praises may go back again,
	Stood challenger on mount of all the age
	For her perfections. But my revenge will come.

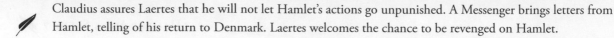
1 Claudius's pleasure is abruptly ended (in pairs)

Claudius makes it clear that he intends to punish Hamlet. He uses an image familiar to Elizabethans: don't let anyone think they can pull my beard and get away with it (lines 32–3). Indeed, at this moment Claudius thinks that on his orders Hamlet will shortly be executed in England. Very soon, he hopes to tell Laertes of Hamlet's death. The letter from Hamlet denies him that pleasure.

a **Reading between the lines** Imagine you are Hamlet writing his letter (lines 43–6) to Claudius. One person reads up to a punctuation mark, then pauses. In each pause, the other person speaks Hamlet's thoughts on what he has just written.

b **Naked** Claudius is puzzled by Hamlet describing himself as 'set naked on your kingdom'. This probably doesn't mean that Hamlet is literally without clothes – but what can it mean? Suggest several explanations for the word that seem to you to be appropriate to the play.

c **Laertes's reaction?** Laertes seems 'lost in it' (line 53). Can you explain why?

Stagecraft

The arrival of the letter

Letters in movies and on stage have the effect of interrupting the action and bringing a different dimension in time as well as character on to the stage or into the foreground. In films, the reading of a letter is often carried out in voice-over, as if it is the inner thoughts of the character reading it, or of a character off stage.

a Which of the following would you advise a director to use, and why? Remember, you do not have to follow the stage directions – they are almost certainly not Shakespeare's.

- The letter read out by Claudius on stage
- Hamlet's disembodied voice.

b What would happen to the letter after it was read? You might like to record your notes in your Director's Journal.

---

flat unfeeling

pastime trivial

we love ourself the natural way in which a king would refer to himself

abuse trick

no such thing no such thing has happened

hand handwriting

character style (or handwriting)

devise help

warms inflames, does good

o'errule me to a peace force me to be friendly

CLAUDIUS   Break not your sleeps for that. You must not think   30
That we are made of stuff so flat and dull
That we can let our beard be shook with danger
And think it pastime. You shortly shall hear more.
I loved your father, and we love ourself,
And that I hope will teach you to imagine –   35

Enter a MESSENGER *with letters*

How now? What news?
MESSENGER   Letters my lord from Hamlet.
This to your majesty, this to the queen.
CLAUDIUS   From Hamlet? Who brought them?
MESSENGER   Sailors my lord they say, I saw them not;
They were given me by Claudio – he received them   40
Of him that brought them.
CLAUDIUS   Laertes, you shall hear them. –
Leave us.

Exit Messenger

[*Reads*] 'High and mighty, you shall know I am set naked on your
kingdom. Tomorrow shall I beg leave to see your kingly eyes, when
I shall, first asking your pardon thereunto, recount th'occasion of   45
my sudden and more strange return.

Hamlet.'

What should this mean? Are all the rest come back?
Or is it some abuse, and no such thing?
LAERTES   Know you the hand?
CLAUDIUS   'Tis Hamlet's character. Naked?   50
And in a postscript here he says alone.
Can you devise me?
LAERTES   I'm lost in it my lord. But let him come –
It warms the very sickness in my heart
That I shall live and tell him to his teeth   55
'Thus didest thou!'
CLAUDIUS   If it be so, Laertes –
As how should it be so? – how otherwise? –
Will you be ruled by me?
LAERTES   Ay my lord,
So you will not o'errule me to a peace.

Claudius begins to hatch a new plot to kill Hamlet. He says that Hamlet envies Laertes, but delays naming the reason for that envy. Instead, Claudius talks of Lamord, an accomplished French soldier.

1 The temptation scene (in pairs)

Claudius realises that his plan to have Hamlet killed in England has failed. Now he sees he can use Laertes's desire for revenge to achieve his aim. Claudius's plot against Hamlet will 'work him / To an exploit … Under the which he shall not choose but fall' (lines 62–4).

Claudius does not immediately tell Laertes of his plan. Instead he talks of 'a quality' of Laertes. When Laertes asks him what that quality is (line 75), Claudius again does not reply directly, but calls the unnamed quality 'A very riband in the cap of youth' (mere ribbon, a decoration on a cap). Yet this quality is 'needful' (or necessary), because it suits youth in the same way that 'health and graveness' suit older people. Claudius then talks about a Frenchman, Lamord.

- Lines 60–161 are often called the 'temptation' scene because Claudius tempts Laertes into a murderous plot. To gain a sense of the conspiracy, sit closely together and quietly speak the lines to each other.

Characters
Further sides to Claudius

In addition to using sophisticated persuasive techniques to motivate Laertes to revenge, Claudius reveals other dimensions to his own character: his enthusiasm for Lamord (which sounds like *la mort* – French for 'death') and his horse-riding skills; his knowledge of Hamlet; and his understanding of Laertes's psychology.

a Do you think Shakespeare is painting the picture of a complex man and king, who is not purely evil but is partially repentant, and also full of earthly enthusiasm and delight – and a good tactician and diplomat? Or are we to read this later episode completely cynically, as the clever operations of a Machiavellian (cunning and opportunist) villain? Discuss this in pairs or small groups, and then report to the class with supporting evidence (look particularly at Act 1 Scene 2, Act 2 Scene 2, Act 3 Scene 1 and Act 3 Scene 3).

b Capture your discussion in the form of an initial character study of Claudius. At this stage, you might write a number of paragraphs on the various sides to his character – and what are, in your view, his prevailing characteristics.

checking at abandoning

an exploit a plot
ripe in my device ready in my scheming

uncharge the practice not suspect trickery

The rather the better
organ agent
falls right falls into place

unworthiest siege least account

sables dark clothes
weeds sober garments

can well are skilful
gallant fashionable young man

incorpsed part of the same body
So far … did his performance outshone even my imagination

brooch jewel in the crown

CLAUDIUS   To thine own peace. If he be now returned,   60
As checking at his voyage, and that he means
No more to undertake it, I will work him
To an exploit, now ripe in my device,
Under the which he shall not choose but fall,
And for his death no wind of blame shall breathe,   65
But even his mother shall uncharge the practice
And call it accident.

[LAERTES   My lord, I will be ruled,
The rather if you could devise it so
That I might be the organ.

CLAUDIUS   It falls right.
You have been talked of since your travel much,   70
And that in Hamlet's hearing, for a quality
Wherein they say you shine. Your sum of parts
Did not together pluck such envy from him
As did that one, and that in my regard
Of the unworthiest siege.

LAERTES   What part is that my lord?   75

CLAUDIUS   A very riband in the cap of youth,
Yet needful too, for youth no less becomes
The light and careless livery that it wears
Than settled age his sables and his weeds
Importing health and graveness.] Two months since   80
Here was a gentleman of Normandy.
I've seen myself, and served against, the French,
And they can well on horseback, but this gallant
Had witchcraft in't. He grew unto his seat,
And to such wondrous doing brought his horse   85
As had he been incorpsed and demi-natured
With the brave beast. So far he topped my thought,
That I in forgery of shapes and tricks
Come short of what he did.

LAERTES   A Norman was't?

CLAUDIUS   A Norman.   90

LAERTES   Upon my life Lamord.

CLAUDIUS   The very same.

LAERTES   I know him well, he is the brooch indeed
And gem of all the nation.

Claudius relates Lamord's praise of Laertes's swordsmanship. Laertes asks what the point of Claudius's words is. Claudius talks of how love fades with time. His words prompt Laertes to seek bloody revenge.

1 Intensifying Laertes's fury (in pairs)

Claudius's two long speeches opposite are intended to work on Laertes's already-inflamed emotions. The first speech reports that Lamord and the best swordsmen in France thought that Laertes was a superior swordsman, outclassing them all. In his long second speech, Claudius reflects on how time kills love, goodness dies of its own excess, and intentions fade away if not quickly carried out. Only when Claudius asks a direct question, 'Laertes, was your father dear to you?' (line 106), does he seem to address what is uppermost in Laertes's thoughts and feelings.

Claudius is deliberately spinning out his story to increase Laertes's resentment against Hamlet: first, by saying that Hamlet envies Laertes's swordsmanship, and wishes to duel with him; second, by implying that Laertes's desire for revenge will fade over time, like love. Claudius wants to work Laertes up into a fury so that he will quickly seize any opportunity to be revenged on Hamlet.

a Experiment with different ways of speaking Claudius's lines opposite. For example, try Claudius always maintaining eye contact with Laertes. Then have Claudius mainly avoiding eye contact, and in his second long speech drifting off into an internal meditation about how love fades with time. Find the style you think is most appropriate.

b Lines 99–101 and 113–22 are in square brackets. They did not appear in the First Folio version of the play (see p. 268). Imagine you are about to put on the play. Will you include these lines or cut them? One of you argues for cutting the lines, the other against. The person arguing to include them might stress how the second bracketed passage echoes the theme of delay. Many of Shakespeare's plays have a long and discursive Act 4, in which key characters deliberate about the action to follow in Act 5. *Macbeth* is a good example of this.

c Laertes's replies are short – indeed curt. Is he a man of action, or simply one who finds it difficult to listen to long passages of persuasive language? Or is there something else on his mind? In your pairs, one of you speaks Laertes's thoughts in response to Claudius's rhetoric, thus elaborating the short responses that he gives in the script. From what you know of Laertes's character in the earlier part of the play, what types of inner responses are most appropriate here?

---

made confession told the truth

art and exercise … defence skill and mastery in swordplay

escrimers master swordsmen

play fence with swords

passages of proof events that bear me out

qualifies moderates, dulls

abate extinguish

is at a like goodness still remains good always

plurisy (disease resulting from) excess

spendthrift tight

to the quick to the heart

CLAUDIUS   He made confession of you,
              And gave you such a masterly report   95
              For art and exercise in your defence,
              And for your rapier most especial,
              That he cried out 'twould be a sight indeed
              If one could match you. [Th'escrimers of their nation
              He swore had neither motion, guard, nor eye,   100
              If you opposed them.] Sir, this report of his
              Did Hamlet so envenom with his envy
              That he could nothing do but wish and beg
              Your sudden coming o'er to play with you.
              Now out of this –
LAERTES   What out of this, my lord?   105
CLAUDIUS   Laertes, was your father dear to you?
              Or are you like the painting of a sorrow,
              A face without a heart?
LAERTES   Why ask you this?
CLAUDIUS   Not that I think you did not love your father,
              But that I know love is begun by time,   110
              And that I see, in passages of proof,
              Time qualifies the spark and fire of it.
              [There lives within the very flame of love
              A kind of wick or snuff that will abate it,
              And nothing is at a like goodness still,   115
              For goodness, growing to a plurisy,
              Dies in his own too much. That we would do,
              We should do when we would, for this 'would' changes,
              And hath abatements and delays as many
              As there are tongues, are hands, are accidents;   120
              And then this 'should' is like a spendthrift sigh,
              That hurts by easing. But to the quick of th'ulcer –]
              Hamlet comes back; what would you undertake
              To show yourself in deed your father's son
              More than in words?
LAERTES   To cut his throat i'th'church.   125

Claudius plans a duel in which one of the swords will not be blunted. Laertes offers to poison the sharpened foil. To make Hamlet's death certain, Claudius proposes to poison Hamlet's drink.

Characters

Insights into character (in pairs)

After careful preparation, Claudius has raised Laertes's hatred of Hamlet to fever pitch. Laertes now plots with Claudius a devious and seemingly foolproof way to murder Hamlet. The two men build upon each other's wickedness in devising ways of ensuring Hamlet's death in a duel. The plot to kill Hamlet involves a duelling sword, sharp ('unbated') and poisoned. With it, Laertes will strike Hamlet in a deceitful thrust ('pass of practice'). A poisoned drink will kill Hamlet if Laertes fails to kill him with his sword.

Take parts and read the script opposite. Then talk together to discover how far you agree with the following statements:

- It is surprising that Laertes has brought a poison ('unction') with him.
- Hamlet is accurately described by Claudius as 'remiss, / Most generous, and free from all contriving' ('remiss' = unsuspecting, 'contriving' = deviousness).
- Claudius has all the details of his plot already in his mind, and only pretends to think up the 'back or second' (the poisoned cup).

1 Another turning point

Act 4 in Shakespeare's plays often marks a turning point. We have already seen that Hamlet is now more focused on revenge in the wake of seeing Fortinbras's army march to fight for a small patch of ground in Poland. Laertes is resolved, and plots with Claudius the downfall and death of Hamlet. In tragedy, the spring has been tightened and now unwinds towards its conclusion.

a See if you can identify the exact line at which the turn takes place for Hamlet and for Laertes.

b At the same time, the movement toward resolution is a slow one. This scene, in particular, unfolds at a sedate and reflective pace. If you were forced to cut part of it, which sections or lines would you eliminate? Make your decisions, then compare notes and discuss in the class as a whole.

sanctuarize protect

keep close stay

in fine finally
wager make bets
remiss careless
peruse the foils
inspect the swords
shuffling indicative of
Claudius's scheming
pass of practice deliberate and
intended thrust
Requite revenge
mountebank quack doctor

cataplasm dressing, antidote
simples medicinal herbs

shape plot, design
drift aim
assayed tried
back or second contingency plan
blast in proof fail

preferred offered
nonce occasion

CLAUDIUS No place indeed should murder sanctuarize;
Revenge should have no bounds. But, good Laertes,
Will you do this, keep close within your chamber;
Hamlet, returned, shall know you are come home;
We'll put on those shall praise your excellence,   130
And set a double varnish on the fame
The Frenchman gave you; bring you in fine together,
And wager on your heads. He being remiss,
Most generous, and free from all contriving,
Will not peruse the foils, so that with ease,   135
Or with a little shuffling, you may choose
A sword unbated, and in a pass of practice
Requite him for your father.

LAERTES   I will do't,
And for that purpose I'll anoint my sword.
I bought an unction of a mountebank,   140
So mortal that but dip a knife in it,
Where it draws blood no cataplasm so rare,
Collected from all simples that have virtue
Under the moon, can save the thing from death
That is but scratched withal. I'll touch my point   145
With this contagion, that if I gall him slightly,
It may be death.

CLAUDIUS   Let's further think of this,
Weigh what convenience both of time and means
May fit us to our shape. If this should fail,
And that our drift look through our bad performance,   150
'Twere better not assayed. Therefore this project
Should have a back or second, that might hold
If this did blast in proof. Soft, let me see.
We'll make a solemn wager on your cunnings –
I ha't!   155
When in your motion you are hot and dry,
As make your bouts more violent to that end,
And that he calls for drink, I'll have preferred him
A chalice for the nonce, whereon but sipping,
If he by chance escape your venomed stuck,   160
Our purpose may hold there. But stay, what noise?

Enter GERTRUDE

How, sweet queen!

Gertrude tells how Ophelia drowned: she fell from a willow as she tried to hang flowers on it, and was pulled under by her clothes. Laertes unsuccessfully fights back tears. Claudius lies about calming Laertes.

▲ *Ophelia* by the Victorian painter Sir John Everett Millais.

1 'There is a willow grows askant a brook'
(in small groups)

Lines 166–83 are much admired for their imaginative and poetic quality. The images of nature reflect Shakespeare's use of flowers in the play. Ophelia's innocence and chanting of 'old lauds' (religious hymns) contrast with Laertes's fall from grace. But Laertes, moments ago a pitiless revenger, is moved to tears.

a Explore different ways of speaking the lines: individually, chorally, echoing, and/or sharing them between you.

b Discuss together: does Gertrude know all the details of Ophelia's death?

Stagecraft
Claudius and Gertrude (in threes)

Claudius lies to his wife, saying he has attempted to calm Laertes. Will she obey his two commands to 'follow'?

a Decide how the three characters will exit, starting with Laertes at line 191 and taking in Claudius's line 'Let's follow, Gertrude'.

b Perform the end of the scene together, indicating through your actions your interpretation of the three characters at this point.

askant leaning over
hoar grey

liberal free-speaking

pendant hanging
cronet coronet, garland
envious in that it wished to hold on to her; or, perhaps, malicious
sliver branch
lauds hymns
incapable of uncomprehending
indued adapted

lay song

trick way

The woman will be out I'll have finished crying
douts douses, extinguishes

GERTRUDE	One woe doth tread upon another's heel,
	So fast they follow. Your sister's drowned, Laertes.
LAERTES	Drowned! Oh where?

165

GERTRUDE	There is a willow grows askant a brook,
	That shows his hoar leaves in the glassy stream.
	Therewith fantastic garlands did she make,
	Of crow-flowers, nettles, daisies, and long purples,
	That liberal shepherds give a grosser name,

170

	But our cold maids do dead men's fingers call them.
	There on the pendant boughs her cronet weeds
	Clamb'ring to hang, an envious sliver broke,
	When down her weedy trophies and herself
	Fell in the weeping brook. Her clothes spread wide,

175

	And mermaid-like awhile they bore her up,
	Which time she chanted snatches of old lauds
	As one incapable of her own distress,
	Or like a creature native and indued
	Unto that element. But long it could not be

180

	Till that her garments, heavy with their drink,
	Pulled the poor wretch from her melodious lay
	To muddy death.

LAERTES	Alas, then she is drowned?
GERTRUDE	Drowned, drowned.
LAERTES	Too much of water hast thou, poor Ophelia,

185

	And therefore I forbid my tears. But yet
	It is our trick; nature her custom holds,
	Let shame say what it will. When these are gone,
	The woman will be out. Adieu my lord,
	I have a speech of fire that fain would blaze,

190

| | But that this folly douts it. | *Exit* |

CLAUDIUS	Let's follow, Gertrude.
	How much I had to do to calm his rage!
	Now fear I this will give it start again.
	Therefore let's follow.

Exeunt

Looking back at Act 4
Activities for groups or individuals

1 Appearance versus reality

All Shakespeare's plays in some way explore the theme of reality versus appearance. To complicate matters, it is not always a case of appearance versus reality, but rather that appearance and reality are indistinguishable at times.

- Identify an example in each scene of Act 4 where things are not as they seem. Present your examples (in the form of references, quotations and events) in an assignment on 'Reality and appearance in Act 4 of *Hamlet*'. You may wish to revisit your work on themes in the earlier acts. Is the issue of appearance and reality the dominant theme in *Hamlet*, or do other themes vie for centrality? More generally, show how a theme is developed through the use of imagery, action and ideas. Use quotations to back up your perceptions.

2 Political matters, family matters: a citizen's view

Act 4 offers reminders of the play's political context. The audience learn in Scene 3 that England, recently defeated by Claudius, is now Denmark's client state. In Scene 4, Hamlet encounters the Norwegian army marching against Poland. In Scene 7, Claudius reveals he has fought against the French. Insurrection briefly threatens Claudius's rule when in Scene 5 the citizens of Denmark ('the rabble') sweep aside the palace guards and call for Laertes to be king.

- Imagine that you are a lifelong Danish citizen, who has served in Denmark's army, heard gossip about court happenings, and seen Laertes's return. Either write your account of what you know, or join a group of other 'citizens' and improvise a discussion about events in Act 4.

3 Honour and revenge

Revenge is both a theme and a plot device in *Hamlet*. It is an idea that pervades the play, resurfacing especially towards the end of the play as the revenge theme begins to drive the plot again. But in Act 4, Hamlet, Fortinbras and Laertes are all concerned with 'honour' and 'manhood' as well as 'revenge'.

a Draw a table to compare their different perspectives (see also the activity on p. 176).

b One of the distinctive features of *Hamlet* is that it is a revenge play with a difference – indeed, with a range of dimensions. Can you characterise what these are?

4 Turning points

During Act 4, both Laertes and Hamlet experience turning points in their trajectories as characters: Hamlet is galvanised into action by witnessing Fortinbras's resolve; and Laertes is spurred to revenge through the machinations of Claudius and his own father's death. The parallels and connections between the two characters are plain to see (both revenge the death of a father).

- Make a comparison, in terms of turning points, with another Shakespeare play that you know well. One example is *Macbeth*, in which Malcolm and Macduff engage in a relatively lengthy deliberation that moves Macduff to take his revenge on Macbeth. Both in *Hamlet* and in *Macbeth*, the turn is a slow one, aided by deliberation, persuasion and a re-orientation on the part of the 'avenger'. At the same time, the action is quickening on a number of fronts via other characters. Write up your comparisons in the form of a short essay. You might find it helpful to map the acts in parallel on a wall – see 'Writing about Shakespeare' on pages 278–9 for more ideas on this.

Throughout the play, Ophelia is dominated by her father, her lover and her brother. Her father makes her reveal her secrets (Act 1) and uses her so that he can spy on Hamlet (Act 2). Hamlet denies he loves her and subjects her to a cruel tongue-lashing (Act 3). Her brother counsels her against Hamlet (Act 1) and is driven to tears by her madness (Act 4). Use the pictures on this page as the basis for an extended essay analysing Ophelia's character and her relationship with the men in the play. You need not necessarily agree that she is dominated by Polonius, Hamlet and Laertes.

Two gravediggers discuss Ophelia's death. They think she committed suicide, but is being allowed a Christian burial because of her high rank.

1 Two gravediggers – alternative perspectives
(in pairs)

After the sombre atmosphere of the previous scene, the mood of the play switches abruptly to comedy – in a graveyard. But Shakespeare is not simply providing comic relief. He is doing here what he does so often: using comedy and ordinary people to provide alternative perspectives on major issues and themes.

a To gain a first impression of the humour, take parts as the two gravediggers (Clown and Other) and read lines 1–50. Afterwards, work out how you would set this scene, and decide how the gravediggers are dressed (see p. 202).

b Invent stage business (actions) to accompany lines 13–17 as the Clown makes clear his meaning.

Write about it
Comic relief

There has not been much comedy in the play so far, apart from Hamlet poking fun at Polonius, Rosencrantz and Guildenstern – and that has been very much as part of the core action, with the main characters and their associates. On the contrary, *Hamlet* seems a dark play with a complex central character. Its unrelenting darkness and prison-like feel ('Denmark's a prison') is reinforced by the fact that most of the action (with the exception of Act 4 Scene 4) takes place in the castle. The comic relief offered by the present scene comes late in the play.

Compare this scene with one other such scene of comic relief, for example the Porter's scene immediately after Duncan's murder in *Macbeth* (Act 2 Scene 3).

* Why do the comic scenes occur where they do?
* Is their function the same or different in each tragedy?
* Do they reinforce or distract from the themes of the plays?

wilfully by her own means (i.e. she has committed suicide, which should prevent her having a Christian burial)

straight immediately, properly (as appropriate to a Christian burial)

crowner … her coroner has held an inquest

se offendendo the gravedigger means 'se defendendo' – in self-defence

Argal 'ergo', therefore

goodman delver gravedigger

will he, nill he willy-nilly (whether he wants to or not)

quest law law of inquest

countenance permission
even-Christen ordinary fellow Christians
Adam the first man

confess thyself be hanged (a proverb)

Act 5 Scene 1

A graveyard near the castle

Enter two CLOWNS *(gravediggers)*

CLOWN   Is she to be buried in Christian burial, when she wilfully seeks her own salvation?

OTHER   I tell thee she is, therefore make her grave straight. The crowner hath sat on her, and finds it Christian burial.

CLOWN   How can that be, unless she drowned herself in her own   5 defence?

OTHER   Why, 'tis found so.

CLOWN   It must be *se offendendo*, it cannot be else. For here lies the point: if I drown myself wittingly, it argues an act, and an act hath three branches – it is to act, to do, to perform. Argal, she drowned   10 herself wittingly.

OTHER   Nay, but hear you goodman delver –

CLOWN   Give me leave. Here lies the water – good. Here stands the man – good. If the man go to this water and drown himself, it is will he, nill he, he goes – mark you that. But if the water come to   15 him, and drown him, he drowns not himself. Argal, he that is not guilty of his own death shortens not his own life.

OTHER   But is this law?

CLOWN   Ay marry is't, crowner's quest law.

OTHER   Will you ha' the truth on't? If this had not been a gentlewoman,   20 she should have been buried out o' Christian burial.

CLOWN   Why, there thou sayst – and the more pity that great folk should have countenance in this world to drown or hang themselves more than their even-Christen. Come, my spade; there is no ancient gentlemen but gardeners, ditchers, and gravemakers; they hold up   25 Adam's profession.

OTHER   Was he a gentleman?

CLOWN   A was the first that ever bore arms.

OTHER   Why, he had none.

CLOWN   What, art a heathen? How dost thou understand the scripture?   30 The scripture says Adam digged. Could he dig without arms? I'll put another question to thee. If thou answerest me not to the purpose, confess thyself –

The gravedigger's question puzzles his mate; the answer praises gravediggers. The gravedigger sings about becoming old. Hamlet speculates on whose skull has been thrown out of the grave.

▼ How can death be considered humorous? Why is this? Use this image to debate the idea. How does your answer fit with Hamlet's approach, and with themes in the play?

1 'the hand of little employment hath the daintier sense'

Do you think lines 58–9 mean that people who don't work have finer feelings than those who do? Or that the less often you do something, the more emotional impact it's likely to have on you? Or is Hamlet echoing the Player King's sentiments that custom deadens the senses (as the previous line suggests: 'property of easiness' = a job that causes him no worry)?

2 Hamlet's return to action

We have not seen Hamlet for a while. He has returned from the journey to England, as we learnt via the letter to Horatio in Act 4 Scene 6. Has he been met by Horatio, and is he now walking 'near the castle' (the given setting for Act 5 Scene 1) on his way back?

- Write a note in your Director's Journal on how you would ask Hamlet to play this re-entry. Fired up and ready for revenge, as appeared the case at the end of Act 4 Scene 4; or calm and purposeful, in a new state of 'readiness'? Or neither of these? How would you account for the change in mood and purpose?

Go to! never!

frame structure (gallows)

unyoke stop work

Mass by the Mass

ass (potential for a pun there!)
mend his pace go faster

Yaughan (no one is quite sure where this place is)
stoup of liquor large jar of beer

behove enjoyment, advantage
meet better

intil into

jowls hurls
Cain (Cain killed his brother Abel with a donkey's jawbone – a subtle reminder of Claudius?)
o'erreaches outwits
circumvent outwit

OTHER	Go to!	
CLOWN	What is he that builds stronger than either the mason, the shipwright, or the carpenter?	35
OTHER	The gallows-maker, for that frame outlives a thousand tenants.	
CLOWN	I like thy wit well in good faith. The gallows does well, but how does it well? It does well to those that do ill. Now, thou dost ill to say the gallows is built stronger than the church; argal, the gallows may do well to thee. To't again, come.	40
OTHER	Who builds stronger than a mason, a shipwright, or a carpenter?	
CLOWN	Ay, tell me that, and unyoke.	
OTHER	Marry, now I can tell.	
CLOWN	To't.	45
OTHER	Mass, I cannot tell.	

Enter HAMLET *and* HORATIO *afar off*

CLOWN	Cudgel thy brains no more about it, for your dull ass will not mend his pace with beating; and when you are asked this question next, say a grave-maker. The houses he makes lasts till doomsday. Go, get thee to Yaughan, fetch me a stoup of liquor.	50

[*Exit Second Clown*]

> In youth when I did love, did love,   *Song*
>   Methought it was very sweet
> To contract-o the time for-a my behove,
>   Oh methought there-a was nothing-a meet.

HAMLET	Has this fellow no feeling of his business? A sings in grave-making.	55
HORATIO	Custom hath made it in him a property of easiness.	
HAMLET	'Tis e'en so, the hand of little employment hath the daintier sense.	

CLOWN			

> But age with his stealing steps   *Song*   60
>   Hath clawed me in his clutch,
> And hath shipped me intil the land,
>   As if I had never been such.

[*Throws up a skull*]

HAMLET	That skull had a tongue in it, and could sing once. How the knave jowls it to th' ground, as if 'twere Cain's jawbone, that did the first murder. This might be the pate of a politician which this ass now o'erreaches, one that would circumvent God, might it not?	65
HORATIO	It might my lord.	

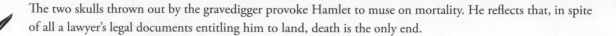

The two skulls thrown out by the gravedigger provoke Hamlet to muse on mortality. He reflects that, in spite of all a lawyer's legal documents entitling him to land, death is the only end.

Themes

Land and its relationship to death (in small groups)

Hamlet's extended reflection on lawyers, their arcane diction and their preoccupation with laws and cases that deal with land and property, introduces a new dimension in the play: the relationship between land and death.

Each group should discuss one the following propositions and then present their comments and conclusions to the whole class, who can contribute further points.

a Hamlet is satirical about the law and lawyers (as were many Elizabethan and Jacobean playwrights, including Shakespere) because they make money from common law disputes, and their language is always impenetrable. You might bring in a present-day statute or legal document to see if anything has changed.

b Land is the earth, which all buried people return to in death. But land is fought over – remember Fortinbras and his army, heading south through Denmark to fight over a patch of land in Poland – because territory is precious. Hamlet and Laertes will soon grapple on the ground over Ophelia's body. Therefore death is tied up not only with Hamlet's reflection on mankind in general, but also with his position as prince of Denmark and as a lover.

c Death is a great leveller. For all the qualities of spirit, soul, heart and mind that have been explored in the play so far, everyone – from a king or queen to a gravedigger – ends up dead. Track Hamlet's preoccupation with death throughout the play, and discuss why he is so fascinated by the work of the gravediggers and their humour. What is his mood in this scene?

d There is a great deal of **dramatic irony** here, which means that the audience knows something that the characters do not. Neither Hamlet nor Horatio seems aware that Ophelia is dead and is about to be buried. Indeed, the gravediggers were talking about her death at the start of the scene. What else does Hamlet not know that is conspiring toward his own death?

e Sex and death: why are these so closely associated in Hamlet's consciousness? See line 77 where he talks about 'breeding'. Is he driven by an excessive puritan morality that sees the body, and physical pleasures, as sinful? Could his education at the Protestant, Lutheran Wittenburg University be influential in this regard? In terms of religion, where does Hamlet stand?

my Lady Worm's my Lady's dead (belonging to Worms)

chopless without jaws

mazard head

revolution change of fortune

breeding conception

loggets skittles (in the Elizabethan game, sticks were thrown at a post)

shrowding sheet funeral shroud

quiddities nuanced meanings

quillets small tracts of land; or quibbles

tenures contracts for land or employment

sconce head

battery assault

statutes legal documents

recognizances (made-up word meaning much the same as statutes)

fines legal documents for ownership of land

vouchers people who vouched for titles to land

recoveries fines

indentures joint agreements

conveyances deeds of land purchase

They are sheep ... in that people who trust in legal documents are stupid

HAMLET	Or of a courtier, which could say 'Good morrow sweet lord, how dost thou sweet lord?' This might be my Lord Such-a-one, that praised my Lord Such-a-one's horse when a meant to beg it, might it not?
HORATIO	Ay my lord.
HAMLET	Why, e'en so, and now my Lady Worm's, chopless, and knocked about the mazard with a sexton's spade. Here's fine revolution, and we had the trick to see't. Did these bones cost no more the breeding but to play at loggets with 'em? Mine ache to think on't.

CLOWN

A pickaxe and a spade, a spade,   *Song*
    For and a shrowding sheet,
Oh a pit of clay for to be made,
    For such a guest is meet.

[*Throws up another skull*]

HAMLET	There's another. Why may not that be the skull of a lawyer? Where be his quiddities now, his quillets, his cases, his tenures, and his tricks? Why does he suffer this rude knave now to knock him about the sconce with a dirty shovel, and will not tell him of his action of battery? Hum, this fellow might be in's time a great buyer of land, with his statutes, his recognizances, his fines, his double vouchers, his recoveries. Is this the fine of his fines and the recovery of his recoveries, to have his fine pate full of fine dirt? Will his vouchers vouch him no more of his purchases, and double ones too, than the length and breadth of a pair of indentures? The very conveyances of his lands will scarcely lie in this box, and must th'inheritor himself have no more, ha?
HORATIO	Not a jot more my lord.
HAMLET	Is not parchment made of sheepskins?
HORATIO	Ay my lord, and of calves' skins too.
HAMLET	They are sheep and calves which seek out assurance in that. I will speak to this fellow. Whose grave's this sirrah?
CLOWN	Mine sir.

(*Sings*)
Oh a pit of clay for to be made
    For such a guest is meet.

HAMLET	I think it be thine indeed, for thou liest in't.
CLOWN	You lie out on't sir, and therefore 'tis not yours. For my part, I do not lie in't, yet it is mine.

70

75

80

85

90

95

100

105

The gravedigger's punning and playing with language prompt Hamlet to reflect on the way peasants imitate courtiers. The gravedigger's remarks reveal that Hamlet is about thirty years old.

Language in the play
Quick-fire dialogue? (in pairs)

The dialogue opposite between Hamlet and the Clown is full of innuendo, wit and humour. Notice that almost all Hamlet's speeches are in the form of questions. Try reading aloud this dialogue in different ways:

- with Hamlet responding quickly, and the gravedigger responding more slowly
- the other way round
- with both of them exchanging utterances at speed
- with some variation throughout the exchange.

Which works best, and why?

1 How old is Hamlet?

Identify the two lines spoken by the Clown that suggest Hamlet is about thirty Then think about whether you imagine Hamlet as thirty, or older or younger. In what senses might he seem adolescent? How old do you imagine Gertrude to be? Claudius? Horatio? (See also p. 271.)

2 Social class (in pairs)

In line 118, Hamlet says that 'the toe of a peasant comes so near the heel of a courtier' (line 118). Earlier in the play, he had expressed the view that 'The time is out of joint'. Does the death of King Hamlet so upset the state of Denmark and of Hamlet's state of mind that social order is turned upside down? Discuss these points with your partner:

- Does social class play a part in Hamlet's attitude towards a) Horatio, b) Ophelia, c) Polonius and d) Rosencrantz and Guildenstern?
- Does Hamlet's status as a prince help or hinder him in relations with other characters in the play? Remember that Hamlet, as a prince, is loved by the people.
- Where would you place Hamlet on a spectrum of political views: as a conservative, a liberal or a socialist? (You may wish to change those categories according to the political system in which you live – they do not mean the same across the world!)

quick living

absolute precise, literal
card letter, or compass (accurately)
equivocation speaking in double (and usually misleading) meanings
picked refined, picky
galls his kibe scuffs his chilblain (treads on his heels)

sexton gravedigger, church caretaker

pocky corses pock-marked corpses
laying in burial
tanner workman who turns animal skins to leather

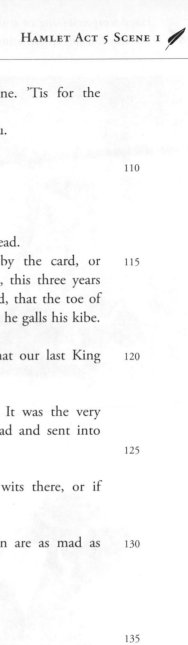

HAMLET	Thou dost lie in't, to be in't and say 'tis thine. 'Tis for the dead, not for the quick, therefore thou liest.	
CLOWN	'Tis a quick lie sir, 'twill away again from me to you.	
HAMLET	What man dost thou dig it for?	
CLOWN	For no man sir,	110
HAMLET	What woman then?	
CLOWN	For none neither.	
HAMLET	Who is to be buried in't?	
CLOWN	One that was a woman sir, but rest her soul she's dead.	
HAMLET	How absolute the knave is! We must speak by the card, or equivocation will undo us. By the lord, Horatio, this three years I have took note of it: the age is grown so picked, that the toe of the peasant comes so near the heel of the courtier, he galls his kibe. How long hast thou been grave-maker?	115
CLOWN	Of all the days i'th'year, I came to't that day that our last King Hamlet o'ercame Fortinbras.	120
HAMLET	How long is that since?	
CLOWN	Cannot you tell that? Every fool can tell that. It was the very day that young Hamlet was born, he that is mad and sent into England.	125
HAMLET	Ay marry, why was he sent into England?	
CLOWN	Why, because a was mad. A shall recover his wits there, or if a do not, 'tis no great matter there.	
HAMLET	Why?	
CLOWN	'Twill not be seen in him there. There the men are as mad as he.	130
HAMLET	How came he mad?	
CLOWN	Very strangely they say.	
HAMLET	How, strangely?	
CLOWN	Faith, e'en with losing his wits.	135
HAMLET	Upon what ground?	
CLOWN	Why, here in Denmark. I have been sexton here man and boy thirty years.	
HAMLET	How long will a man lie i'th'earth ere he rot?	
CLOWN	Faith, if a be not rotten before a die, as we have many pocky corses nowadays that will scarce hold the laying in, a will last you some eight year, or nine year. A tanner will last you nine year.	140
HAMLET	Why he more than another?	

Hamlet expresses disgust at the thought that Yorick, once so full of tricks and laughter, is now merely a skull. The physical corruption brings his mother (or women in general) bitterly to his mind.

Which of these three depictions of Hamlet comes closest to your own idea of him at this point in the play?

hide skin

whoreson poxy (expressing contemptuous familiarity)
lien you lain

Rhenish Rhine wine

fancy imagination

My gorge rises I am sickened
gibes jokes
gambols horseplay
were wont ... roar made everyone at dinner laugh uproariously
chop-fallen miserable (down in the mouth)
favour appearance
Alexander Alexander the Great, 356–323 BC, a conqueror who ruled a vast empire

base uses trivial purposes return be recycled

too curiously over-complicatedly

CLOWN   Why sir, his hide is so tanned with his trade, that a will keep
               out water a great while, and your water is a sore decayer of your   145
               whoreson dead body. Here's a skull now: this skull hath lien you
               i'th'earth three and twenty years.

HAMLET   Whose was it?

CLOWN   A whoreson mad fellow's it was. Whose do you think it was?

HAMLET   Nay I know not.   150

CLOWN   A pestilence on him for a mad rogue, a poured a flagon of
               Rhenish on my head once. This same skull sir, was Yorick's skull,
               the king's jester.

HAMLET   This?

CLOWN   E'en that.   155

HAMLET   Let me see. [*Takes the skull.*] Alas poor Yorick! I knew him
               Horatio, a fellow of infinite jest, of most excellent fancy, he hath
               borne me on his back a thousand times – and now how abhorred
               in my imagination it is! My gorge rises at it. Here hung those lips
               that I have kissed I know not how oft. Where be your gibes now?   160
               your gambols, your songs, your flashes of merriment that were wont
               to set the table on a roar? Not one now, to mock your own grinning?
               Quite chop-fallen? Now get you to my lady's chamber, and tell her,
               let her paint an inch thick, to this favour she must come. Make her
               laugh at that. – Prithee Horatio, tell me one thing.   165

HORATIO   What's that my lord?

HAMLET   Dost thou think Alexander looked o' this fashion i'th'earth?

HORATIO   E'en so.

HAMLET   And smelt so? Pah!   [*Puts down the skull*]

HORATIO   E'en so my lord.   170

HAMLET   To what base uses we may return, Horatio! Why may not
               imagination trace the noble dust of Alexander, till a find it stopping
               a bunghole?

HORATIO   'Twere to consider too curiously to consider so.

Hamlet reasons that death transforms great kings into trivial objects. A Priest tells Laertes that Claudius's command has granted Ophelia a Christian funeral. As a suicide, the Church would deny her burial.

1 Laertes (in threes)

The last time we saw Laertes, he was in tears at the news of Ophelia's death and suppressing an immediate urge to avenge his sister's death. Now he follows her coffin to her burial. It is not so much the Priest's views on the kind of burial she is allowed, but Laertes's persistent questioning, that is dramatically significant here.

a Take lines 190–208 and prepare Laertes's background thoughts behind each of the questions he asks. You might write these in prose or verse as asides, or simply as his thoughts. Aim for ten or so lines, which you can act out, to represent his background thinking for each question.

b Then perform the dialogue, complete with thoughts expressed aloud by the third person. Which way will the third person face? Will the third person be less or more incensed than Laertes? Will the dialogue increase in intensity – and if so, how will lines 205–8 be delivered?

2 'Her death was doubtful'

It looks as though the Priest has found a compromise: 'virgin crants' and 'maiden strewments' are to be thrown in the grave, instead of the customary stones and broken fragments of a suicide burial.

a What evidence can you find in the script that Ophelia did commit suicide?

b As a class, debate contemporary attitudes toward suicide, as well as religious beliefs and taboos about it.

flaw storm
Aside stand aside

maimèd rites incomplete ritual

Fordo destroy
estate high rank
Couch hide

obsequies funeral rites
warranty authority

ground unsanctified unconsecrated ground
last trumpet Doomsday
Shards pottery fragments
crants wreaths of flowers, garlands
strewments flowers strewn on the grave

profane disrespect
sage requiem solemn music for the dead

HAMLET No faith, not a jot, but to follow him thither with modesty 175
enough, and likelihood to lead it, as thus: Alexander died, Alexander
was buried, Alexander returneth to dust, the dust is earth, of earth
we make loam, and why of that loam whereto he was converted
might they not stop a beer barrel?

    Imperious Caesar, dead and turned to clay, 180
    Might stop a hole, to keep the wind away.
    Oh that that earth which kept the world in awe
    Should patch a wall t'expel the winter's flaw!
But soft, but soft! Aside – here comes the king,
The queen, the courtiers.

Enter CLAUDIUS, GERTRUDE, LAERTES, *and a coffin,* [*with* PRIEST]
and LORDS *attendant*

    Who is this they follow? 185
And with such maimèd rites? This doth betoken
The corse they follow did with desperate hand
Fordo it own life. 'Twas of some estate.
Couch we awhile and mark.   [*Retiring with Horatio*]

LAERTES What ceremony else? 190

HAMLET That is Laertes, a very noble youth. Mark.

LAERTES What ceremony else?

PRIEST Her obsequies have been as far enlarged
As we have warranty. Her death was doubtful,
And but that great command o'ersways the order, 195
She should in ground unsanctified have lodged
Till the last trumpet. For charitable prayers,
Shards, flints, and pebbles should be thrown on her.
Yet here she is allowed her virgin crants,
Her maiden strewments, and the bringing home 200
Of bell and burial.

LAERTES Must there no more be done?

PRIEST   No more be done.
We should profane the service of the dead
To sing sage requiem and such rest to her
As to peace-parted souls.

1 Gertrude's wish (in pairs)

Talk together about how lines 210–13 add to your knowledge of Gertrude. Begin by telling each other whether her wish for Hamlet and Ophelia to marry came as a surprise to you. Do you think her words are genuine?

Stagecraft

Where do they fight – in or out of the grave?

In some productions, Hamlet leaps into the grave and Laertes struggles with him there. The directors of these productions argue that the fight in the grave is dramatically symbolic. Other directors feel strongly that Laertes should climb out of the grave to attack Hamlet.

- What is your view? Draw up a list of the advantages and disadvantages of each practice. Use the list to reach a conclusion about your own preferences.

Language in the play

A heightened state (in pairs)

Although we know that Claudius has persuaded Laertes to fight with Hamlet in a duel with a poisoned sword and chalice, the chance opportunity to fight comes earlier as they encounter each other over (and/or in) Ophelia's grave. Consider the language in this encounter.

a Look at each of the six sentences Laertes speaks in the script opposite. For each, write two words expressing the emotional tone of the sentence (the first might be 'tender, loving').

b 'This is I, / Hamlet the Dane' Hamlet seems to be claiming the throne: 'the Dane' usually means 'King of Denmark'. Suggest how he speaks the first half of line 225 and how each main character (Claudius, Gertrude, Laertes, Horatio) should react.

c In lines 213–25, both Laertes and Hamlet use the hyperbolic (exaggerated) language of the traditional hero of revenge tragedy. Take parts and read the lines aloud, emphasising this heroic style of language.

churlish ignorant

ministering looking after my and others' souls

liest howling suffer in hell

decked decorated

thy most ingenious sense your delicate intelligence

quick living

Pelion, Olympus mountains in Thessaly, Greece, where the gods lived

Bears such an emphasis is so prominent

Conjures the wandering stars bewitches the planets

splenitive hot tempered

LAERTES	Lay her i'th'earch,	205

LAERTES   Lay her i'th'earch,   205
And from her fair and unpolluted flesh
May violets spring. I tell thee, churlish priest,
A ministering angel shall my sister be
When thou liest howling.

HAMLET   What, the fair Ophelia!

GERTRUDE Sweets to the sweet, farewell.   [*Scattering flowers*]   210
I hoped thou shouldst have been my Hamlet's wife.
I thought thy bride-bed to have decked, sweet maid,
And not t'have strewed thy grave.

LAERTES   Oh treble woe
Fall ten times treble on that cursèd head
Whose wicked deed thy most ingenious sense   215
Deprived thee of. Hold off the earth awhile
Till I have caught her once more in mine arms.
                Leaps in the grave
Now pile your dust upon the quick and dead
Till of this flat a mountain you have made
T'o'ertop old Pelion or the skyish head   220
Of blue Olympus.

HAMLET [*Advancing*]   What is he whose grief
Bears such an emphasis? whose phrase of sorrow
Conjures the wandering stars, and makes them stand
Like wonder-wounded hearers? This is I,
Hamlet the Dane.
        [*Laertes climbs out of the grave*]

LAERTES   The devil take thy soul. [*Grappling with him*] 225

HAMLET Thou pray'st not well.
I prithee take thy fingers from my throat,
For though I am not splenitive and rash,
Yet have I in me something dangerous
Which let thy wisdom fear. Hold off thy hand.   230

CLAUDIUS Pluck them asunder.

GERTRUDE   Hamlet, Hamlet!

ALL   Gentlemen!

HORATIO Good my lord, be quiet.
         [*The Attendants part them*].

HAMLET Why, I will fight with him upon this theme
Until my eyelids will no longer wag.

Hamlet rants that his love for Ophelia was infinitely greater than Laertes's, and that he can match any action, however improbable. He leaves with an enigmatic remark. Claudius takes control.

1 'I'll rant as well as thou' (in pairs)

On page 212, you were invited to speak in the exaggerated style of the traditional revenger. Hamlet continues in that bombastic manner. In lines 236–51, he rants furiously against Laertes's love for his sister.

a Speak the lines to each other several times in an over-the-top way, using gestures.

b Talk together about Hamlet's motivation for using such extravagant language. Is it to convince Claudius he is mad? Discuss what Hamlet's final lines 258–9 might mean (no one can be totally sure).

c Why does Hamlet exit early, and how? See the 'Stagecraft' box below for more exploration of the exits from the stage.

2 What is Claudius actually thinking? (in pairs)

Events may be overtaking Claudius's plans. One person speaks Claudius's five sentences in lines 260–6. After each sentence, the other person voices what Claudius has in mind (and notice he says 'your son', not 'our son' or 'my son' as earlier).

Stagecraft

'*Exeunt*' – everyone leaves the stage (in small groups)

The action has suddenly accelerated, after a period at the beginning of this scene that was more reflective, humorous and appeared to bring some light relief. Given that much of the play has proceeded slowly, driven by Hamlet's procrastination and reflection, the scene is now set for a tumultuous descent to the end of the play.

a Invent a piece of business (an action) for each character as they exit. Perhaps some actions take place over Ophelia's grave. Each character's wordless action expresses their feelings about what has happened in the scene. Don't forget the Clown (gravedigger) and the Priest.

b If you have not yet read to the end of the play, make predictions about what fate and the plot will bring to each of Claudius, Gertrude, Hamlet, Laertes and Horatio.

---

theme issue

forbear him leave him alone

Woo't would you (wilt thou)
eisel vinegar
eat a crocodile crocodiles were thought to shed false tears
outface outdo

prate rant, bluster
our ground ... zone until the height of our mountain touches the sun
Singeing his pate burning the crown of his head
Ossa mountain in Greece

her golden couplets in this case, her eggs

the present push immediate action

living lasting

GERTRUDE	O my son, what theme?	235
HAMLET	I loved Ophelia; forty thousand brothers	
	Could not with all their quantity of love	
	Make up my sum. What wilt thou do for her?	
CLAUDIUS	Oh he is mad Laertes.	
GERTRUDE	For love of God forbear him.	240
HAMLET	'Swounds, show me what thou't do.	
	Woo't weep, woo't fight, woo't fast, woo't tear thyself?	
	Woo't drink up eisel, eat a crocodile?	
	I'll do't. Dost thou come here to whine,	
	To outface me with leaping in her grave?	245
	Be buried quick with her, and so will I.	
	And if thou prate of mountains, let them throw	
	Millions of acres on us, till our ground,	
	Singeing his pate against the burning zone,	
	Make Ossa like a wart. Nay, and thou'lt mouth,	250
	I'll rant as well as thou.	
GERTRUDE	This is mere madness,	
	And thus awhile the fit will work on him;	
	Anon, as patient as the female dove	
	When that her golden couplets are disclosed,	
	His silence will sit drooping.	
HAMLET	Hear you sir,	255
	What is the reason that you use me thus?	
	I loved you ever – but it is no matter.	
	Let Hercules himself do what he may,	
	The cat will mew, and dog will have his day.	*Exit*
CLAUDIUS	I pray thee good Horatio wait upon him.	260

Exit Horatio

(*To Laertes*) Strengthen your patience in our last night's speech;
We'll put the matter to the present push. –
Good Gertrude, set some watch over your son. –
This grave shall have a living monument.
An hour of quiet shortly shall we see, 265
Till then in patience our proceeding be.

Exeunt

Hamlet tells Horatio how he could not sleep on the ship. He searched in Rosencrantz and Guildenstern's cabin for the letter from Claudius. It ordered that he should be executed immediately on arrival in England.

1 Hamlet's story (in pairs)

It can be considered strange that Hamlet's retelling of his experience on the ship to England comes after the events of the previous scene. But, as the 'Themes' box below asks, perhaps there is a significant development in the depiction of Hamlet's character at this point – and it could be that Ophelia's burial and the contemplation of death has focused his mind.

Retell the story, so that you are clear about what happened en route to England from Denmark, in one of a number of ways:

- as a told tale, in role as Hamlet
- as a storyboard for a filmic sequence
- in a dialogue between the prosecuting lawyer and Hamlet in a court of law
- as if Horatio were retelling it to Marcellus and Barnardo afterwards
- in mime.

mutines in the bilboes mutineers in their chains

indiscretion instinct, intuition

Themes

'There's a divinity that shapes our ends'

'Divinity' is the will of God, a type of Christian plan that determines people's lives. Hamlet says that important matters are decided by a divine force, however much humans try to plan their lives: an individual has little power over what they will become.

With lines 10–11 in mind, write a paragraph on each of the following:

- Is Hamlet's fate in the play shaped by a 'divinity' or by other factors (his character, chance, other people's actions and so on)?
- Do you believe 'There's a divinity that shapes our ends, / Rough-hew them how we will'? (However you plan and act, what will happen to you is not in your power to determine.)
- How do these two lines signify a development in Hamlet's character? And how do they relate to previous soliloquies?
- How does this world view compare with Horatio's? Is Horatio's reply ('That is most certain') one of deferential agreement, or a real meeting of minds and ideologies between him and Hamlet? Find evidence to prove your case.

Fingered their packet pickpocketed their letter

in fine in conclusion

Larded decorated, elaborated

Importing concerning

bugs and goblins ... life horrors that would follow if I lived

supervise first reading

no leisure bated no time spared

Act 5 Scene 2
The Great Hall of Elsinore Castle

Enter HAMLET *and* HORATIO

HAMLET	So much for this sir, now shall you see the other.
	You do remember all the circumstance?
HORATIO	Remember it my lord!
HAMLET	Sir, in my heart there was a kind of fighting
	That would not let me sleep. Methought I lay 5
	Worse than the mutines in the bilboes. Rashly,
	And praised be rashness for it – let us know,
	Our indiscretion sometime serves us well
	When our deep plots do pall, and that should learn us
	There's a divinity that shapes our ends, 10
	Rough-hew them how we will –
HORATIO	That is most certain.
HAMLET	Up from my cabin,
	My sea-gown scarfed about me, in the dark
	Groped I to find out them, had my desire,
	Fingered their packet, and in fine withdrew 15
	To mine own room again, making so bold,
	My fears forgetting manners, to unseal
	Their grand commission; where I found, Horatio –
	O royal knavery! – an exact command,
	Larded with many several sorts of reasons, 20
	Importing Denmark's health, and England's too,
	With ho! such bugs and goblins in my life,
	That on the supervise, no leisure bated,
	No, not to stay the grinding of the axe,
	My head should be struck off.
HORATIO	Is't possible? 25
HAMLET	Here's the commission, read it at more leisure.
	But wilt thou hear now how I did proceed?
HORATIO	I beseech you.

Hamlet tells how he wrote a substitute letter commanding the execution of Rosencrantz and Guildenstern. He feels no remorse for their death, dismissing them as mere instruments of Claudius.

1 Activities on Hamlet's story (in small groups)

In the script opposite, Hamlet describes the letter from Claudius to the king of England, asking the latter to execute Rosencrantz and Guildenstern.

a Write the letter 'fair' (neatly), using lines 31–47 as a guide. Seal it with wax and the imprint of a ring, or design your own seal.

b Hamlet sends Rosencrantz and Guildenstern to their death without a qualm of conscience (line 58). Talk together about whether the two courtiers deserve their fate. What does the decision and his lack of remorse suggest about Hamlet's character?

c Tom Stoppard's play *Rosencrantz and Guildenstern Are Dead* acts out lines 4–55, in which Hamlet describes the theft, the forging, his escape, and how Rosencrantz and Guildenstern sail on to England and death. The 1990 Zeffirelli movie also shows the sequence (and the beheading of the two courtiers in England). Write and/or enact the scene that awaits Rosencrantz and Guildenstern in England.

Themes

'mighty opposites'

So far in the play, we have identified a number of interlocking themes that have arisen from the action and speeches.

a Refer back to your notes on these themes, and now see if you can cast them as opposites – for example 'love and its relationship with death', 'the personal and the public', 'kingship and ignominy'; and 'action and inaction'. What others are there?

b Does 'oppositional thinking' like this help clarify your thoughts – or does it limit them? Do all themes have to be expressed in conflicting opposites?

c Does Hamlet mean in lines 60–2 that it was dangerous for Rosencrantz and Guildenstern to come between his plans and those of Claudius (as represented by Laertes in the forthcoming duel)? Is he being prescient (seeing what is to come) and/or just making a larger and more general point?

benetted trapped

Or … to my brains before I could think

statists politicians

yeoman loyal attendant

conjuration solemn promise, plea
tributary lesser and dependent state
the palm symbol of peace
comma pause

debatement consideration

shriving time opportunity to confess their sins
ordinant directing, ordaining
signet ring

gave't th'impression sealed it

was sequent followed

insinuation devious intervention
baser nature inferior people
pass thrust
fell incensèd points deadly sword points

HAMLET	Being thus benetted round with villainies,
	Or I could make a prologue to my brains, 30
	They had begun the play. I sat me down,
	Devised a new commission, wrote it fair.
	I once did hold it, as our statists do,
	A baseness to write fair, and laboured much
	How to forget that learning; but sir, now 35
	It did me yeoman's service. Wilt thou know
	Th'effect of what I wrote?
HORATIO	Ay good my lord.
HAMLET	An earnest conjuration from the king,
	As England was his faithful tributary,
	As love between them like the palm might flourish, 40
	As peace should still her wheaten garland wear,
	And stand a comma 'tween their amities,
	And many suchlike as-es of great charge,
	That on the view and knowing of these contents,
	Without debatement further, more, or less, 45
	He should those bearers put to sudden death,
	Not shriving time allowed.
HORATIO	How was this sealed?
HAMLET	Why, even in that was heaven ordinant.
	I had my father's signet in my purse,
	Which was the model of that Danish seal; 50
	Folded the writ up in the form of th'other,
	Subscribed it, gave't th'impression, placed it safely,
	The changeling never known. Now, the next day
	Was our sea-fight, and what to this was sequent
	Thou know'st already. 55
HORATIO	So Guildenstern and Rosencrantz go to't.
HAMLET	Why man, they did make love to this employment.
	They are not near my conscience. Their defeat
	Does by their own insinuation grow.
	'Tis dangerous when the baser nature comes 60
	Between the pass and fell incensèd points
	Of mighty opposites.
HORATIO	Why, what a king is this!

Hamlet argues that he is well justified in killing Claudius. He regrets his behaviour towards Laertes, seeing him as a fellow revenger. Hamlet comments dismissively on Osric, and mocks him. Osric tells of a wager.

Write about it
Four reasons for revenge

Hamlet lists four reasons for revenge in lines 63–6: Claudius has killed his father ('my king'), slept with his mother, pushed in front of Hamlet's own claim to the throne ('Popped in between th'election and my hopes'), and plotted Hamlet's death.

- Write the four reasons in order of their importance to Hamlet. Add a paragraph explaining why you have chosen that order.

Language in the play
Explanatory versus dramatic language (in pairs)

In the script opposite, Hamlet acknowledges that he has only a short time to kill Claudius. But he thinks the advantage is briefly with him because Claudius has not yet learned the news from England. Hamlet expresses regret that he overreacted to Laertes's grief, and recognises that they have a similar motive for revenge. He wishes to make peace with Laertes, and says Laertes's exaggerated grief caused his own outburst.

a Match each sentence in the paragraph above with the appropriate lines in the script, then talk together about the ways in which Shakespeare's language is so much more dramatic and suited to performance than the bare description given above.

b The explanatory prose is in the third person, as past 'reported' speech; Hamlet speaks from his own experience, in the first person. Try rewriting the passage in first-person explanatory prose to gauge the further difference that dramatic verse makes.

1 Osric: character or caricature?

A character might have many sides, but a caricature is usually two-dimensional, emphasising one trait.

- What is your impression of Osric so far? What dramatic function do you think he will serve?

Does it … stand me now upon don't you think I now must

angle fishing hook (plotted)
cozenage deceit, trickery
quit him kill him
canker of our nature disease of humanity

to say 'one' a brief moment

the image of my cause (i.e. revenge)
portraiture reflection
court his favours be more polite in future

crib … mess even a beast will be able to sit at the king's table if he has enough land
chough jackdaw
spacious generous

HAMLET	Does it not, think thee, stand me now upon –
	He that hath killed my king, and whored my mother,
	Popped in between th'election and my hopes,
	Thrown out his angle for my proper life,
	And with such cozenage – is't not perfect conscience
	To quit him with this arm? And is't not to be damned
	To let this canker of our nature come
	In further evil?
HORATIO	It must be shortly known to him from England
	What is the issue of the business there.
HAMLET	It will be short. The interim's mine,
	And a man's life's no more than to say 'one'.
	But I am very sorry, good Horatio,
	That to Laertes I forgot myself,
	For by the image of my cause, I see
	The portraiture of his. I'll court his favours.
	But sure the bravery of his grief did put me
	Into a towering passion.
HORATIO	Peace, who comes here?

65

70

75

80

Enter young OSRIC

OSRIC	Your lordship is right welcome back to Denmark.
HAMLET	I humbly thank you sir. – Dost know this water-fly?
HORATIO	No my good lord.
HAMLET	Thy state is the more gracious, for 'tis a vice to know him. He hath much land and fertile; let a beast be lord of beasts, and his crib shall stand at the king's mess. 'Tis a chough, but as I say, spacious in the possession of dirt.
OSRIC	Sweet lord, if your lordship were at leisure, I should impart a thing to you from his majesty.
HAMLET	I will receive it sir with all diligence of spirit. Put your bonnet to his right use, 'tis for the head.
OSRIC	I thank your lordship, it is very hot.
HAMLET	No believe me, 'tis very cold, the wind is northerly.
OSRIC	It is indifferent cold my lord, indeed.
HAMLET	But yet methinks it is very sultry and hot for my complexion.
OSRIC	Exceedingly my lord, it is very sultry, as 'twere – I cannot tell how. But my lord, his majesty bade me signify to you that a has laid a great wager on your head. Sir, this is the matter –

85

90

95

Osric praises Laertes as an outstanding model of a gentleman. He uses such affected language that Hamlet makes fun of him by responding in a style that is even more elaborate and obscure.

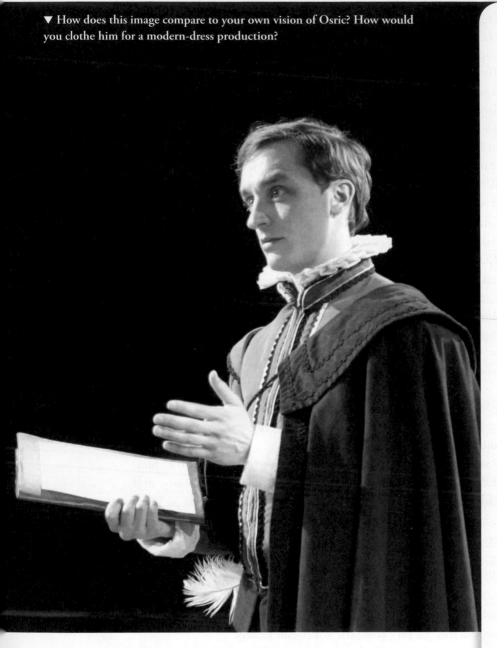

▼ How does this image compare to your own vision of Osric? How would you clothe him for a modern-dress production?

excellent differences gifted accomplishments

soft society good manners

the card or calendar the one everyone wants a date with

continent ... see the major part or attribute a gentleman seeks

perdition loss

yaw zig-zag

infusion qualities

dearth uniqueness

semblable likeness

umbrage shadow

concernancy the matter

what imports the nomination? what is the significance?

meed merit, achievements

1 Mocking Osric – without drawing breath

Hamlet obviously detests Osric's affected manner and language. In lines 106–12, Hamlet makes up words ('definement' = definition, 'inventorially' = as an inventory/list), uses pompous phrases ('the verity of extolment' = the truth of praising), and mocks Osric's praise of Laertes.

* These lines can be spoken at high speed, emphasising the flamboyant nature of the speech. Try it yourself!

HAMLET   I beseech you remember.

[Hamlet moves him to put on his hat]

OSRIC   Nay good my lord, for my ease in good faith. Sir, [here is newly   100
come to court Laertes; believe me an absolute gentleman, full of
most excellent differences, of very soft society and great showing.
Indeed, to speak feelingly of him, he is the card or calendar of
gentry, for you shall find in him the continent of what part a
gentleman would see.   105

HAMLET   Sir, his definement suffers no perdition in you, though I know
to divide him inventorially would dozy th'arithmetic of memory,
and yet but yaw neither in respect of his quick sail. But in the verity
of extolment, I take him to be a soul of great article, and his infusion
of such dearth and rareness as, to make true diction of him, his   110
semblable is his mirror, and who else would trace him, his umbrage,
nothing more.

OSRIC   Your lordship speaks most infallibly of him.

HAMLET   The concernancy, sir? Why do we wrap the gentleman in our
more rawer breath?   115

OSRIC   Sir?

HORATIO   Is't not possible to understand in another tongue? You will
to't sir, really.

HAMLET   What imports the nomination of this gentleman?

OSRIC   Of Laertes?   120

HORATIO   His purse is empty already, all's golden words are spent.

HAMLET   Of him sir.

OSRIC   I know you are not ignorant –

HAMLET   I would you did sir, yet in faith if you did, it would not much
approve me. Well sir?]   125

OSRIC   You are not ignorant of what excellence Laertes is.

[HAMLET   I dare not confess that, lest I should compare with him in
excellence, but to know a man well were to know himself.

OSRIC   I mean sir for his weapon; but in the imputation laid on him
by them, in his meed he's unfellowed.]   130

HAMLET   What's his weapon?

OSRIC   Rapier and dagger.

HAMLET   That's two of his weapons, but well.

1 'How if I answer no?'

In this exchange of wit and engagement with Osric's frothy verbiage, there is a line that stands out as potentially of a different tone: 'How if I answer no? (line 151)

a Experiment with different ways of speaking this line. For example, try it as if Hamlet does not want to fight the duel, or as if he doesn't care what happens, or with defiance. Try leaving a long pause between 'answer' and 'no' to experience the dramatic effect it makes.

b Decide which style of speaking you think is most appropriate, and write notes advising an actor on your preferred style of delivery.

Characters

Osric's character – and is he in on the plot?

Horatio sees Osric as a precocious (very forward) juvenile: 'This lapwing runs away with the shell on his head.' A lapwing chick leaves its nest very shortly after hatching, often with parts of its shell still sticking to its head.

Hamlet suggests that no one else is likely to praise Osric ('there are no tongues else for's turn') so he does well 'to commend it [his duty] himself'. He compares Osric to a baby that 'did comply with his dug' (made a deal with his mother's breast). Hamlet goes on to say that Osric is typical of the flock ('bevy') of frothy, superficial people fashionable in these frivolous ('drossy') times. They burst like bubbles when they face some real test. The 'fanned and winnowed opinions' are the lightweight opinions that people like Osric simply ignore.

a List Osric's character traits, finding lines to support your ideas. Try to think of someone in public life today who is like Osric.

b Imagine Osric knows of Claudius's murderous plan. How would that affect his performance? How likely is it that he knows?

c Write a short character (or caricature) study of Osric: drawing on evidence from the script will be good practice for a longer study of one of the major characters later. Are there any reasons an audience might feel sympathy for Osric?

Barbary Arab

impawned wagered

six French rapiers … and so equipment wagered by Laertes

liberal conceit fanciful decoration

edified by the margent enlightened by an explanation (as in the margin of a book)

germane relevant

vouchsafe the answer accept the challenge

trial duel

breathing exercise

redeliver you take your message back

for's turn on his part

lapwing … head (a metaphor for reckless and silly youthfulness)

dug nipple

yesty collection yeasty (frothy) brew, trivial people

fanned and winnowed light, insubstantial

OSRIC   The king sir hath wagered with him six Barbary horses, against   135
          the which he has impawned, as I take it, six French rapiers and
          poniards, with their assigns, as girdle, hangers, and so. Three of
          the carriages in faith are very dear to fancy, very responsive to the
          hilts, most delicate carriages, and of very liberal conceit.

HAMLET   What call you the carriages?

HORATIO   I knew you must be edified by the margent ere you had done.   140

OSRIC   The carriages sir are the hangers.

HAMLET   The phrase would be more germane to the matter if we could
          carry a cannon by our sides; I would it might be hangers till then.
          But on, six Barbary horses against six French swords, their assigns,
          and three liberal-conceited carriages – that's the French bet against   145
          the Danish. Why is this impawned, as you call it?

OSRIC   The king sir, hath laid sir, that in a dozen passes between yourself
          and him, he shall not exceed you three hits. He hath laid on twelve
          for nine. And it would come to immediate trial, if your lordship
          would vouchsafe the answer.   150

HAMLET   How if I answer no?

OSRIC   I mean my lord, the opposition of your person in trial.

HAMLET   Sir, I will walk here in the hall. If it please his majesty, it is
          the breathing time of day with me. Let the foils be brought, the
          gentleman willing, and the king hold his purpose, I will win for   155
          him and I can. If not, I will gain nothing but my shame and the
          odd hits.

OSRIC   Shall I redeliver you e'en so?

HAMLET   To this effect sir, after what flourish your nature will.

OSRIC   I commend my duty to your lordship.   160

HAMLET   Yours, yours.

                                                              [*Exit Osric*]

          He does well to commend it himself, there are no tongues else for's
          turn.

HORATIO   This lapwing runs away with the shell on his head.

HAMLET   A did comply with his dug before a sucked it. Thus has he,   165
          and many more of the same bevy that I know the drossy age dotes
          on, only got the tune of the time and outward habit of encounter,
          a kind of yesty collection, which carries them through and through
          the most fanned and winnowed opinions; and do but blow them
          to their trial, the bubbles are out.   170

                              [*Enter a* LORD

A lord asks if Hamlet will duel with Laertes now or later. Hamlet is ready. Horatio warns that he will lose, and offers to give his apologies, but Hamlet feels the time is ripe. He asks Laertes to pardon him.

Characters

From 'To be, or not to be' to 'Let be' (in pairs)

Hamlet has been on a long emotional journey from the anxiety of 'To be, or not to be' to the simple acceptance of 'Let be.' He does not think he will lose the duel, but feels foreboding ('how ill all's here about my heart'). However, he is resolute, and sees 'special providence in / the fall of a sparrow' (an image from St Matthew's Gospel, suggesting the seemingly insignificant nature of the small bird).

Hamlet seems ready to accept whatever fate has in store for him. Whether death comes sooner or later, it will come. What matters is the frame of mind to meet death: 'the readiness is all'. Since no one really knows the meaning of life or what he will miss by dying young, what does it matter to die early ('betimes')?

a Talk together about how Hamlet's mood at this point contrasts with that earlier in the play.

b Experiment with ways of speaking the lines. How might Hamlet vary his tone from thought to thought?

c After the first two sentences, Hamlet uses almost only monosyllables ('If it be now … Let be.'). Speak the lines, making each monosyllable sharp and clear. Discuss the dramatic effect of such simple words.

d 'The readiness is all'. In reflecting on life, death and whether fate plays a part or not in one's existence, Hamlet seems to have come to a state in which he is ready for death, and for life. His balanced, focused, calm position stands between the two, making him (in some eyes) a great tragic figure. Discuss what you think 'the readiness is all' means, and whether you agree with the statement that Hamlet is achieving greatness.

e 'I am punished / With a sore distraction'. How seriously do we take Hamlet's gracious confession to Claudius? Has Hamlet really been punished, and have his actions during the play been the result of a form of melancholy that has caused him distraction and delay? Or is he purposely overstating this to Claudius, keeping up the pretence of madness while engineering a moment to kill him?

commended him sent his compliments

attend await

If his fitness speaks if he is ready

In happy time just at the right time (spoken ironically?)

gentle entertainment courteous greetings

at the odds according to the wager

gaingiving misgiving (gainsaying)

repair hither coming here

augury predictions of the future

betimes early

This presence everybody here

sore distraction melancholy

exception grievance, wish for revenge

LORD	My lord, his majesty commended him to you by young Osric, who brings back to him that you attend him in the hall. He sends to know if your pleasure hold to play with Laertes, or that you will take longer time.
HAMLET	I am constant to my purposes, they follow the king's pleasure. 175 If his fitness speaks, mine is ready; now or whensoever, provided I be so able as now.
LORD	The king and queen, and all, are coming down.
HAMLET	In happy time.
LORD	The queen desires you to use some gentle entertainment to 180 Laertes, before you fall to play.
HAMLET	She well instructs me.]

[Exit Lord]

HORATIO	You will lose, my lord.
HAMLET	I do not think so. Since he went into France, I have been in continual practice; I shall win at the odds. But thou wouldst not 185 think how ill all's here about my heart – but it is no matter.
HORATIO	Nay good my lord –
HAMLET	It is but foolery, but it is such a kind of gaingiving as would perhaps trouble a woman.
HORATIO	If your mind dislike anything, obey it. I will forestall their 190 repair hither, and say you are not fit.
HAMLET	Not a whit, we defy augury. There is special providence in the fall of a sparrow. If it be now, 'tis not to come; if it be not to come, it will be now; if it be not now, yet it will come – the readiness is all. Since no man of aught he leaves knows, what is't 195 to leave betimes? Let be.

A table prepared, with flagons of wine on it. Trumpets, Drums and Officers with cushions. Enter CLAUDIUS, GERTRUDE, LAERTES *and* LORDS, *with other Attendants with foils, daggers and gauntlets*

CLAUDIUS	Come Hamlet, come and take this hand from me.
	[Hamlet takes Laertes by the hand]
HAMLET	Give me your pardon sir, I've done you wrong;
	But pardon't as you are a gentleman.
	This presence knows, 200
	And you must needs have heard, how I am punished
	With a sore distraction. What I have done,
	That might your nature, honour and exception
	Roughly awake, I here proclaim was madness.

Hamlet claims that his madness, rather than he himself, was to blame for the death of Polonius. Laertes, with reservations, accepts Hamlet's apology. Hamlet praises Laertes's fencing skills. They choose rapiers.

1 True or false? Laertes's reply (in pairs)

Laertes intends, secretly and treacherously, to kill Hamlet. In lines 216–24, he says he is satisfied as far as natural feelings go ('in nature'), but he must obey a higher moral code (that of vengeance, his 'terms of honour') to keep his reputation pure ('name ungored'). He promises not to wrong Hamlet's love.

- One person reads lines 216–24, pausing at each punctuation mark. In each pause the other person, as Laertes, says either 'true' or 'false', and explains what his secret thoughts really are at that moment.

Stagecraft

The choosing of foils – how is it performed?

The choosing of the foils is an important dramatic moment, as notwithstanding the skill or luck of each contestant, life or death hangs upon the choice.

- Write notes in your Director's Journal for actors performing lines 226–38. Your aim is to make the choosing of the foils as dramatically effective as possible. Remember: Laertes knows one has an unblunted blade, so how does he ensure he gets the right rapier?

2 Resorting to honour

There is a strong emphasis on honour and making peace with each other before the duel. We know that Laertes, despite his protestations of honour, is in league with Claudius; but Hamlet acts, for the moment, according to the highest principles of honour and selflessness.

Despite there being 'special providence in the fall of a sparrow', there is the potential downfall of a major heroic figure here. Hamlet's 'readiness' in Act 5 has been noticeable – part of the tragic trajectory in this play (it is not the same in all) is for Hamlet to reach a peak of dignity and honour just before the fall from greatness, or just before death.

- Draw a graph, act by act, to show Hamlet's trajectory as a tragic hero. You can annotate it with quotations and comments. Compare your graph and annotations with someone else's in the class, and see if you both agree on the line of the graph. What is its high point? And where are its lows? Discuss and debate any variations between your graphs.

faction party

disclaiming ... evil (Hamlet is exonerating himself from blame for what is to come)

I have shot ... brother I have hurt you accidentally

some elder ... honour qualified experts

voice ... peace judgement in favour of reconciliation

Stick fiery off stand out brilliantly

bettered improved

likes me pleases me

all a length all the same length

228

	Was't Hamlet wronged Laertes? Never Hamlet.	205
	If Hamlet from himself be tane away,
	And when he's not himself does wrong Laertes,
	Then Hamlet does it not, Hamlet denies it.
	Who does it then? His madness. If't be so,
	Hamlet is of the faction that is wronged,	210
	His madness is poor Hamlet's enemy.
	Sir, in this audience,
	Let my disclaiming from a purposed evil
	Free me so far in your most generous thoughts,
	That I have shot my arrow o'er the house	215
	And hurt my brother.
LAERTES	I am satisfied in nature,
	Whose motive in this case should stir me most
	To my revenge; but in my terms of honour
	I stand aloof, and will no reconcilement
	Till by some elder masters of known honour	220
	I have a voice and precedent of peace
	To keep my name ungored. But till that time
	I do receive your offered love like love,
	And will not wrong it.
HAMLET	I embrace it freely,
	And will this brother's wager frankly play.	225
	Give us the foils, come on.
LAERTES	Come, one for me.
HAMLET	I'll be your foil Laertes. In mine ignorance
	Your skill shall like a star i'th'darkest night
	Stick fiery off indeed.
LAERTES	You mock me sir.
HAMLET	No, by this hand.	230
CLAUDIUS	Give them the foils, young Osric. Cousin Hamlet,
	You know the wager?
HAMLET	Very well my lord.
	Your grace has laid the odds a'th'weaker side.
CLAUDIUS	I do not fear it, I have seen you both.
	But since he is bettered, we have therefore odds.	235
LAERTES	This is too heavy, let me see another.
HAMLET	This likes me well. These foils have all a length?

Claudius orders wine and celebrations if Hamlet is successful. He will drink a toast if Hamlet wins, and put a pearl in the wine. Hamlet makes two hits. Claudius offers the poisoned cup, but Hamlet declines to drink.

1 The poisoned cup

Imagine you are directing a rehearsal of the play. You are asked two questions by the actors:

- Is Hamlet suspicious about the drink at line 260?
- How should Claudius say 'Gertrude, do not drink!' at line 268?

Invent your replies, and write them down as notes for the actors.

▼ Identify which is Hamlet and which is Laertes in this production photograph.

stoups flagons, large jars (see stage direction after line 196)

quit win
ordnance cannons

an union a pearl

kettle kettle-drum

wary watchful

palpable tangible, definite

Stay wait

fat unfit, sweaty (Gertrude often shows affection for Hamlet here)
carouses drinks (is she suspicious? See p. 232)

OSRIC   Ay my good lord.

Prepare to play

CLAUDIUS   Set me the stoups of wine upon that table.
            If Hamlet give the first or second hit,   240
            Or quit in answer of the third exchange,
            Let all the battlements their ordnance fire.
            The king shall drink to Hamlet's better breath,
            And in the cup an union shall he throw
            Richer than that which four successive kings   245
            In Denmark's crown have worn. Give me the cups,
            And let the kettle to the trumpet speak,
            The trumpet to the cannoneer without,
            The cannons to the heavens, the heaven to earth,
            'Now the king drinks to Hamlet!' Come, begin,   250
            And you the judges bear a wary eye.

Trumpets the while

HAMLET   Come on sir.
LAERTES   Come my lord.

They play

HAMLET   One.
LAERTES   No.   255
HAMLET   Judgement.
OSRIC   A hit, a very palpable hit.
LAERTES   Well, again.
CLAUDIUS   Stay, give me drink. Hamlet, this pearl is thine.
            Here's to thy health.

Drum, trumpets sound, and shot goes off

                                Give him the cup.   260
HAMLET   I'll play this bout first, set it by awhile.
            Come.

[They play]

            Another hit. What say you?
LAERTES   A touch, a touch, I do confess't.
CLAUDIUS   Our son shall win.
GERTRUDE   He's fat and scant of breath.
            Here Hamlet, take my napkin, rub thy brows.   265
            The queen carouses to thy fortune, Hamlet.
HAMLET   Good madam.
CLAUDIUS   Gertrude, do not drink!

Gertrude drinks from the poisoned cup. Laertes wounds Hamlet. In a scuffle, they exchange rapiers and Hamlet wounds Laertes. The queen falls and dies. Laertes reveals the treacherous plot.

Stagecraft

Staging the duel (in small groups)

The duel and its bloody outcome last only around sixty lines. But Shakespeare provides opportunities to create thrilling stage action. In many productions Laertes wounds Hamlet deceitfully at line 280, a moment that Hamlet thinks is an interval in the fight.

a Act out a non-contact but dramatic fight scene, weaving the words of the script into the action.

b Are you sure that Laertes acts dishonourably? To make your decision clear to an audience, work out how you would stage: the wounding of Hamlet by Laertes; the scuffle that follows; the exchange of rapiers; and the wounding of Laertes.

do but dally waste time

pass thrust

make a wanton of me treat me as a spoilt child

1 The death of Gertrude: accident or suicide?
(in pairs)

The queen dies by drinking from the poisoned cup that Claudius intended for her son. Every actor playing Gertrude thinks hard about whether she knows the cup is poisoned and therefore whether her death is an accident or suicide (see line 269). If the actor decides that Gertrude suspects the cup is poisoned, to be theatrically convincing she should be seen distancing herself from Claudius in earlier scenes (she may point to Claudius as she speaks her final words).

incensed inflamed, mad, out of control

- One partner argues for Gertrude committing suicide. The other argues for Gertrude not knowing the drink is poisoned. How could 'I will, my lord' be said in different ways to show either her ignorance or her knowledge? How do these different interpretations affect our empathy towards Gertrude? Look at her words carefully to determine your answers.

as a woodcock … springe like a foolish bird, caught in my own trap

sounds swoons

Themes

Does divinity shape their ends? (in small groups)

The tragic end to this play is unfolding via a treacherous plot by Claudius to kill Hamlet. Unwittingly, or perhaps deliberately on Claudius's part, Laertes and Gertrude (and he) will die too.

- On page 216, you wrote about the extent to which divine force controls the characters in *Hamlet*. Read through this answer, and make notes on whether or not you still agree with what you wrote.

Unbated and envenomed sharp and poisonous

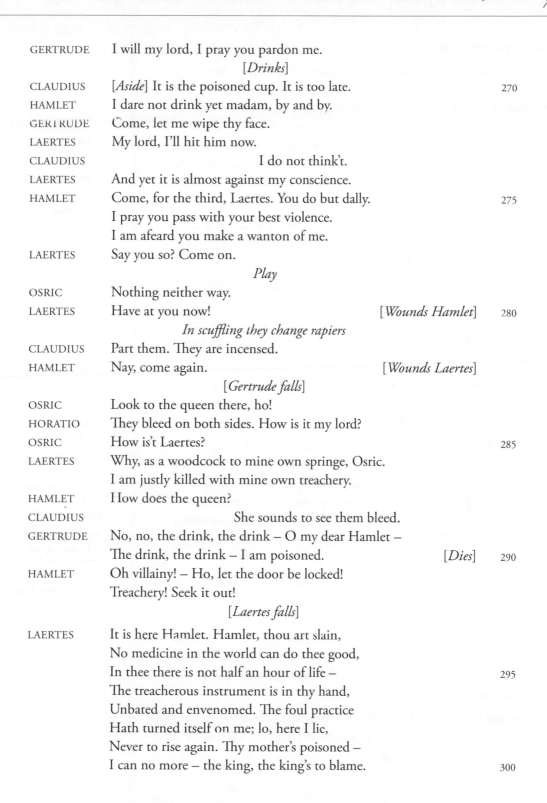

GERTRUDE	I will my lord, I pray you pardon me.		
	[Drinks]		
CLAUDIUS	*[Aside]* It is the poisoned cup. It is too late.		270
HAMLET	I dare not drink yet madam, by and by.		
GERTRUDE	Come, let me wipe thy face.		
LAERTES	My lord, I'll hit him now.		
CLAUDIUS	I do not think't.		
LAERTES	And yet it is almost against my conscience.		
HAMLET	Come, for the third, Laertes. You do but dally.		275
	I pray you pass with your best violence.		
	I am afeard you make a wanton of me.		
LAERTES	Say you so? Come on.		
	Play		
OSRIC	Nothing neither way.		
LAERTES	Have at you now!	*[Wounds Hamlet]*	280
	In scuffling they change rapiers		
CLAUDIUS	Part them. They are incensed.		
HAMLET	Nay, come again.	*[Wounds Laertes]*	
	[Gertrude falls]		
OSRIC	Look to the queen there, ho!		
HORATIO	They bleed on both sides. How is it my lord?		
OSRIC	How is't Laertes?		285
LAERTES	Why, as a woodcock to mine own springe, Osric.		
	I am justly killed with mine own treachery.		
HAMLET	How does the queen?		
CLAUDIUS	She sounds to see them bleed.		
GERTRUDE	No, no, the drink, the drink – O my dear Hamlet –		
	The drink, the drink – I am poisoned.	*[Dies]*	290
HAMLET	Oh villainy! – Ho, let the door be locked!		
	Treachery! Seek it out!		
	[Laertes falls]		
LAERTES	It is here Hamlet. Hamlet, thou art slain,		
	No medicine in the world can do thee good,		
	In thee there is not half an hour of life –		295
	The treacherous instrument is in thy hand,		
	Unbated and envenomed. The foul practice		
	Hath turned itself on me; lo, here I lie,		
	Never to rise again. Thy mother's poisoned –		
	I can no more – the king, the king's to blame.		300

Hamlet wounds Claudius and forces him to drink from the poisoned cup. Claudius dies. Laertes forgives Hamlet, then dies. Hamlet prevents Horatio from suicide, and asks him to report his (Hamlet's) story.

1 Key moments

a **Staging the death of Claudius** The killing of Claudius is often a savage affair. Hamlet runs him through with his sword, then, without pity, forces him to drink poison. The courtiers cry 'Treason, treason!' but do nothing. Some productions have Hamlet chasing a terrified Claudius, who tries to hide behind the courtiers. Others have portrayed Claudius facing death with calm dignity. How would you stage lines 301–6? Write notes on how Hamlet, Claudius and the courtiers behave (in line with your view of Hamlet's and Claudius's characters).

b **Treachery! Seek it out!** In line 292 of this scene, Hamlet's final act appears not to be a vengeful one, but an act for his country's honour. In pairs, talk about how this affects your view of him.

c **'Wretched queen adieu'** Hamlet's three-word farewell to his mother at line 112 is often turned into a poignant moment in performance. In one production, Hamlet crawled across to Gertrude and kissed her as he spoke. Write notes on how you would turn those three words into a memorable theatrical episode.

d **'Exchange forgiveness with me'** Laertes turns against Claudius, asking Hamlet for mutual forgiveness. Discuss how Laertes's last speech relates to *Hamlet* as revenge tragedy.

e **'A wounded name'** Hamlet forbids Horatio to take the poison and commit suicide, because he wants Horatio to 'report me and my cause aright / To the unsatisfied' (those who do not know the full story). Hamlet wants to ensure that his 'name' (reputation) is remembered. List six words you think Hamlet would wish to be included in Horatio's description of him. Then list six words of your own to describe how you see Hamlet. Do the two lists match?

f **'March afar off, and shot within'** This stage direction heralds the arrival of the Norwegian force and the ambassadors from England, and with a single offstage sound effect takes the action back into a wider political frame. It is a reminder that this scene marks not only the death of Hamlet but also the end of the reign of Hamlet's entire line. Decide whether you wish to make the sound effect small scale and intimate, or large scale and epic.

g **Act it out** Lines 302–40 constitute a tremendous part of the scene to act out. In groups of four or five, take parts and rehearse the lines for presentation to the rest of the class.

union precious pearl

is justly served has received his just deserts
tempered mixed

chance mischance
mutes silent watchers
fell cruel

the unsatisfied those who wish to know the whole story

antique Roman ancient Roman who would rather commit suicide than live dishonourably

ha't have it
wounded name dishonoured name and reputation

Absent thee from felicity leave happiness behind

HAMLET	The point envenomed too! Then, venom, to thy work!
	Hurts the king
ALL	Treason, treason!
CLAUDIUS	Oh yet defend me friends, I am but hurt.
HAMLET	Here, thou incestuous, murderous, damnèd Dane,
	Drink off this potion. Is thy union here? 305
	Follow my mother. *King dies*
LAERTES	He is justly served,
	It is a poison tempered by himself.
	Exchange forgiveness with me, noble Hamlet.
	Mine and my father's death come not upon thee,
	Nor thine on me. *Dies* 310
HAMLET	Heaven make thee free of it! I follow thee.
	I am dead, Horatio. Wretched queen adieu.
	You that look pale, and tremble at this chance,
	That are but mutes or audience to this act,
	Had I but time, as this fell sergeant death 315
	Is strict in his arrest, oh I could tell you –
	But let it be. Horatio, I am dead,
	Thou livest; report me and my cause aright
	To the unsatisfied.
HORATIO	Never believe it.
	I am more an antique Roman than a Dane. 320
	Here's yet some liquor left.
HAMLET	As th'art a man,
	Give me the cup. Let go, by heaven I'll ha't.
	O God, Horatio, what a wounded name,
	Things standing thus unknown, shall live behind me!
	If thou didst ever hold me in thy heart, 325
	Absent thee from felicity awhile,
	And in this harsh world draw thy breath in pain
	To tell my story.
	March afar off, and shot within
	What warlike noise is this?

Before dying, Hamlet declares Fortinbras to be his choice as king of Denmark. Fortinbras wonders at the sight of so many dead bodies. The English ambassador reports that Rosencrantz and Guildenstern are dead.

1 'the rest is silence' (in pairs)

Hamlet dies – seemingly undramatically, although his death is soon followed by the entrance of Fortinbras and the English ambassadors – and his final words are as much political as personal. He wishes Fortinbras, whom he prophesises will take over as king, to know what has led up to this moment. But characteristically, he entwines the personal with the political.

* Discuss the nature and impact of Hamlet's death. Compare your thoughts with the rest of the class.

▼ In the 1990 Zeffirelli movie, Hamlet dies beside his mother. How would you stage Hamlet's death?

warlike volley gunfire salute

o'ercrows triumphs over

prophesy … Fortinbras predict Fortinbras will be chosen as king of Denmark

he has my dying voice in death, he has my vote and support

th'occurrents more and less all the events

solicited brought about (my vote); Hamlet does not complete his sentence

quarry heap of dead bodies
cries on suggests
toward being prepared

OSRIC   Young Fortinbras, with conquest come from Poland,
To the ambassadors of England gives   330
This warlike volley.

HAMLET   Oh I die, Horatio,
The potent poison quite o'ercrows my spirit.
I cannot live to hear the news from England.
But I do prophesy th'election lights
On Fortinbras; he has my dying voice.   335
So tell him, with th'occurrents more and less
Which have solicited – the rest is silence.   *Dies*

HORATIO   Now cracks a noble heart. Good night sweet prince,
And flights of angels sing thee to thy rest. –
Why does the drum come hither?   340

Enter FORTINBRAS *and* ENGLISH AMBASSADORS, *with drum, colours
and Attendants*

FORTINBRAS   Where is this sight?

HORATIO   What is it you would see?
If aught of woe or wonder, cease your search.

FORTINBRAS   This quarry cries on havoc. O proud death,
What feast is toward in thine eternal cell
That thou so many princes at a shot   345
So bloodily hast struck?

I AMBASSADOR   The sight is dismal,
And our affairs from England come too late.
The ears are senseless that should give us hearing,
To tell him his commandment is fulfilled,
That Rosencrantz and Guildenstern are dead.   350
Where should we have our thanks?

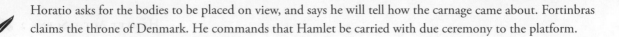

Horatio asks for the bodies to be placed on view, and says he will tell how the carnage came about. Fortinbras claims the throne of Denmark. He commands that Hamlet be carried with due ceremony to the platform.

1 Tell Horatio's story (in small groups)

In lines 359–64, Horatio lists seven incidents he proposes to relate. In role, and moving from person to person in the group, tell the story Horatio intends to tell, in any of a number of ways: as an anecdote; as an epic tale; as a tragedy; or as a murder mystery.

Stagecraft

'The end is everything'

Aristotle, the ancient Greek philosopher and critic, commented that in Greek tragedy 'the end is everything'. The suggestion is that in any story, the end reflects back on the story as a whole. Comedies in Shakespeare often end in marriage, dance and jollity; tragedies end in despair, downfall and possible renewal. Undertake the following activities, leading towards a presentation of the final two pages of the script (and perhaps continuing the final activity on p. 234).

a The moment captured in the script opposite is one of transition: from the past, which Horatio will tell 'to th'yet unknowing world' (line 358), to the future, represented by Fortinbras, whom we know is a young soldier of honour. Work out positions on stage and postures for Horatio and Fortinbras, either in a tableau or in a more dynamic performance, and write notes in your Director's Journal.

b There is a calmness and shocked silence at the close of the play, perhaps echoing Hamlet's dying words, 'the rest is silence'. How sinister is this silence? Even though there are words from Horatio and Fortinbras, and 'a peal of ordnance are shot off', what part does silence play towards the end?

c Why are Hamlet's last words (331–7) so seemingly modest? And what does he mean by them?

d What image and soundscape would you wish to leave in the audience's mind as the play ends and people leave their seats?

e What part will lighting play in the final moments? Most of the play has been dark, much of it in the castle. Do the final moments bring some light and fresh air to the stage, or does the sombre atmosphere continue to the end?

f When you have considered the points above, work in groups to stage the final moments of the play.

HORATIO   Not from his mouth,
    Had it th'ability of life to thank you;
    He never gave commandment for their death.
    But since, so jump upon this bloody question,
    You from the Polack wars, and you from England,   355
    Are here arrived, give order that these bodies
    High on a stage be placèd to the view,
    And let me speak to th'yet unknowing world
    How these things came about. So shall you hear
    Of carnal, bloody, and unnatural acts,   360
    Of accidental judgements, casual slaughters,
    Of deaths put on by cunning and forced cause,
    And in this upshot, purposes mistook
    Fallen on th'inventors' heads. All this can I
    Truly deliver.

FORTINBRAS   Let us haste to hear it,   365
    And call the noblest to the audience.
    For me, with sorrow I embrace my fortune.
    I have some rights of memory in this kingdom,
    Which now to claim my vantage doth invite me.

HORATIO   Of that I shall have also cause to speak,   370
    And from his mouth whose voice will draw on more.
    But let this same be presently performed,
    Even while men's minds are wild, lest more mischance
    On plots and errors happen.

FORTINBRAS   Let four captains
    Bear Hamlet like a soldier to the stage,   375
    For he was likely, had he been put on,
    To have proved most royal; and for his passage,
    The soldier's music and the rite of war
    Speak loudly for him.
    Take up the bodies. Such a sight as this   380
    Becomes the field, but here shows much amiss.
    Go bid the soldiers shoot.

Exeunt marching, after the which a peal of ordnance are shot off

Looking back at the play
Activities for groups or individuals

1 Love in *Hamlet*

'forty thousand brothers / Could not with all their quantity of love / Make up my sum' cries Hamlet as he rages against Laertes beside Ophelia's grave. In all the writing about *Hamlet*, 'love' is less discussed than 'revenge' or 'madness'. Yet it plays a vital part in the tragedy in many ways.

* Consider each major character and identify who (or what – Polonius loves the sound of his own voice) they love, and if that love is returned or if it changes. Use your findings to write an extended essay: 'The importance of love in *Hamlet*'. Remember to back up your observations with quotations.

2 What caused the tragedy?

Write at least a paragraph on each of the following, analysing how it contributes to the tragedy of *Hamlet*:

* the personality of Hamlet (perhaps a fatal flaw; see pp. 254–8)
* the personality of Claudius (see p. 259)
* fate – the inevitability of destiny, and whether it comes from 'outside' or is a flaw of character
* the supernatural – ghostly intervention
* Denmark (a corrupt society is perhaps the major cause of the tragedy)
* chance and accident (e.g. the encounter with the pirate ship).

3 Modern relevance

Write down all the factors you would include in an argument that *Hamlet* is relevant to today's world. Discuss this as a whole class, and move the discussion to a formal debate if you wish.

4 'the rest is silence' – an 'early' ending

Some productions have ended at Act 5 Scene 2, line 337: Hamlet's 'the rest is silence.'

* Give your view on that practice, identifying what is lost or gained dramatically by ending the play at that line; and what an early ending would mean for our view of Horatio's role in the play.

5 The structure of the whole play

Hamlet is Shakespeare's longest play. If we look at the relative length of the scenes, we can see that, in this edition, Acts 1 and 3 take up about twenty-five pages each and Acts 2, 4 and 5 about twenty. You might like to undertake a more granular analysis, and work out the balance of the play scene-by-scene within each act.

a What do you think are the reasons for the length, and are they justified? Is it principally to do with Hamlet's procrastination, or do the complexities of the plot and the personal/public dimensions require such length?

b If you were asked, as a director, to cut the play, where would you make the cuts and why?

c See if you can stage or present the whole of *Hamlet* in two minutes. Use your inventiveness to compress the action (and inaction) into the timeframe. Afterwards, watch Tom Stoppard's *15-Minute Hamlet*.

These images from a 2006 production by the Royal Shakespeare Company show the intimacy and passion of the final struggle between Claudius and Hamlet. Compare them to any production(s) you have seen, to your imagined ending, and/or to images you can collect from the Internet.

241

Perspectives and themes

What is the play about?

Millions of words in thousands of books and articles have been written on *Hamlet*. They stand in ironic contrast to Hamlet's final words: 'the rest is silence.' The character of Hamlet himself has attracted most critical commentary. In the nineteenth century, he appealed to the romantic melancholic mood and was interpreted as the noble doomed hero. From the second half of the twentieth century, more attention has been given to his contradictions and unpleasantness: a man who can speak great poetry yet revile a young woman, stab her father in a sudden violent moment and send two old friends to their death without a twinge of conscience.

the purpose of playing as to show 'the very age and body of the time his form and pressure', so every society reproduces *Hamlet* to mirror itself. Thus a German production in the 1970s presented Ophelia as a Baader–Meinhof terrorist. A Romanian production in the late 1980s portrayed Denmark as a totalitarian police state in Eastern Europe. And in 2004, London's Old Vic Theatre presented Hamlet as a contemporary disturbed, neurotic adolescent. In a Lithuanian production at Shakespeare's Globe in London's 2012 World Shakespeare Festival, the director's interpretation was described as 'engag[ing] with the diversity of human nature, at once funny and violent, visceral and light-hearted, and always deeply compelling'.

One way of answering the question 'What is *Hamlet* about?' could be to think of it as the dramatisation of a story. Denmark is under threat of invasion by Fortinbras of Norway. Young Hamlet, Prince of Denmark, is deeply depressed. His father, the king, has recently died in mysterious circumstances. His mother Gertrude has quickly married his uncle Claudius, whom Hamlet detests. Claudius, not Hamlet, has become king. Hamlet's father returns as a ghost and tells Hamlet that Claudius is responsible for his murder. Hamlet desires revenge and pretends to be mad to achieve that end. But he is uncertain whether the Ghost is honest, or is an agent of the devil, tempting him to do evil.

There is something universal about *Hamlet*. It absorbs the interests and anxieties of any culture and any age. When manifested in performance and criticism, it renders back those interests and preoccupations as 'abstracts and brief chronicles of the time'. Just as Hamlet described

He delays taking revenge. The visit of a group of travelling actors gives him an idea: he will have them perform a murder before Claudius. If Claudius reacts guiltily, it will prove the Ghost has spoken the truth. And that is what happens.

But Hamlet's assumed madness has disastrous consequences. He violently insults Ophelia, the young woman we suppose that he had loved. Then, confronting his mother, he kills Polonius, Ophelia's father, thinking him to be Claudius. The result is that Ophelia is actually driven mad, and Hamlet is sentenced to be exiled to England, where Claudius plans Hamlet's execution. But a chance encounter with a pirate ship enables Hamlet to return to Denmark, where he learns that Ophelia has drowned. Ophelia's brother Laertes plots with Claudius to kill Hamlet deceitfully in a duel using a poisoned sword and drink. Their plan backfires, and Gertrude drinks the poison and dies. Laertes, fatally wounded, reveals the truth. Hamlet, wounded by the poisoned sword, kills Claudius, and then he too dies. Fortinbras arrives, to become king of Denmark.

Such a brief telling of the story, however, seems inadequate to answer the question 'What is *Hamlet* about?' It has become customary to attempt to answer the question by considering the themes of the play. Themes are ideas or concepts (such as 'delay' or 'surveillance') that recur throughout the play. They suggest that Shakespeare was preoccupied by such ideas as he wrote, and sought to explore them through drama that would entertain his audiences – and make them think. Major themes include: the relationship between the individual, politics and society; revenge in relation to honour and justice; madness and melancholia; sin and salvation; acting and theatre; confinement, responsibility and freedom; the nature of existence; sexuality; and connections between all of these.

◆ Look back at the diagram that you began on page 12, showing how the different themes are interconnected. Is there one dominant theme? In small groups, discuss whether you think there is a hierarchy of themes.

Politics and society – 'Denmark's a prison'

The play is set in a politically and culturally interconnected Europe: Denmark, Norway, Poland, France, Germany, England. Elsinore is not a remote backwater, but a vital strategic place in European political and social life. Its young aristocrats are educated at Wittenberg University and it claims England as one of its dependent states, subdued by bloody combat (Act 4 Scene 3, lines 54–60).

But Claudius's Denmark is insecure. When the play opens, it is a country feverishly preparing for war. The nervous anxiety of that preparation is evident in the very first words spoken: 'Who's there?' Barnardo, the relieving sentry, mistakenly challenges Francisco, when military discipline requires Francisco to challenge the newcomer. When the Ghost appears, it may be a visitor from the supernatural world, but its meaning is political: it 'bodes some strange eruption to our state' (Act 1 Scene 1, line 69).

There are echoes of an older, feudal world of the dead fathers (old Hamlet and old Fortinbras) who settled disputes by personal combat guided by a chivalric code ('law and heraldy'). But that older society of honour is giving way to the new world under Claudius. He is a smooth negotiator, an efficient, unscrupulous schemer who prepares for war but settles territorial quarrels by dispatch of ambassadors and formal treaties. He is truly a 'politician' of the type Hamlet reviles in the graveyard: 'one that would circumvent [outwit] God' (Act 5 Scene 1, line 67).

The people of Denmark barely appear in the play, but Claudius increasingly sees them as a threat to his rule. They are 'the distracted multitude', 'the rabble', 'false Danish dogs' who favour Hamlet, or who call for Laertes to be king. All such unreliable people must be closely watched, even more so those who are a direct threat to Claudius's rule, such as Hamlet. It would be dangerous to allow Hamlet to return to Wittenberg, so Claudius refuses permission. He keeps Hamlet under surveillance at home, with the devious words: 'Here in the cheer and comfort of our eye' (Act 1 Scene 2, line 116). That comforting eye will shortly employ two of Hamlet's close friends to spy on him. When Hamlet tells Rosencrantz and Guildenstern 'Denmark's a prison' (Act 2 Scene 2, line 234), he is not simply speaking metaphorically.

The chief minister of state, Polonius, is a willing instrument of Claudius's desire to keep his subjects under surveillance. In the England of Queen Elizabeth I, Polonius's equivalent

▼ **Lord Burghley was the chief advisor to Queen Elizabeth I for most of her reign.**

was Lord Burghley, who also believed in close surveillance to maintain order.

Just as Burghley maintained an extensive network of spies, so Polonius is infected by the desire to overhear in secret, to keep all potential dissidents under surveillance. He spies on Hamlet, using his own daughter as bait. Even his own family must be watched. Although Polonius utters conventional decencies to Laertes ('these few precepts'), he sets a spy on his own son. It is hardly surprising that rumours circulate in Denmark. After the death of Polonius, there is no shortage of 'buzzers' (rumour-mongers) to infect Laertes's ears.

For all the ordered formalities of Claudius's court and the seemingly close domesticity of Polonius's family, a sense of corruption grows throughout the play. 'Something is rotten in the state of Denmark' says Marcellus (Act 1 Scene 4, line 90), and the stench of decay at the heart of personal and social life increasingly infects the language. The madness that Hamlet displays and into which Ophelia descends is the individual symptom of a deeper social malaise. Hamlet projects his disgust onto a variety of targets: Claudius, his mother's and Ophelia's sexuality, death itself. But his words mirror the deeper social corruption that pervades Denmark: 'foul deeds', 'maggots', 'carrion', 'offal', 'rank corruption, mining all within', 'the ulcerous place', 'an unweeded garden'. However civilised outward appearances are, the routine oppressions of a police state prevent natural social interaction.

The two women in the play are little more than pawns in a patriarchal world of sexual exploitation. Gertrude has been 'taken to wife' by Claudius. Just as he has seized Denmark, so too he appropriates her body. She has no real power, but is a possession to be fought over by king and prince, husband and son. Ophelia is even more of an object manipulated by men. Her brother lectures her, seeking to control her sexuality. Her father uses her as bait in a spy trap: 'I'll loose my daughter to him' (Act 2 Scene 2, line 160). Hamlet takes out on her a misogynistic (women-hating) side of his character. The masculine brutalities of Denmark quite literally drive Ophelia mad.

Hamlet, with his reflective self-questioning, is as much a modern man as a Renaissance prince. His preoccupation with notions of sin and salvation (see pp. 249–50) shows he is the product of a feudal world where religion is used as an instrument of control. But his style of thought marks him out as a true individual. He is trapped in this changing world and subject to its contradictions. Hamlet can both reflect 'What a piece of work is a man!' (Act 2 Scene 2, line 286) and casually dismiss Rosencrantz and Guildenstern to their deaths.

As well as being a personal quest for justice and/or revenge, Hamlet's vendetta against Claudius is also a struggle for political power, just as Claudius's murder of old Hamlet was a political assassination. Such political struggles mirrored the anxieties of Shakespeare's England. Elizabeth's reign might have seemed on the surface to be stable and secure, but it was always subject to threats of overthrow by a powerful faction of the nobility. At the end of the play, Fortinbras and his army take over. This is not the harmonious end of a domestic tragedy, with order restored by a benevolent ruler. Rather, it is the brutal realpolitik (politics based on practical or material reasons rather than theoretical ideas) of a society that, at base, rests on the dominance of a state by a small but militarily powerful minority.

The *quietus* (peace in death) that Hamlet finally achieves might represent private fulfilment, but it is politically empty and futile. Such a way of coming to terms with death might be seen as a weak submission that masks the harsh realities of political and social life in Hamlet's Denmark.

◆ Use the information in this section as the basis for an extended essay that answers this question: 'In what ways might a production of *Hamlet* explore the political and social implications of the play?'

Revenge, and revenge tragedy – 'Oh, vengeance!'

Today, many people consider revenge immoral because it means taking the law into one's own hands. It is seen as a profoundly unsocial act. But it seems to be a very human impulse: to exact retribution from someone who has done wrong to you or your family. Revenge follows the Old Testament maxim 'an eye for an eye, a tooth for a tooth'. Revenge is still central to some criminal codes of honour (e.g. the vendetta among the Sicilian mafia).

In Shakespeare's time, revenge was a crime in law and was also an irreligious act. For the Church of the late sixteenth century, revenge was a sin. The revenger's soul was damned, condemned to suffer everlasting torment in hell. That thought preoccupies Hamlet for much of the play. (See the image on p. 44.)

Francis Bacon, a contemporary of Shakespeare, called revenge 'a kind of wild justice'. He wrote in 1625 in an essay on revenge:

The most tolerable sort of revenge is for those wrongs which there is no law to remedy, but then let a man take heed the revenge be such as there is no law to punish; else a man's enemy is still beforehand, and it is two for one. Some, when they take revenge, are desirous the party should know whence it cometh. This is the more generous. For the delight seemeth to be not so much in doing the hurt as in making the party repent … This is certain, that a man that studieth revenge keeps his own wounds green, which otherwise would heal and do well. Public revenges are for the most part fortunate, as that for the death of Caesar. But in private revenges it is not so. Nay rather, vindictive persons live the life of witches, who, as they are mischievous, so end they infortunate.

◆ Write a reply to Bacon. Begin 'In Hamlet's case …', and argue the points Bacon makes in his essay. You could also write a reply that argues with Bacon's position from your own point of view.

◆ Write a brief outline of a modern revenge story or play. Then write the opening chapter of the story, or the first scene of the play.

◆ Write a paragraph responding to each of the following statements:

- Revenge is always wrong.
- *Hamlet* is not so much a revenge play as a play about revenge.
- The play suggests that revenge does not pay.
- *Hamlet* is more a tragedy than a revenge play: its focus is on the fall of a hero rather than on the execution of a pledge to revenge.
- The revenge plot of *Hamlet* is one of the least important elements in the play.

Revenge tragedy was hugely popular when Shakespeare began his playwriting career. The central feature of each revenge play was a hero (or villain) who sought to avenge a wrong. Elizabethan playwrights served up a rich diet of madness, melancholy and retribution. In the ten years before *Hamlet* was performed, enthusiastic crowds flocked to see Thomas Kyd's *The Spanish Tragedy*, Christopher Marlowe's *The Jew of Malta*, and Shakespeare's *Titus Andronicus*.

Shakespeare also knew a twelfth-century revenge story about Amleth, Prince of Denmark. In the tale, a brother murders the king and marries his wife. The son, Amleth, pretends to be mad to pursue revenge. He slays one of his uncle's spies, forges a letter to have the king's two accomplices executed in England, and finally kills his uncle and becomes king.

Elizabethan revenge tragedy contained typical ingredients:

- a melancholy hero/avenger
- a hesitating avenger (without hesitation the play would be over too quickly)
- a villain who was to be killed in revenge
- complex plotting
- murders (usually from sexual motives) and other physical horrors

- a play-within-a-play
- sexual obsession and lust related to the passion for revenge
- a ghost who calls for revenge
- real or feigned madness
- the death of the revenger.

The plays were usually set in Italy or Spain, but the Elizabethans seemed able to relate the wider themes of each play to their own world.

The typical revenge tragedy had five parts:

- **exposition** usually by a ghost (providing motivation for revenge)
- **anticipation** in which detailed planning of the revenge takes place
- **confrontation** between avenger and intended victim
- **delay** as the revenger hesitates to perform the killing
- **completion** of the revenge (often with the death of the revenger).

Hamlet has four revenge plots. Hamlet vows to revenge his father's death at the hands of Claudius. Laertes swears to avenge his father's death at the hands of Hamlet. Fortinbras seeks to avenge his father's death at the hands of King Hamlet. Another son seeking revenge is Pyrrhus in the play-within-a-play: he slaughters Priam, whose son had killed Pyrrhus's father.

Hamlet has many elements of Elizabethan revenge tragedy. Merely telling the story makes it sound very sensational: eight deaths, a mad woman, a fight in a grave, and so on. But *Hamlet* has outlived most other revenge plays and is still immensely popular. Why?

◆ Use the information given above to identify in what ways *Hamlet* can be regarded as an Elizabethan revenge tragedy. Then suggest reasons why *Hamlet* continues to hold great appeal after 400 years.

For more on *Hamlet* as a tragedy, see the section on 'The nature of tragedy' on page 259.

Madness and melancholia – 'This is mere madness'

Today, doctors and psychiatrists rarely use the words 'mad' or 'lunacy'. Instead, they use such expressions as 'manic depression' (violent mood swings), 'schizophrenia' (deranged perceptions and emotions), 'suffering from a nervous breakdown', 'psychotic' (suffering from delusions, dangerously out of contact with reality), 'emotionally disturbed' and 'mentally ill'. Shakespeare's audiences had few qualms about using the term 'mad'. Often, when people were considered mad they were thought to be possessed by devils, and were confined to asylums. Visiting such places to watch the behaviour of 'mad' men and women was considered a source of amusement.

Madness was one of the conventions of revenge tragedy. Following that convention, Hamlet proposes to 'put an antic disposition on' (Act 1 Scene 5, line 172). From then on, the question of whether he is merely feigning madness, or has indeed descended into real mental derangement, has divided critics and audiences alike. Every new production of the play raises the issue afresh.

Some of Hamlet's behaviour, particularly his verbal assault on Ophelia in Act 3 Scene 1 ('To a nunnery, go'), is extreme. Ophelia's lament 'Oh what a noble mind is here o'erthrown!' seems a well-judged comment on what she has experienced, and she thinks Hamlet 'Blasted with ecstasy [madness].' But her earlier description of his behaviour, 'Pale as his shirt, his knees knocking each other' (Act 2 Scene 1, line 79) makes him sound rather like a man putting on an act. Yet as he prepares for the duel with Laertes, Hamlet offers an apology – apparently sincere – in which he claims he was indeed mad: 'His madness is poor Hamlet's enemy' (Act 5 Scene 2, line 211).

▲ Albrecht Dürer's engraving of *Melancholia* (1514). Dürer's engraving has often been used in programmes for stage productions of *Hamlet*. Give some reasons why you think it is frequently chosen as a powerful picture to illustrate the play.

The one person in the play who is without doubt driven to mental breakdown is Ophelia. Her two 'mad episodes' (in Act 4 Scene 5) are both poignant and bizarre, 'A document in madness'. The terrible blow of her father's death has tipped her over the edge, and her songs display a curious mixture of innocence and sexuality, sense and nonsense.

247

Her evident dementia stands in contrast to the constant
puzzle that attends all instances of Hamlet's 'madness':
is he just 'putting it on'?

◆ Step into role in turn as Claudius, Gertrude, Polonius,
Ophelia, Horatio, Rosencrantz and Guildenstern. Give
each character's response, with reasons, to the question
'Is Hamlet mad?' Then speak Hamlet's own answer to that
question.

◆ An Elizabethan medical text described the symptoms of
melancholy: 'sad and fearful … distrust, doubt, diffidence
or despair, sometimes furious, and sometimes merry …
sardonian [sardonic], and false laughter … every serious
thing for a time, is turned into a jest, and tragedies into
comedies' (Timothy Bright, *Treatise on Melancholy*, 1586).
How accurately does each of these words or phrases
describe Hamlet?

▼ Use these images of Ophelia to help you define the nature and
manifestation of her own madness. She is often depicted as a
helpless victim – but madness can present itself in many ways.

Sin and salvation – 'What form of prayer / Can serve my turn?'

In Shakespeare's day, the threat of hell and eternal damnation was much more sharply felt than it is today. Most Elizabethans cared passionately about their religion and the state of their souls. They were obsessed by what would happen to them after death. They believed that one of three possibilities awaited them. If they died in a state of grace, with all their sins confessed, they would go to heaven and enjoy eternal peace. If none of their sins was confessed and forgiven, they would go to hell and endure eternal suffering. The third possibility was purgatory, where those who had not made full confession would go. There they suffered until their unconfessed sins were burnt away (purged). Suicides were bound for hell in whatever state they died.

Hamlet explores this obsession with the afterlife. In his first soliloquy Hamlet longs for the peace of death ('O that this too too solid flesh would melt'), but recognises that suicide is forbidden by God ('Or that the Everlasting had not fixed / His canon 'gainst self-slaughter'). In his 'To be, or not to be' soliloquy, he broods on the uncertainty of what will happen after death. It is 'the dread of something after death' that makes us endure the oppressions of life (Act 3 Scene 1, lines 56–82).

Later in the play, the consequences of religious attitudes to suicide are highlighted as the gravediggers' talk reveals that suicides are normally denied the right to 'Christian burial' in a churchyard. Ophelia should be denied the full rites of such burial because it is thought she has taken her own life ('Her death was doubtful'). The Priest at her funeral says that only Claudius's command prevented what she should properly receive as a suicide: not 'charitable prayers', but 'Shards, flints, and pebbles should be thrown on her'. Such was the pronouncement of the Church on suicides.

The Ghost tells how he suffers in purgatory: 'confined to fast in fires, / Till the foul crimes done in my days of nature / Are burnt and purged away' (Act 1 Scene 5, lines 11–13). Because he died without having a chance to confess his sins, he must undergo torment before he can earn a place in heaven, reconciled to God. But Hamlet cannot be sure whether the Ghost is good or bad: 'Be thou a spirit of health, or goblin damned' (Act 1 Scene 4, line 40).

The question of whether the Ghost is to be trusted or not haunts Hamlet for much of the play. It reflects the Elizabethan view that some ghosts were benign, others evil, tempting humans to behave badly and so damn themselves to an afterlife of torment in hell. Hamlet fears what he has seen may be a devil who 'Abuses me to damn me'.

To test whether it is a 'damned ghost' sent to lure his own soul to eternal damnation, Hamlet contrives the play in which he hopes to 'catch the conscience of the king'. When Claudius reveals his guilt by his reaction to the Mousetrap play, Hamlet is convinced the Ghost has spoken true: 'I'll take the ghost's word for a thousand / pound' (Act 3 Scene 2, lines 260–1). And in the play's final scene, Hamlet declares his conviction that heaven guides him (Act 5 Scene 2, lines 10–11).

Hamlet's delay in avenging his father's murder can be partly explained by his beliefs about sin and salvation. Shortly after the play-within-the-play, Hamlet finds Claudius at prayer, hoping God will pardon him. The fact that Claudius is praying stops Hamlet from instantly killing him. Hamlet's own father suffers after death because Claudius killed him at a moment when he was unprepared for heaven, not having confessed his sins. Now Hamlet wishes Claudius to experience the same horrible suffering after death. He therefore sheathes his sword and decides to wait, to catch Claudius at a moment 'That has no relish of salvation in't'. That moment will be when Claudius is committing a sin: 'drunk asleep, or in his rage, / Or in th'incestuous pleasure of his bed, / At game a-swearing' (Act 3 Scene 3, lines 89–91). Killing him at such a moment, when he has no thoughts of heaven in his mind, will surely send Claudius to hell, to eternal damnation. Ironically, as Claudius reveals, he has not been successfully praying at all: 'My words fly up, my thoughts remain below. / Words without thoughts never to heaven go' (Act 3 Scene 3, lines 97–8).

Dr Johnson, an eighteenth-century essayist, poet and Shakespeare critic, believed Hamlet's thoughts when he found Claudius at prayer 'too terrible to be read or uttered'. Johnson's view influenced productions for over 100 years. Hamlet's speech (Act 3 Scene 3, lines 73–96) was either cut in performance or interpreted as not expressing Hamlet's real intentions, but simply an excuse to procrastinate, to delay the action.

◆ Talk together about what you think of Dr Johnson's view in the preceding paragraph.

◆ Imagine you are Hamlet and write a paragraph about each of the following characters: Polonius, Rosencrantz and Guildenstern, Ophelia, Laertes, Gertrude, Claudius. Say whether you feel responsible for their death, whether each one deserved to die, and what you think will happen to each character after death.

Acting and theatre – 'The play's the thing'

Hamlet richly displays Shakespeare's interest both in his own profession as actor and playwright, and in the London theatres at the end of the reign of Queen Elizabeth I. *Hamlet* is an intensely theatrical play, with many references to playing and acting. Play-acting is part of a puzzle that obsesses Hamlet: the difference between appearance and reality, truth and falsehood. Hamlet uses a company of travelling players to perform a stage murder. The performance traps Claudius into revealing his guilty conscience: a fiction has discovered the 'truth' of the Ghost's story.

The play resonates with the language of theatre: 'play', 'act', 'show', 'perform', 'applaud', 'prologue', 'shape' (costume), 'part' and 'stage' (see p. 265). Hamlet's soliloquies are like those of an actor reflecting on the part he has to play.

He sees the players as 'the abstract and brief chronicles of the time', and the purpose of acting as holding 'the mirror up to nature'. For Hamlet, the function of drama is to portray the nature of society: 'to show virtue her own feature, scorn her own image, and the very age and body of the time his form and pressure' (Act 3 Scene 2, lines 19–20).

On Hamlet's first appearance he denies he is playing a part: 'I know not seems.' His grief is real. But he puts on 'an antic disposition', and throughout the play muses (or rages) about deceptive appearance: 'Smiling, damned villain!' Other characters dissemble, most obviously Claudius. Rosencrantz and Guildenstern put on an act of friendship, and even Ophelia is instructed to 'show' to enable her father and Claudius to eavesdrop on Hamlet.

The play is filled with highly dramatic scenes: the Ghost's five appearances; Hamlet's raging at Ophelia and Gertrude; the dumb-show; the fight in the grave. The final scene has abundant theatrical opportunities and references: the duel between Hamlet and Laertes; the many deaths, witnessed by 'mutes or audience to this act'; the entry of Fortinbras (preceded by 'March afar off, and shot within'); Horatio's 'give order that these bodies / High on a stage be placed to the view'; Fortinbras's order that 'four captains / Bear Hamlet like a soldier to the stage'; and the final stage direction: *'Exeunt marching, after the which a peal of ordnance are shot off'*.

The 'tragedians of the city'

Shakespeare's own company of players was sometimes forced to tour when plague closed the London theatres. The players' appearance at Elsinore echoes the experience of troupes of London actors as they toured the English provinces or Europe. On tour, they performed in the great halls of country houses or on makeshift stages in inn-yards or town squares.

Around the time Shakespeare wrote *Hamlet*, an acting company of boy players was enjoying great success in London. For a short time, these 'little eyases' (unfledged hawks) threatened the livelihood of some adult professional acting companies. The adult players were forced to tour because they could not attract London audiences. Hamlet's exchanges with Rosencrantz and Guildenstern in Act 2 Scene 2, lines 295–333, are thought to be about these boy players and the 'war of the theatres' (see p. 84). There was a brief but intense rivalry between adult companies as their resident playwrights mocked each other in their plays ('much throwing about of brains').

The members of Shakespeare's acting company (The King's Men, originally The Lord Chamberlain's Men) worked together closely for over twenty years. They knew each other very well and may have contributed to Shakespeare's script. Because of his fascination with acting, Shakespeare may have put into *Hamlet* private jokes and theatrical references that would have amused his fellow players at the Globe Theatre on London's Bankside:

- 'you hear this fellow in the cellarage' (the space under the Globe stage?) Act 1 Scene 5, line 151
- 'this distracted globe' (the Globe Theatre? Hamlet's head? The world?) Act 1 Scene 5, line 97
- 'I did enact Julius Caesar' (the actor who played Polonius may well have created the title role in *Julius Caesar,* written by Shakespeare shortly before *Hamlet.*) Act 3 Scene 2, line 91
- 'this majestical roof fretted with golden / fire' (the sky, or the painted 'heavens' of the Globe's stage?) Act 2 Scene 2, lines 284–5
- 'thy face is valanced [bearded] since I saw thee last'; 'Pray God your voice … be not cracked' (was Shakespeare joking at his fellow actor's changed appearance, and the thought that the boy actors who played the female parts would all too soon grow up?) Act 2 Scene 2, lines 386–90

◆ Collect quotations from the play about actors, acting or the theatre. Use them to write an essay (or written dialogue in question-and-answer form) in response to the following: '*Hamlet* is a tragedy dominated by the idea of the play. Discuss'.

Further themes

In addition to the themes discussed above, ideas of confinement, responsibility and freedom, attitudes towards sex, and the nature of existence pervade the play.

Confinement manifests itself in terms of the prison-like nature of Denmark for Hamlet, who seems trapped and shackled by his presence there. He is back from university, and finds the transition to home difficult ('For your intent / In going back to school in Wittenberg / Is most retrograde to our desire', Act 1 Scene 2, lines 112–14) – particularly because his mother has married Claudius and the Ghost indicates that his father has been murdered. Some productions of the play emphasise Denmark's dark, prison-like nature and the sense that Hamlet has limited choice in his actions. His stature as prince of Denmark also constrains him.

Responsibility and freedom are closely related to Hamlet's position as prince. On the one hand, Hamlet has freedoms and privileges – he appears not to have to work or account for his time, and can afford to sink into melancholy with only gentle chiding from his mother ('Good Hamlet cast thy nighted colour off', Act 1 Scene 2, line 68). But at the same time, he has responsibilities weighing upon him as successor to the throne of Denmark. The sight of Fortinbras passing through the country with his army reminds Hamlet of his inaction and his need to put things right.

Hamlet's attitude towards sex (Act 3 Scene 1, Act 3 Scene 2 and Act 3 Scene 4) has been described as Oedipal, warped, frustrated and cruel. He treats Ophelia with impunity, urging her to 'Go thy ways to a nunnery'. Freudian analyses of Hamlet's state of mind might suggest that his horror of the sexual relationship between Claudius and Gertrude, his solitude, his obsession with his mother, and even his inability to act until late in the play, are evidence of imbalance – perhaps also contributing to his 'madness'. (For more on this, see p. 255)

The nature of existence is a theme that recurs through the play. First, the appearance of the Ghost raises questions of perception and the afterlife for Horatio and the Watch; once verified by Horatio, it threatens doom and inspires revenge. Second, and in contrast, the very existence of the physical self in the world preoccupies Hamlet, who muses on the relationship of life and death. Third, the loneliness of the human on the planet ('existentialism') creeps into Hamlet's consciousness, as does a sense of the inevitability of – and preparedness for – death: 'There is special providence in the fall of a sparrow … the readiness is all' (Act 5 Scene 2, lines 192–5).

◆ Take three or four themes as identified in this section, and work out how they are related to each other in the play. You might find it helpful to discuss their relationship in groups first, then as a class, as you will touch on some complex philosophical issues. Then, using appropriate evidence from the script, write an essay on the relationship between your chosen themes.

What relevance does *Hamlet* have to a young, contemporary audience?

The part of Hamlet is often played by an actor in his late twenties or early thirties – perhaps to suggest Hamlet himself is around that age, maybe also because it is a long and difficult part for a younger actor to take on. But Hamlet as a character appeals to younger age groups (those in their teenage years or early twenties) because of his rebelliousness, his shifting moods, his anger and frustration at oppression and confinement, and his complicated sexuality and identity (or his search for some sense of solid identity).

◆ Look at the photographs of Hamlet in this edition of the play, and in pairs discuss which of them you find the most appropriate for your own vision of how he should appear. Rank the best three and the worst three, from your point of view, and then debate your preferences with the rest of the class.

◆ Look at the photographs from a young persons' workshop on the opposite page. Which moments from the play do you think are being enacted?

◆ Imagine you are producing *Hamlet* for an audience younger than you. What parts would you cut? Which themes would you emphasise? How can you ensure that the audience will be engaged by the play, and that they will see something of their own lives, problems and preoccupations in your production? Juliet in *Romeo and Juliet* can be played as a thirteen-year-old, according to the script. How young can you play Hamlet and Ophelia? You could put on a performance as a community play for a younger year group, a partner school or a young people's group in your area.

▶ *Hamlet* in workshop performance with the Royal Shakespeare Company's Young People's Shakespeare in 2010. Can you identify the characters in each photo?

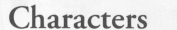

Characters

▼ Which of Hamlet's characteristics do you think are most evident in this 2010 performance?

Hamlet

Hamlet's words to Guildenstern – 'you would pluck out the heart of my mystery' – describe what thousands of books and articles have tried to do since *Hamlet* was first performed. But Hamlet's character remains elusive. He plays many roles throughout the play: alienated outsider, potential suicide, actor, swordsman, joker, friend of Horatio, angry son, bloodthirsty revenger, lacerating self-critic. His mood swings from depression to elation, from extreme self-loathing to quiet acceptance of his fate in 'the readiness is all'.

Hamlet has been seen as an ironic commentator on mortality and sin, a man with acute sexual problems, a genuine madman, a clever impersonator of madness, a man tortured by irreconcilable moral dilemmas, an unhappy adolescent, a puritanical fundamentalist, a dreamer, a philosopher and a truly noble prince.

The script shows that Hamlet is a great listener. He listens intently to what is said to him and often seizes on a word or phrase to construct his own reply. His very first words: 'A little more than kin, and less than kind' (Act 1 Scene 2, line 65), imply that Claudius is too presumptuous in calling him 'son' (kin), and that his nature (kind) is unlike Claudius's. His next line 'I am too much i'th'sun' puns on Claudius's 'son'. His following two replies to Gertrude pun ironically on her use of 'common' and 'seems'.

In many ways, Hamlet is something of a chameleon – he changes colour in relation to those he is with, and/or in relation to the situation in which he finds himself. Another way of putting this is in modern social-psychological terms: he varies the presentation of his self in everyday life. In other words, he is a character who is made up of different selves, and the desire to see him as a single self (either by the other characters in the play or by ourselves as audience) is doomed to failure.

Hamlet revels in how the slipperiness of language gives potential for bitter or comic puns or ironic retorts. He uses puns to great effect, picking up a speaker's words and giving them back with a different meaning (look at Act 3 Scene 2, 82–112 for an example). The Clown/gravedigger is the only other character in the play to use this style of deliberate misunderstanding. He gives Hamlet a taste of his own medicine.

◆ Identify examples of this linguistic technique of Hamlet's. Against which characters does he use it most frequently?

◆ Hamlet not only listens carefully to others, he also listens intently to himself and comments on his own thoughts. Identify passages in his soliloquies in which he comments on his own thoughts and feelings (e.g. with self-disgust or reproof).

◆ Use your findings in the two activities above to compile an assignment on what aspects of Hamlet's character are revealed by how he listens to others and to himself.

◆ Track Hamlet's appearances throughout the play. Identify one or two moods from each appearance, and then create a graph of his changing states of mind across the play as a whole. Does he present the trajectory of a typical tragic hero – the rise and fall of a great person? Or is his trajectory different? If so, in what respects and why? (See the notes on tragedy on p. 258.)

◆ What is the significance of Horatio for Hamlet? At a simple level, he is a trusted friend in a world of deceit, intrigue and falsity. But there is more to Horatio. Identify the scenes in which Horatio and Hamlet appear together. Highlight their dialogue, and examine how they talk together. What does a friendship with Horatio tell us about Hamlet – how is Hamlet reflected in Horatio?

Hamlet's sexual identity

What is Hamlet's attitude towards the two women in the play? Some productions have suggested that Hamlet is sexually obsessed by his mother. Other productions imply that he truly loves Ophelia. Almost every possibility about Hamlet's sexuality has been explored on stage, on film and in print.

- **An Oedipus complex?** Hamlet is in love with his mother and is violently jealous of Claudius, his stepfather. This Oedipus complex makes him unable to have a loving relationship with Ophelia, whom he treats badly. His hatred for Claudius is based on sexual jealousy, since Claudius has usurped not only his father's crown but also his mother's bed.

- **A Puritan?** Hamlet is severely puritanical about love and sex. He is appalled by what he sees as the lust that drives the relationship between Claudius and Gertrude (see Act 3 Scene 4, lines 92–4). His disgust at his mother's sexuality makes him despise all women. Hamlet therefore subjects Ophelia to violent verbal abuse, full of sexual innuendo.

- **A true lover?** Hamlet genuinely loves Ophelia. He urges her to go to a nunnery to escape the torturous, prison-like nature of love in the world that Denmark represents. His harsh words cover his deep love for her, and he is being 'cruel only to be kind'.

- **An immature boy?** Hamlet is not ready for love. His sexual bantering with Polonius, Rosencrantz and Guildenstern is immature male behaviour. He is unable to understand his mother's sexual life or to appreciate Ophelia's innocent and more mature affection for him.

- **A split personality?** Hamlet both loves and hates Ophelia, and simultaneously admires and abhors his mother. His sexual feelings for Ophelia and his mother fight against his other feelings. His rational mind attempts to reconcile these sexual and emotional tensions, but thought itself makes him unable to act.

- **Private love versus public office?** Hamlet's sexual confusion arises not from his personality but from his position as prince of Denmark. He may not choose for himself in marriage but must think first of his responsibility to the country.

▼ 'I loved Ophelia'. In this Royal Shakespeare Company production, Hamlet displayed his genuine love for Ophelia by leaping into her grave for a final embrace.

◆ Find two or more quotations from the script to support each of the viewpoints listed on page 255. Arrange the six interpretations in order of which you find the most convincing, using the evidence in the play.

◆ Undertake some research into Freud's theories of sexuality and depression, and then do a Freudian analysis of Hamlet. You can do this in two stages: a dramatised analysis of Hamlet as a client of Freud's in his clinic in Vienna or London; and a written set of case notes on Hamlet, compiled after a number of sessions with him.

◆ Step into role as Hamlet. Imagine, just before you die, that you have the chance for a longer, cooler and more reasoned reflection on your behaviour and attitudes to Gertrude and Ophelia. Either write this out as a prose or verse soliloquy, or respond to questions and accusations from Gertrude, Ophelia and Horatio.

◆ In another possible world, or different story (one in which the present play stops before the 'closet' scene), imagine that Hamlet, after the erratic behaviour of the first half of the play, marries Ophelia. You can stage the marriage and perhaps the reception afterwards with as many characters as you wish (six, to include Gertrude, Claudius, Polonius and Laertes; or a larger wedding party to include the other characters in the play). In particular, write the best man's speech (Horatio?); the father of the bride's speech (Polonius); and the groom's and bride's speeches.

▼ Do you think that Hamlet shows an unhealthy, negative attitude towards the women in the play? In this production, Ophelia was visibly upset when Hamlet insulted her.

Hamlet: a tragic hero?

'Tragedy' is the conventional description of a play that portrays human suffering and the decline and death of a hero or heroine. Traditionally the hero or heroine is of high status, and the fall from grace immense. But some modern tragedies, like Arthur Miller's *Death of a Salesman*, have an ordinary person as their tragic hero. To help your thinking about Hamlet's character, consider the following interpretations of Hamlet as a tragic hero.

- **Tragic flaw?** The hero's downfall is caused by a tragic flaw or blemish in his character. Hamlet's weakness may be that he 'thinks too much' and cannot make up his mind. The resulting inaction leads to his death. But Hamlet's tragic flaw ('vicious mole of nature', Act 1 Scene 4, line 24) may be some other feature in his character responsible for his downfall.

- **A tragedy of fate?** The hero has no real control over his destiny. Once the spring of *Hamlet*'s tragic narrative is released, it unwinds inevitably towards its conclusion: the death of Hamlet. His fate is predetermined. As Hamlet says, 'There's a divinity that shapes our ends'.

- **A tragedy of chance?** Accident and bad luck determine the fate of the hero. The unplanned chance encounter with the pirate ship, for example, brings Hamlet back to Denmark. Hamlet accidentally kills Polonius. The tragic hero is the victim of random events.

- **Irreconcilable opposites?** The hero's character comprises sets of irreconcilable forces. Hamlet's mind and feelings are filled with such tensions: reason battles with passion, love is contrasted with lust, action is inhibited by thought. Hamlet struggles with a wish to die and an urge to live. *Hamlet* can be read as the tragedy of a man trapped between such contraries.

- **Hero as paragon?** The tragic hero has an excess of virtues. This nineteenth-century Romantic view of Hamlet as a Renaissance prince suggests that he is more noble and refined than ordinary people, and that his nobility and purity carry the seeds of their own destruction. Hamlet cannot live in the world because he is too 'good' for it. His sensitivity and noble qualities lead to his downfall.

◆ Find evidence (quotations or actions in the play) to support each of the above viewpoints. Decide which interpretation you favour most. Rank the rest in order, dismissing any you think are not plausible or not supported by evidence. Then write your own view of Hamlet as a tragic hero.

The nature of tragedy

Aristotle's *Poetics* contains some ancient Greek insights into tragedy, which was then emerging as a major new genre to challenge the epic form. For example:

*Tragedy is an imitation of an action that is admirable, complete and possesses magnitude ... [it effects] through pity and fear the purification [or **catharsis**] of such emotions*

The events, i.e. the plot, are what tragedy is there for, and that is the most important thing of all.

Translated by Malcolm Heath, Penguin, 1996

According to Aristotle's theory, a tragic character needs four qualities: to be moral, to behave appropriately, to be realistic and to be consistent. He defines four kinds of tragedy:

- a simple tragedy with a straightforward plot of the rise and fall of a great person
- a complex tragedy, depending entirely on reversal and recognition, so that there is some degree of self-knowledge gained by the protagonist
- a tragedy of suffering, which often marks the slow decline of a person who experiences loss, despair and hopelessness
- a tragedy of character that identifies the 'tragic flaw' mentioned above.

These refer to different types of plot, and at least three may be present in any one play.

◆ Use these definitions from Aristotle to shed light on *Hamlet* and on its eponymous hero. Which of them apply to Hamlet?

◆ Which of the following characteristics and dramatic devices of tragedy might apply to *Hamlet*? Give reasons and evidence for your answers.

- **Hubris:** pride or arrogance in the over-estimation of one's powers, usually followed by a fall and humiliation.

- **Catharsis:** the revelation brought about by purgation, clarification and/or purification; a moment of insight and release from emotional tension, usually in an audience but sometimes in a character.
- **Anagnorisis:** a critical discovery by a character in a play.
- **Peripeteia:** a reversal and turning point for a key character in a play.

Claudius

Claudius has committed an evil deed to become king, murdering his own brother. He plans similar evil as the play unfolds, plotting to have Hamlet killed in England. When that fails, he lures Laertes into a scheme to kill Hamlet in a deceitful duel. He lies about his 'love' for Hamlet and tells Gertrude that he tried to calm Laertes, when in fact he deliberately fuelled Laertes's rage. Hamlet condemns Claudius as a drunkard and sees him as the source of corruption in Denmark: 'this canker of our nature'.

Claudius's hypocrisy is evident throughout the play (see p. 14 on the devious eloquence of his first speech). But he seems a competent king, intelligent and quick witted. There is no hint that the nobles of Denmark challenge his right to the throne. He appears to love Gertrude and to respect Polonius, willing to accept his advice. He knows that he does wrong, and is racked by conscience, struggling unsuccessfully to pray to find some way of absolving his murderous guilt: 'Oh my offence is rank, it smells to heaven.' He bravely stands up to Laertes's threats, but his noble words 'There's such divinity doth hedge a king' are hypocritical, because he himself has killed a king, his own brother.

◆ Write a character study of Claudius, describing in particular how Shakespeare portrays his hypocrisy. Consider ways in which Shakespeare complicates the view that Claudius is simply 'a villain' in order to make him sympathetic and human.

▼ Glenn Close as Gertrude in
Franco Zeffirelli's 1990 film.
What aspects of her character
are suggested by this image?

Gertrude

A puzzle that all productions of the play face is the question of whether Gertrude knows that Claudius is a murderer. She seems in thrall to Claudius for the first half of the play, and is genuinely distressed by her son's bizarre behaviour. But Shakespeare gives Gertrude lines in and after her encounter with Hamlet in her chamber that suggest she progressively distances herself from her second husband.

Critics have often judged Gertrude as a weak, selfish and innocent woman, caught up in conflicts she does not fully understand. Her hasty marriage to Claudius so soon after her first husband's death disgusts Hamlet, and seems to indicate her pliability or perhaps her powerlessness as the widow of a dead king. That capacity to be easily persuaded is evident when she allows Polonius to use her private chamber to spy on Hamlet.

Gertrude feels compassion for both Polonius and Ophelia, and she may well love Claudius, at least for the first half of the play. She tries to protect him from Laertes's aggression. But what are Gertrude's feelings towards Hamlet? Ever since Laurence Olivier's film portrayed Hamlet's incestuous desire for his mother, productions have to decide just how to present her affection for Hamlet.

Polonius

Polonius is the king's counsellor, Claudius's chief minister of state. He is evidently filled with a sense of self-importance, and is proud of the service he has given to the king. Claudius acknowledges him as 'a man faithful and honourable'.

Polonius seeks to control public life. He also wishes to control his family. He hands out good advice to his son Laertes ('these few precepts in thy memory'), but then sends Reynaldo to spy on him in France. He orders Ophelia to avoid Hamlet and to return his love tokens. He even uses her as an accomplice to eavesdrop on Hamlet, an action that results in his daughter being savagely insulted by Hamlet. Polonius offers no word of comfort to the distraught Ophelia.

He conceals himself behind the arras in Gertrude's chamber, only to be killed by Hamlet, who mistakes the hidden figure for the king.

In spite of his pomposity and authoritarianism, Polonius is loved by his children. Shakespeare enables the actor to play Polonius not simply as a spymaster and over-strict father, but also as a character who can gain audience sympathy as a well-meaning father and loyal counsellor.

◆ **What aspects of parenthood are embodied in Polonius? Use the theme of the father–son relationship to explore how Polonius's relationship with Laertes mirrors or contrasts with that of Claudius and Hamlet.**

◆ **As a comparison, talk about the father–daughter relationship. How does Polonius interact with Ophelia?**

Ophelia

Many critics have judged Ophelia as a beautiful, innocent but essentially passive character. Increasingly, however, actors have sought to bring out her strength and knowledge of the world. In the past, she was often played as obedient to her father, and touchingly poignant in her madness. Modern productions tend to emphasise how she rebukes Laertes after his long catalogue of advice, and show her unwillingly or resentfully following her father's instructions.

Ophelia feels deeply for Hamlet, and his apparent rejection affects her grievously, 'Oh woe is me / T'have seen what I have seen, see what I see.' When he jokes with her at the play scene, she seems fully aware of his sexual meanings. The songs she sings in her madness reveal not simply the depth of her love for her father, but also an uninhibited sexual awareness that her mental derangement has allowed to surface.

There are parallels between Ophelia and Hamlet. Both have fathers who have been violently killed. Both feel let down by a person they deeply love. Both suffer the distress of madness, whether it is real and/or assumed.

◆ Use the photographs of Ophelia in this book to explore her character. Is she the passive victim of her father, brother and lover as she is often portrayed? What evidence can you find in the script to show that there is more to her than passivity?

◆ As the only young woman in the play (without a foil or friend that she can define herself against), what clothes and look would you provide for her as a costume/make-up designer for your production? Does Ophelia obediently follow court custom, as Polonius's daughter; or is she more rebellious?

◆ In relation to Hamlet, and in her own development as a young woman, how would Ophelia account for herself? Write her diary, or her version of a psychiatric appointment with Freud (see activity on p. 256), before her death.

Laertes

From his first speech (Act 1 Scene 2, lines 50–56), Laertes seems straight, honourable, dutiful and a potential foil to Hamlet – who is not the opposite embodiment of these traits, but is a darker, more complex character burdened by melancholy. Laertes does not dwell on his feelings inwardly, but manifests them in direct expression. Interestingly, he 'bookends' the play by appearing near the start and near the end, and so provides a frame of reference for Hamlet's procrastination. He also provides his own revenge motives in response to Hamlet's treatment of Ophelia and the killing of Polonius.

Despite this, there is something hypocritical about Laertes. His invocation to his sister to be wary of Hamlet's approaches (Act 1 Scene 3) while she retorts that he himself must live by his own precepts (lines 45–51); his willingness, in Act 4 Scene 7, to go along with Claudius's devious scheme to poison the rapiers for the duel with Hamlet; and his thrust at the apparently off-guard Hamlet with the poisoned rapier in Act 5 Scene 2, line 280. All these instances point to a character who is not entirely honourable and who, like all the characters in the play – with perhaps the exception of Horatio and Ophelia – is tainted somewhat by the corruption of Denmark.

◆ Do you see Laertes as merely representative of certain values (honour, duty, loyalty) or as a rounded character in his own right? Take sides in a debate. One side argues that Laertes is a victim of circumstance, a largely honourable young man (without a mother) whose sister and father fall prey to a disturbed and reckless prince. The other side argues that he is a corrupt, weak-minded, easily angered and hypocritical character who pales in comparison to Hamlet.

◆ Imagine the play without Laertes. Would it work?

The language of *Hamlet*

Imagery – 'the morn in russet mantle clad'

Hamlet abounds in **imagery**: vivid words and phrases that conjure up emotionally charged pictures or associations in the mind. When Hamlet thinks of how the First Player would perform if he had suffered such grief as Hamlet, he declares, 'He would drown the stage with tears'. The image passionately conveys the depth of Hamlet's feelings. Similarly, Polonius abruptly dismisses Hamlet's 'holy vows' of his love to Ophelia as 'springes to catch woodcocks': merely traps to snare innocent and foolish birds.

Imagery carries powerful significance, far deeper than its surface meanings. Images enrich particular moments, as when Claudius agonises that his hand is stained with his brother's blood: 'Is there not rain enough in the sweet heavens / To wash it white as snow?' Imagery repeatedly illuminates the themes of the play such as revenge or madness (as when Gertrude describes Hamlet as 'Mad as the sea and wind, when both contend / Which is the mightier.').

Imagery stirs the audience's imagination and deepens the impact of particular moments or moods. It provides insight into character, and intensifies meaning and emotional force. In *Hamlet* the imagery is sometimes so brilliantly complex that, although it can be analysed and understood, it defies any final 'explanation', as in Hamlet's words:

> *Whether 'tis nobler in the mind to suffer*
> *The slings and arrows of outrageous fortune,*
> *Or to take arms against a sea of troubles,*
> *And by opposing end them.*
>
> Act 3 Scene 1, lines 57–60

All Shakespeare's imagery uses metaphor, simile or personification. All are comparisons that in effect substitute one thing (the image) for another (the thing described).

A **simile** compares one thing to another using 'like' or 'as'. Ophelia describes Hamlet's derangement as 'Like sweet bells jangled, out of tune and harsh'. The Ghost tells how the poison spread through his body 'swift as quicksilver'.

A **metaphor** is also a comparison, suggesting that two dissimilar things are actually the same or have something in common. The distraught Hamlet speaks of his head as 'this distracted globe'. He describes one play as 'caviary to the general' (caviar to ordinary people – too good for them). To put it another way, a metaphor borrows one word or phrase to express another.

Personification turns all types of things into persons, giving them human feelings or attributes. In the quotation from Act 3 Scene 1, 'fortune' is personified. The dying Hamlet memorably personifies death itself as a cruel officer of the law: 'this fell sergeant death / Is strict in his arrest'.

Certain image clusters recur through the play, notably those of corruption and disease, the theatre and acting.

Corruption and disease

In the play's opening moments Francisco's 'I am sick at heart' is the first indication of the many images of infection that pervade *Hamlet*. Marcellus declares that 'Something is rotten in the state of Denmark.' Hamlet is haunted by the corruption of his mother's incest, seeing it as an infectious disease: 'the ulcerous place / Whiles rank corruption, mining all within, / Infects unseen.' Claudius thinks of Hamlet as a fever: 'like the hectic in my blood he rages'. Hamlet describes Claudius as 'a mildewed ear' and as 'this canker of our nature'. Watching Fortinbras's army marching towards death, Hamlet reflects that 'This is th'impostume [abscess] … That inward breaks, and shows no cause without / Why the man dies' (Act 4 Scene 4, lines 27–9). This final image refers to an inner problem, like the development of cancerous cells, that cause death without there being any visible signs of the disease.

Theatre and acting

Page 250 describes how the language of theatre and acting recurs in the play: 'play', 'act', 'cue', 'prompted', 'mutes' and so on. Shakespeare's fascination with his own professional world is evident in *Hamlet*: the players, the play-within-a-play that reveals Claudius's guilt, the talk of the 'little eyases' (boy actors). In Hamlet's first appearance he uses 'actions', 'play' and 'show' as he angrily denies that his grief is reflected only in his outward appearance (Act 1 Scene 2, lines 84–5):

> For they are actions that a man might play,
> But I have that within which passes show –

The notion of acting as a pretence that somehow convinces finds expression in Hamlet's amazement that an actor can weep for a fictional character: 'And all for nothing? / For Hecuba!'

Lastly, imagery is intimately and deeply connected with the themes in the play. In many ways, it operates to indicate the themes, as in the clusters of images mentioned immediately above – along with what the actors explicitly say and do (the plot). It points towards unconscious connections in the play, and the preoccupations of the characters who express their thoughts.

◆ Identify a dozen images in the play that especially appeal to you. Write an analysis of how they operate, both for immediate effect in the scene and in the play as a whole, reinforcing and complicating its themes.

Antithesis

Antithesis is the opposition of words or phrases against each other, as in 'To be, or not to be', and 'I must be cruel only to be kind'. This setting of the word against the word ('To be' versus 'not to be', 'cruel' versus 'kind') is one of Shakespeare's favourite language devices. He uses it extensively in all his plays. Why? Because antithesis powerfully expresses conflict through its use of opposites, and conflict is the essence of all drama. In *Hamlet*, conflict occurs in many forms. Claudius versus Hamlet, revenge versus justice, son versus mother, and dark shadows versus a more colourful presence (for example, in the acting troupe that visits Elsinore). Antithesis intensifies the sense of conflict and definition.

Claudius's many antitheses in his first speech (Act 1 Scene 2) suggest a man attempting to balance conflicting emotions and values as he tells of his marriage to Gertrude – for example, lines 11–13:

> With one auspicious and one dropping eye,
> With mirth in funeral and with dirge in marriage,
> In equal scale weighing delight and dole

For an Elizabethan audience the antithesis 'With one auspicious and one dropping eye' implied deviousness, because a contemporary proverb held that a false man looked up with one eye and down with the other. The other antitheses imply a similar two-facedness: someone who can simultaneously express joy and sorrow, or show an inappropriate emotion at a funeral or a marriage. In Act 3 Scene 1, lines 51–3, Claudius uses an image full of antitheses to acknowledge that a prostitute's use of make-up is similar to how he hypocritically conceals his evil deed behind a mask:

> The harlot's cheek, beautied with plastering art,
> Is not more ugly to the thing that helps it
> Than is my deed to my most painted word.

Laertes's passionate desire for revenge on Hamlet ('To cut his throat i'th'church') is given additional emotional power by the opposition of the bloodiness of the action with the sanctity of the holy place. In the very last moments of the play (Act 5 Scene 2, lines 380–1), Fortinbras opposes the appropriateness of dead bodies on the battlefield ('field') with their inappropriateness in the court ('here'): 'Such a sight as this / Becomes the field, but here shows much amiss.'

◆ Collect between ten and twenty examples of antithesis in the play script. Use them in an essay showing how antithesis helps create a sense of conflict and paradox in *Hamlet*.

Verse and prose

Just under three quarters of the play is in verse, and just over one quarter in prose. How did Shakespeare decide whether to write in verse or prose? A rough rule of thumb is that aristocrats speak verse, and low-status and comic or mad characters speak prose. But context is very important. Thus the players (low status) speak verse in the Gonzago play to emphasise that they are playing aristocratic characters. Hamlet and Ophelia (high status) express madness in prose.

Verse was thought more suitable than prose to moments of high dramatic or emotional intensity. So 'serious' scenes are likely to be in verse, 'comic' episodes in prose. Hamlet uses prose with Rosencrantz and Guildenstern, the Gravedigger and Osric. Hamlet's 'What a piece of work is a man' speech (Act 2 Scene 2, lines 286–91) is also in prose, but has all the qualities claimed for poetry.

Hamlet is written mainly in **blank verse**: unrhymed verse written in **iambic pentameter**. This is a rhythm, or **metre**, in which each line has five unstressed syllables (/) alternating with five stressed syllables (×) (often expressed as da-DUM da-DUM da-DUM da-DUM da-DUM), as in Act 3 Scene 2, line 196:

> / × / × / × / × / ×
> But die thy thoughts when thy first lord is dead

By the time he wrote *Hamlet*, Shakespeare had become very flexible in his use of iambic pentameter. He often uses **enjambement** (running on), where one line flows on into the next, seemingly with little or no pause. Lines may have more or fewer than ten syllables.

◆ Choose a verse speech and speak it to emphasise the metre. Then speak it as if it were prose, then as you feel it should be delivered on stage. Finally, write eight lines of your own in any form of verse.

◆ Choose a passage of verse from the play and 'translate' it into prose. What is gained or lost in translation? How do the effects of each differ?

(See also the activities on pp. 92 and 184.) Why is this exercise not so satisfactory or useful if you are asked to convert prose to verse?

Questions

Hamlet is full of questions. Barnardo's opening challenge 'Who's there?' sets the questioning tone that characterises the whole play. Virtually every character wishes to find out something. On almost every page questions are asked. Hamlet is often self-questioning.

◆ Turn to any page of the script. Identify the questions on that page, and check how many are answered. Repeat for several more pages. Decide which questions can be answered, and which cannot. Then make up a few questions of your own about the play. Try to answer them in a small group. Put any you cannot answer to the class as a whole – and to the teacher!

Soliloquies

Hamlet is famous for his **soliloquies**. A soliloquy is a kind of internal debate spoken by a character who is alone on stage (or believes themselves to be alone). Soliloquies reveal the character's true thoughts and feelings. Hamlet's soliloquies, in parts, give the impression of a man discovering what he thinks as he speaks.

◆ Hamlet's soliloquies appear at the following points in the play:
  • Act 1 Scene 2, lines 254–7
  • Act 1 Scene 5, lines 92–112
  • Act 2 Scene 2, lines 501–58
  • Act 3 Scene 1, lines 56–90
  • Act 3 Scene 3, lines 349–60
  • Act 3 Scene 3, lines 73–96
  • Act 4 Scene 4, lines 32–66

Select one and work out a dramatic presentation. You could share the lines around your group, and have several people echoing key lines or phrases. Try speaking it as a conversation, or to the audience, or to a portrait of another character, or to a stage prop. Experiment with styles of delivery (for example, as an observer disgusted with the human condition, or as a bloodthirsty revenger).

◆ Divide the class into seven groups. Each group takes one soliloquy. First, in your groups, enlarge a copy of your text so that you can see the whole speech in one poster or banner. Annotate it with verbal commentary and with images. Have two of the group stand by the poster while the others in your group visit the other posters/banners and pose questions about the nature of the soliloquies.

◆ If you wish to explore the meaning differently and perhaps in more depth, perform a dialogic version of the soliloquy using more than one voice, and employing techniques such as choral presentation, question and answer, and emphasis of key words and phrases.

Doubling language: a cause of delay?

All kinds of 'doubling' go on in *Hamlet*: the two sentries at the play's beginning; Rosencrantz and Guildenstern; Cornelius and Voltemand; two English ambassadors; two kingly brothers, Claudius and old Hamlet. Furthermore, Hamlet and Laertes are both students, sons, revengers and opponents.

Such doubling is strikingly reflected in the play's language. It appears in repetition of words and phrases: 'Tush tush', 'Speak, speak', 'this too too solid flesh', 'To be, or not to be' and so on. Polonius seems to say everything twice: 'You have me, have you not?' Most commonly the doubling is by means of the conjunction 'and'. When Laertes requests Claudius for permission to return to France, he uses 'leave and favour', 'thoughts and wishes', 'leave and pardon'.

Hamlet contains around 250 examples of such 'doublings'. In Act 3 Scene 1, lines 144–55, Ophelia's lines lamenting Hamlet's treatment of her ('Oh what a noble mind is here o'erthrown!') includes doubling of single words

(observed/observers, quite/quite, seen/seen, see/see), together with six examples of doubles using 'and':

• expectancy and rose of the fair state
• glass of fashion and the mould of form
• deject and wretched
• noble and most sovereign reason
• out of time and harsh
• form and feature.

A special type of such doubling is known as **hendiadys** (pronounced hen-die-a-dees), a technical term meaning 'one through two'. Here, the two words express a single idea. They duplicate the sense rather than amplify or modify each other, as these few examples from the script show:

• food and diet
• grace and mercy
• spark and fire
• cheer and comfort
• lecture and advice
• flash and outbreak
• pith and marrow
• duty and obedience
• native and indued
• book and volume
• heat and flame
• strange or odd.

This tendency to use two words when one would be sufficient to convey meaning contributes to dramatic effect. It lengthens the play, adding to the sense of delay. In its suggestion of 'one through two' it echoes the play's concern with marriage and incest (the union of separate or *like* selves).

◆ Search through the play for examples of these 'doubling' devices. Talk together about their dramatic effect and how they provide insights into character and situation.

What did Shakespeare write?

Shakespeare probably wrote *Hamlet* around 1601. But there are problems in knowing exactly what he wrote (let alone what he intended). First, he was a playwright, and undoubtedly had second thoughts as he worked with the actors rehearsing and performing the play. Second, there are three versions of the play, from which all editors make their choices as they prepare their own edition for publication.

- **The First Quarto** (Q1: the 'bad quarto'), published in 1603 and thought to be a pirated (unauthorised) version, put together by some actors and sold for a quick profit. It has 2154 lines.
- **The Second Quarto** (Q2: the 'good quarto'), published in 1604 and thought to be Shakespeare's response to the 'bad quarto', in order to establish the 'correct' version. It has 3674 lines.
- **The First Folio** (F1), published in 1623. This is thought to be Shakespeare's version of the play to make it even more suitable for the stage. But remember that Shakespeare died in 1616, and the First Folio was compiled seven years later by two actors in his company. It has 3535 lines (including 83 that do not appear in Q2).

Some lines of the script are in square brackets [ ]. These are the lines in Q2 that were cut out of F1. It is thought that Shakespeare cut these lines to make a more actable version of the play.

- ◆ Find several examples of lines in square brackets (for example, Act 1 Scene 4, lines 17–38, Act 3 Scene 4, lines 203–21 and Act 4 Scene 7, lines 113–22). Discuss possible reasons why Shakespeare cut them. But remember – no one can be certain that Shakespeare himself did so. Would you cut the lines in performance? Give reasons for your decision.

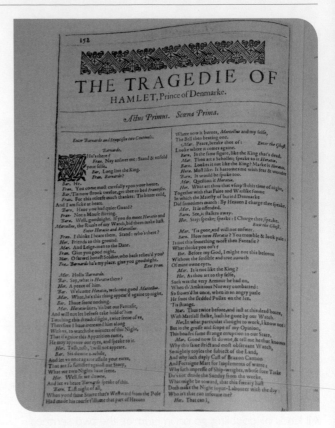

▲ The first page of *Hamlet* from a facsimile edition of the First Folio of Shakespeare's plays, published in 1623.

Quick-fire dialogue

As well as seven soliloquies, there is a great deal of (potentially) fast dialogue in the play, usually associated with Hamlet's wit. For example, Hamlet's dialogue with Polonius in Act 2 Scene 2, lines 169–212, or with Gertrude, Claudius and Ophelia in Act 3 Scene 2, lines 210–30.

- ◆ Find other examples, and divide the class into the same number of groups as the total number of quick-fire dialogues you can find (including the two examples listed here). Each group (or members of the group) tries acting out a section at various paces – with both or all characters talking at speed; with Hamlet as the fastest; and with some variation within the dialogues.

◆ Can you find any examples of 'stichomythic' dialogue, when single alternating lines, or half-lines, are given to alternating characters? What is the effect of such rapid-fire exchanges?

◆ When you have experimented with pace, ask yourselves (and answer the questions as best you can): which versions work best, and why? What do we learn about Hamlet's mind and his impatience and/or wit as a result of these dialogues?

The language of the First Player

When the players first arrive at Elsinore, Hamlet asks the First Player to recite a speech that he 'chiefly loved' in which Aeneas speaks of Priam's slaughter (Act 2 Scene 2, line 405 onwards). Hamlet starts the speech (lines 410–22) then asks the Player to continue it (lines 426 onwards). Shakespeare's contemporary, Christopher Marlowe, writes in this grander style in some of his plays (e.g. *Tamburlaine*, *Dido Queen of Carthage*), and it is possible that Shakespeare is both mocking the style and appreciating it at the same time. The style is characterised by archaic diction ('couchèd in the ominous horse', line 412); epithets ('hellish Pyrrhus', 'revered Priam', lines 421 and 437); an excess of doubling ('wrath and fire', line 419; 'baked and impasted', line 417); numerous classical references (Pyrrhus, Priam, Ilium); circumlocution ('th'Hyrcanian beast', line 408); and over-dramatic grandeur ('anon the dreadful thunder / Doth rend the region', lines 444–5). It is a far cry from the colloquial language of much of Shakespeare's prose.

◆ From line 410 to 476, divide the speech into constituent sentences (there are twelve in all). Individually, in pairs or in threes, take a sentence and compare it to sentences in any of Hamlet's soliloquies – choose two or three from Hamlet's speeches that you think will make a good comparison. Undertake a close analysis of Hamlet's and the Player's 'acting' language on the one hand and that of Hamlet in his soliloquies on the other. See if you can characterise the similarities and differences in style. As a starting point, think of how the Player's performance demonstrates epic as a form of narrative (an epic is a lengthy story in the grand style, involving heroism and adventure); and how Hamlet's soliloquies follow his thoughts. There are different functions here – but how are those functions revealed in the language used?

Hamlet's last lines

Between the wounding of Hamlet at line 280 in Act 5 Scene 2, and his death at line 337, there are over fifty lines spoken, more than half by Hamlet himself. And yet as Hamlet becomes aware that he is soon to die, his language is not epic or dramatically 'tragic' or over-imbued with emotion. Rather, it is measured, conscious of his fate and his reputation ('report me and my cause aright / To the unsatisfied' and 'tell my story'), dignified and, finally, political ('I do prophesy th'election lights / On Fortinbras; he has my dying voice').

In some ways, it is surprising that Shakespeare did not give Hamlet some grander lines to end with, reflecting on human nature, existence, his father's revenge and his own relation to death and the 'divinity that shapes our ends'.

◆ Write the 'missing' speech by Hamlet in which he does reflect on the grander themes, and as a misunderstood, wronged and complex figure, takes his leave from the world.

◆ Perform that speech, inserting it where you see fit in the closing part of the play.

Hamlet in performance

Hamlet through history

Hamlet has always been a popular play. Since it was written around 1601, it has rarely been absent from the stage for long. There is even a record of a version acted on a ship off the coast of Sierra Leone in 1608. Quotations from the play (such as 'To be, or not to be') have become utterly familiar, even to those who have never seen the play. But in every age the text has been cut, altered and added to. For over 400 years audiences have watched and heard very different versions of *Hamlet*. For example, throughout the eighteenth and nineteenth centuries Fortinbras disappeared from most productions – this tradition still influences modern productions. Also, performances occasionally end with Hamlet's death: 'the rest is silence'.

The example of the famous eighteenth-century actor-manager David Garrick shows there is no such thing as the 'authentic' *Hamlet*. Garrick wanted to portray Hamlet as a truly noble prince, and to make the play into what he saw as a genuine tragedy. He therefore cut anything that detracted from a heroic image of Hamlet, and removed what he called 'the rubbish of the fifth act': Ophelia's funeral and the gravediggers. Garrick's audiences did not hear how Hamlet sent Rosencrantz and Guildenstern to their deaths, nor the 'Now might I do it pat' speech (in which Hamlet wishes for Claudius to suffer in hell), because Garrick thought both speeches diminished Hamlet's noble nature. Laertes did not poison his sword, or Claudius the drink. Gertrude died off stage in guilt-ridden insanity, Fortinbras did not appear, and Laertes survived to rule over Denmark jointly with Horatio.

Productions in the nineteenth century usually presented romantic interpretations of Hamlet as a sane, intellectual, sensitive prince, unable to sweep swiftly to revenge. Sets often attempted to create the illusion of a historically accurate castle of Elsinore. For example, Edmund Kean played Hamlet between 1814 and 1833, removing much of the blank verse and replacing it with prose. His attitude to the Ghost was more one of welcome than of terror, and he also treated Ophelia with tenderness rather than bitterness. In the USA, Edwin Booth performed the part in a production at Burton's Theater in New York in 1857: apparently an introspective and mild performance, eschewing the more melodramatic style that was popular at the time.

Modern productions have increasingly portrayed Hamlet as disturbed and alienated, and have abandoned realistic sets. They rely more on 'symbolic' settings or bare stages with a minimum of scenery. This can be seen as a return to the conditions of Shakespeare's own Globe Theatre stage, which was not dependent on theatrical illusion. The first mention of Hamlet in the play is as 'young Hamlet' and, from what the gravedigger says, he seems to be about thirty. But for over 400 years Hamlet has been played by actors of all ages.

▼ **Christopher Eccleston as Hamlet in a production at the West Yorkshire Playhouse, Leeds, 2002.**

Notable productions

In 2004, a twenty-three-year-old Ben Whishaw played Hamlet at The Old Vic in London (see right). One reviewer said: 'Far from being a robust young man, haunted by anger and revenge that is only held back by uncertainty, this Hamlet [was] skinny and frail in stature, raw and idealistic in nature', considering suicide with a penknife and a bottle of pills as he recited 'To be or not to be'. The youthful appearance of Hamlet's mother in this production dramatically heightened his confused feelings towards her. Alongside this, nineteen-year-old Samantha Whittaker played Ophelia as a teenage girl with a crush on Hamlet. It is possible, as has been suggested in this edition, to play Hamlet as an even younger character, and for younger actors to play him – though the demands are considerable.

Richard Burbage, the first actor ever to play Hamlet (in 1601), was thirty-four when he filled the role. Other actors have played the part when they were well past forty. Sarah Bernhardt, a French actress, played him when she was fifty-six. In the eighteenth century, Thomas Betterton played the part when he was over seventy.

A number of features create the impression of a youthful Hamlet. He faces familiar problems of adolescence: relations with the opposite sex, coming to terms with responsibility, finding one's own personality. He seems rebellious and misunderstood, and is constantly self-questioning, unsure whom to trust, and feeling betrayed by former friends. He has problems with his mother and stepfather, and with coming to terms with the death of his own father.

In 2001, Sam West took the title role in the Royal Shakespeare Company's uncut four-hour version of *Hamlet,* which emphasised the bleak, modernistic dimensions of the play. In 2008, another RSC production of the play starred David Tennant as a witty, graceful Hamlet who compulsively mimicked other characters rather than looking inwards at his conflicted self.

In 2012, *Hamlet* was produced at the Utah Shakespeare Festival, directed by Marco Barricelli and characterised as a 'powerful examination of the human psyche … [Shakespeare's] most mature, and chilling, revenge tragedy'. In London in the same year, the play was performed in Lithuanian as *Hamletas* in the Globe World Shakespeare Festival. This production's frantic pace was set by the jerky, deranged physical movements of the characters, and Hamlet displayed his madness by lying completely still in the midst of this manic scene.

Hamlet at the Globe Theatre

In Shakespeare's lifetime, *Hamlet* was almost certainly performed at the Globe Theatre. It was a round theatre, open to the sky. The audience standing in the pit, the 'groundlings', got wet if it rained. Those in the galleries (who paid more), and the actors on stage, were protected from the worst of the weather.

The original Globe Theatre audiences expected and enjoyed a noisy display of drums, trumpets and the firing of cannon. *Hamlet* richly fulfils that expectation. In the play's second scene, Claudius promises that 'the great cannon' will sound to heaven itself to celebrate his drinking. That boastful ritual is heard as Hamlet awaits the Ghost's appearance ('The kettle-drum and trumpet thus bray out'), and in Act 5 Scene 2 before the duel Claudius orders 'let the kettle to the trumpet speak, / The trumpet to the cannoneer without, / The cannons to the heavens'. His order is obeyed as *'Drum, trumpets sound, and shot goes off'.*

In Shakespeare's day, Gertrude and Ophelia were played by boys. Although there were no elaborate sets on the bare stage of the Globe Theatre, the actors dressed in attractive and expensive costumes, usually the fashionable dress of the times. Only a few props were used – swords, goblets and so on.

The 2000 production of *Hamlet* at Shakespeare's Globe presented the play in that 'authentic' style. Actors were dressed in the fashion of the Danish court in the late sixteenth century (similar to Elizabethan costume). The royal family wore red and gold, and their coat of arms was visible on stage. To suggest the freezing cold on the gun platform, sheepskin cloaks were worn. The players in the play-within-a-play wore what Elizabethans would have thought of as Roman dress.

In Dominic Dromgoole's stripped-down and touring production of *Hamlet* at Shakespeare's Globe in 2012, the emphasis was on 'political intrigue and sexual obsession, philosophical reflection and violent action, tragic depth and wild humour'.

Performing *Hamlet*

Consider what your own production of *Hamlet* would be like. There are various aspects to putting on a performance, and you can choose from the following activities – whether you work on *Hamlet* as a full production, whether you create a stripped-down version, or whether you simply undertake some of the activities as a way of engaging with and interrogating the script itself.

◆ Take the whole script (which, as we have seen, can take four hours and more if performed in its entirety). Cut it down, either to half its length or to a minimal version that would take forty-five minutes to an hour to perform. What would you retain and what would you cut?

◆ Look at examples of set design, in the images throughout this book and on the Internet. Decide whether you wish to have an elaborate design set in a particular period, or whether you prefer the more minimal approach. You can work with a shoebox for your initial designs, or you can construct a more ambitious model.

◆ Costume design often follows the stage and set design. Traditionally, *Hamlet* is performed in dark colours to reflect the sombre, melancholy mood of the play. But there is room for contrasts, eccentricity and extravagance in parts of the play. Choose a section where the action is particularly exciting, and draw designs for the costumes of one or more characters on stage at this point.

◆ On the left-hand pages of this book, there has often been reference to a Director's Journal in which you have been encouraged to write guidance for actors, notes about stage directions and other reflections about performing *Hamlet*. As a director, look back at your notes and sketch out your grand plan as to your conception of the play and how you would like to see it performed.

All-female and all-male performances

In an article in the *Guardian* newspaper on 20 November 2012, the actress Harriet Walter stated, 'When you play Hamlet, you become, as it were, humanity. You stand for humankind.' Yet women are not often given the centrality and status of Hamlet in Shakespeare's plays (Rosalind in *As You Like It* may be the exception). The practice of having women play Shakespeare's male roles seeks to explore and interrogate this issue and its related assumptions.

In November 2012, there was an all-female production of *Julius Caesar* at the Donmar Warehouse, London, directed by Phyllida Lloyd. The drive to an all-female cast in the professional theatre is partly a feminist wish to redress imbalances in casting over centuries, and to provide a counterpoint to the frequent all-male casts in Shakespearean productions. Of the 900 and more characters in Shakespeare, only fifteen per cent are female.

▼ Asta Nielsen as Hamlet in the 1920 movie version of the play.

In some all-girl schools, an all-female cast presents an opportunity and a challenge. Why not attempt plays like *Julius Caesar* and *Hamlet*, which look male dominated, but in which an all-female production would give a very different perspective? The Sydney Theatre Company cast a female Hamlet for their 2010 production. As their notes to the production stated:

> The 'female Hamlet' has become an enigma. Ever since the late eighteenth century, leading actresses such as Sarah Bernhardt (also the first Hamlet on film, 1899), Sarah Siddons, Asta Neilsen and more recently Diane Venora (1983) and Angela Winkler (1999) have played the role of Hamlet. Many of these performers have been involved in radical politics and theatre movements in Stalinist Russia, Poland, and Germany.

> In theatre, film, and radio, women have challenged the notion of Hamlet as exclusive to the male gender. The opportunity to play this cultural icon for many is viewed as a political act drawing attention to gender inequity, the lack of substantial roles for women and the often unspoken 'femininity' of Hamlet.

◆ Think of the major male characters in *Hamlet*: Hamlet himself, Claudius, Polonius, Horatio. What challenges, and what particular characteristics would need to be addressed and considered carefully if casting only women in the play? What would it mean to the dynamic of the play as a whole?

Women can also play female roles in Shakespeare in ways that subvert the traditional associations of passivity and marginalisation. In a Canadian production of *Hamlet*, Ophelia was played by a woman dressed in black – like Hamlet himself – and her madness was represented by violent movements with a sword, presaging the duel between her brother and her lover.

All-male productions have been common since Shakespeare's day. Single-sex schools tend to choose the plays that give the boys or girls the most accessible parts to play. And yet an all-male version of *Hamlet* presents interesting problems for those playing Gertrude and Ophelia, as consideration of sexuality is never far from the surface.

Hamlet on the radio

Think of a production of *Hamlet* on the radio. In many
ways, it is well suited to the medium: its dark, inactive
(until the final act) nature; the speaking Ghost on the
battlements; the clanking chains of the prison that is
Denmark; the doors opening and shutting, or remaining
half-opened as spies keep account of the developing
behaviour of Hamlet himself. All these qualities lend an
air of internal mental anguish to the play, and are ideal for
the interior soundscape of radio. There are many great
recordings of *Hamlet*, but why not make your own?

◆   Split into groups, and have each group take a scene
    or two of the play to work with – there are twenty
    scenes in the play as a whole, of uneven length.
    Larger groups could take an act each. Record a

radio version of the selected play section, with
each member of the group taking responsibility for
a certain element – direction, voice acting roles,
sound effects and so on. Mood can be created by
emphasising variations in speech (tone, volume,
spoken asides, soliloquies, public statements), sound
effects and atmospheric background soundtracking.

Hamlet in the movies

Laurence Olivier's 1948 movie of *Hamlet* began with
the statement, 'This is the tragedy of a man who could
not make up his mind', and strongly implied that Hamlet
felt incestuous desire for his mother. Another famous
black-and-white film of *Hamlet* is the 1964 version by
the Russian director, Grigori Kozintsev, which stresses the
political aspects of the play.

In 1990, Mel Gibson played Hamlet in a colour movie
that used only about one third of Shakespeare's script.
Fortinbras is cut from this version, as well as scenes
with Claudius as a political diplomat. In contrast,

Kenneth Branagh's 1996 film lasted four hours, using virtually all the script, although a shortened two-hour version is available. Branagh's use of late nineteenth-century costumes contrasts with a 2000 modern-dress American movie in which Hamlet is a New York businessman. In 2010, David Tennant played Hamlet in a BBC production in which surveillance was the key motif, and in which the madness was emphasised.

Films provide close-ups, tracking shots and cinematic spectacle not available on stage. In the 1964 Russian movie Fortinbras's army marches along a real sea coast (see p. 166). The sea symbolises the possibility of freedom from Elsinore's prison-like atmosphere. Movies can even suggest moral perspectives, as when Olivier uses high-angle shots to look down on Claudius's court as if in moral judgement.

▲ Modern films sometimes make sly or obvious reference to *Hamlet*, as in Arnold Schwarzenegger's *Last Action Hero* from 1993.

◀ This image and the one on page 210 both show how Ophelia's funeral has been presented in stage versions of *Hamlet*. How would you adapt the funeral scene for a film version of the play? Think about how you could use different shots and camera angles to show the characters' reactions at this point to the greatest effect.

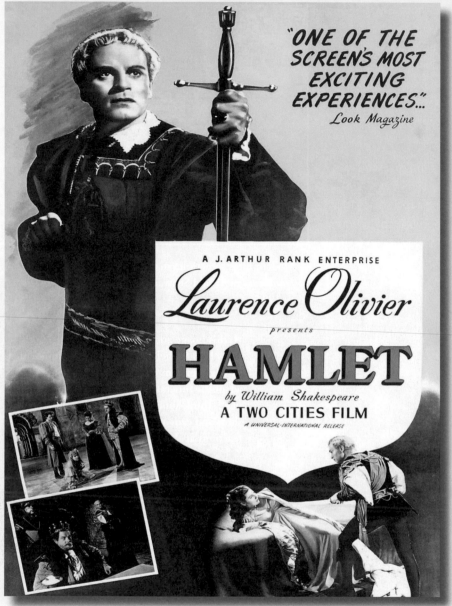

▲ The poster for the 1948 movie.

Some final activities in relation to *Hamlet* in performance

◆ Consider in detail the different design and content elements of the poster shown on this page. Source other posters of movies or stage productions of *Hamlet*. Then create your own poster, perhaps using inspiration from the existing posters you think are most striking and effective.

◆ Write programme notes for a production, including the usual features in programmes: a narrative of the action of the play; background thematic material; and some character analysis.

◆ Create a list of props you will need for an actual or imagined production, and write a note for the stage manager as to how they will be used.

◆ Go to see a stage production of *Hamlet* – or more than one, if possible. Write reviews of each production you see.

◆ Take one of the soliloquies from the play (e.g. 'To be or not to be' and compare clips of performances online. Rate the different versions and justify your decisions.

◆ Write a comparative review of as many movie productions of *Hamlet* as you can see. In addition to those mentioned so far, there is a 2000 movie directed by Michael Almereyda with Ethan Hawke as Hamlet, Diane Venora as Gertrude, Bill Murray as Polonius and Kyle MacLachlan as Claudius. This version is set in corporate, urban America, with Hamlet as an independent filmmaker trying to find his way through the corruption of contemporary culture.

◆ Write or produce a satirical and subversive version of *Hamlet* that compresses the play into a very short space of time – at most, ten minutes.

Several such works exist, ranging from *The Skinhead Hamlet* (1982), which reduces the play to a series of grunts, exclamations and expletives, to the *Bouncy Castle Hamlet* performed at the Edinburgh Festival.

◆ There are productions of *Hamlet* worldwide, in movies and on stage. One example is *The Banquet* (also known as *Legend of the Black Scorpion*, directed by Feng Xiaogang, China, 2006), a Kung Fu movie adaptation. The opera *Revenge of the Prince*, produced by the Shanghai Peking Opera, is set in ancient China, complete with acrobatic and dance elements. Eastern European productions of *Hamlet* have often accentuated the play's political significance.

◆ Several manga editions of *Hamlet* exist, as well as other comic book versions. Seek them out and carry out a comparison to determine which is the best.

◆ Several puppet versions of *Hamlet* are available on the Internet; watch a few, and decide whether you think the play is suitable for this approach. Not all these puppet versions are light-hearted. See, for example, kabuki (Japanese dance-drama), which sometime includes puppetry, or bunraku, which involves puppets of about half-life-size. You might like to produce your own puppet version of a shortened *Hamlet* in the style you think appropriate (or inappropriate!).

▼ A scene from the kabuki version of *Hamlet*, Mermaid Theatre, London, 1991.

Writing about Shakespeare

The play as text

Shakespeare's plays have always been studied as literary works – as words on a page that need clarification, appreciation and discussion. When you write about the plays, you will be asked to compose short pieces and also longer, more reflective pieces like controlled assessments, examination scripts and coursework – often in the form of essays on themes and/or imagery, character studies, analyses of the structure of the play and on stagecraft. Imagery, stagecraft and character are dealt with elsewhere in this edition. Here, we concentrate on themes and structure. You might find it helpful to look at the 'Write about it' boxes on the left-hand pages throughout the play.

Themes

It is often tempting to say that the theme of a play is a single idea, like 'death' in *Hamlet*, or 'the supernatural' in *Macbeth*, or 'love' in *Romeo and Juliet*. The problem with such a simple approach is that you will miss the complexity of the plays. In *Romeo and Juliet*, for example, the play is about the relationship between love, family loyalty and constraint; it is also about the relationship of youth to age and experience; and the relationship between Romeo and Juliet is also played out against a background of enmity between two families. Between each of these ideas or concepts there are tensions. The tensions are the main focus of attention for Shakespeare and the audience; this is also how the best drama operates – by the presentation of and resolution of tension.

Look back at the 'Themes' boxes throughout the play to see if any of the activities there have given rise to information that you could use as a starting point for further writing about the themes of the specific play you are studying.

Structure

Most Shakespeare plays are in five acts, divided into scenes. These acts were not in the original scripts, but have been included in later editions to make the action more manageable, clearer and more like 'classical' structures. One way to get a sense of the structure of the whole play is to take a printed version of the play (not this one!) and cut it up into scenes and acts. Then display each scene and act, in sequence, on a wall, like this:

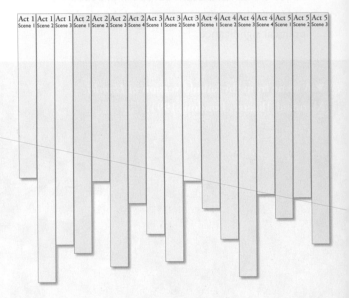

As you set out the whole play, you will be able to see the 'shape' of each act, the relative length of the scenes, and how the acts relate to each other (such as whether one of the acts is shorter, and why that might be). You can annotate the text with comments, observations and questions. You can use a highlighter pen to mark the recurrence of certain words, images or metaphors to see at a glance where and how frequently they appear. You can also follow a particular character's progress through the play.

Such an overview of the play gives you critical perspective: you will be able to see how the parts fit together, to stand back from the play and assess its shape, and to focus on particular parts within the context of the whole. Your writing will reflect a greater awareness of the overall context as a result.

The play as script

There are different, but related, categories when we think of the play as a script for performance. These include *stagecraft* (discussed elsewhere in this edition and throughout the left-hand pages), *lighting*, *focus* (who are we looking at? Where is the attention of the audience?), *music and sound*, *props and costumes*, *casting*, *make-up*, *pace and rhythm*, and other *spatial relationships* (e.g. how actors move around the stage in relation to each other). If you are writing about stagecraft or performance, use the notes you have made as a result of the 'Stagecraft' boxes throughout this edition of the play, as well as any information you can find about the plays in performance.

What are the key points of dispute?

Shakespeare is brilliant at capturing a number of key points of dispute in each of his plays. These are the dramatic moments where he concentrates the focus of the audience on difficult (sometimes universal) problems that the characters are facing or embodying.

First, identify these key points in the play you are studying. You can do this as a class by thinking about what you consider to be the key points in small groups, then debating the long-list as a whole class, and then coming up with a short-list of what the class thinks are the most significant. (This is a good opportunity for speaking and listening work.) They are likely to be places in the play where the action or reflection is at its most intense, and which capture the complexity of themes, character, structure and performance.

Second, drill down at one of the points of contention and tension. In other words, investigate the complexity of the problem that Shakespeare is exploring. What is at stake? Why is it important? Is it a problem that can be resolved, or is it an insoluble one?

Key skills in writing about Shakespeare

Here are some suggestions to help you organise your notes and develop advanced writing skills when working on Shakespeare:

- Compose the title of your writing carefully to maximise your opportunities to be creative and critical about the play. Explore the key words in your title carefully. Decide which aspect of the play – or which combination of aspects – you are focusing on.
- Create a mind map of your ideas, making connections between them.
- If appropriate, arrange your ideas into a hierarchy that shows how some themes or features of the play are 'higher' than others and can incorporate other ideas.
- Sequence your ideas so that you have a plan for writing an essay, review, story – whichever genre you are using. You might like to think about whether to put your strongest points first, in the middle, or later.
- Collect key quotations (it might help to compile this list with a partner), which you can use as evidence to support your argument.
- Compose your first draft, embedding quotations in your text as you go along.
- Revise your draft in the light of your own critical reflections and/or those of others.

The following pages focus on writing about *Hamlet* in particular.

Writing about *Hamlet*

More has been written about *Hamlet* than about any other work in literature. It is sometimes said that at least one article or review about this play is published per day. Given its popularity as a play for study in schools, colleges and universities, there are probably many essays and other types of writing produced in academic contexts every day. What can you write about that will make your piece distinctive; and how will you go about expressing that new perspective? First, here is some guidance to help you in the preparation for your writing on *Hamlet*.

Look back over the writing you have done in the course of reading, acting and studying the play – in particular at your Director's Journal and your responses to the 'Write about it' activities. You may already have a good deal of material in the form of paragraphs, notes and reflections on the play.

In addition, some of the work you have undertaken in relation to the 'Themes', 'Characters' and 'Language' boxes will contribute to the substantial and reflective writing you might now do.

◆ This edition has emphasised the importance of embedded quotations in your writing. You will have already collected quotations that illustrate your sense of the complexity of themes and character in the play. Go back over the play to see if you can add to that collection of quotations.

Second, an important stage in preparing to write about *Hamlet* is standing back and looking at the play as a whole. The activity on page 278, which involves cutting out the play and displaying it on a wall, is one way of achieving a sense of the whole play. This act of standing back is particularly important in *Hamlet*, given its length.

◆ Here are some short statements about the play to help you decide your own perspective on it. Rank these in order of importance to you. Gather supporting evidence for the issue you have ranked as most important; also consider how you could structure an argument for this issue – based on cause (why you believe it to be true) and effect (how it is represented in the play). Then discuss your order with a partner or with a larger group.

a Hamlet is clearly central to the play. He is the eponymous hero (i.e. the play is named after him) and that makes his actions and his inner psyche the main focus of attention.

b The play is principally a political drama in which the succession to the throne of Denmark is the paramount concern. The line of succession from old Hamlet through Claudius, bypassing young Hamlet and moving on to Fortinbras, is the main strand.

c Essentially, this is a revenge tragedy with an extra dimension: that dimension is the procrastination that Hamlet experiences throughout the play – the result of a combination of reason, humanity, impulsiveness, feigned madness and conscience.

d The women in the play are victims: Ophelia is subject to her father's, brother's and lover's bullying; Gertrude is often in the dark about what is going on around her. They are caught up in a male-dominated world of confinement and corruption.

You can also disagree with these statements; amend their wording to suit your own perspectives; and adapt them as titles for your own writing as you see fit, and in discussion with your peers and teacher.

Third, you can decide which genre or type of text you wish to use in writing about *Hamlet*. Here are some alternatives to the conventional essay that might suit *Hamlet* in particular:

◆ An extended review of film or stage or radio productions (to do all three would require a dissertation or thesis). Such a review should be done with close reference to the script, using quotations as you would in a conventional essay. You can collect resources for such a review online, in libraries and via other means. Remember to consider the nature of the medium (the hardware, the context, the frame) as well as the modes of expression (sound, the spoken word, action) and the affordances of the medium you have chosen (what does it allow, what are its characteristics, and what aspects of *Hamlet* does it foreground?).

◆ Dialogues, in question-and-answer format, between the characters and an interrogator. For example, as has been suggested, Hamlet or Ophelia could be interviewed by a psychiatrist; Horatio could be interviewed by a judge and/or panel that is investigating the death of Hamlet, Laertes, Gertrude, Ophelia and Laertes.

◆ A Socratic dialogue, in which an interrogator (like Socrates – look up an example) has a thesis that he or she wishes to prove via questioning. Often the questions are designed to catch out the person or character being questioned – who could be an actor, a character in the play, a director or some other figure who will need to draw on the script to provide evidence.

Finally, some examples of essay questions that you are likely to encounter in writing about *Hamlet*:

◆ 'Hamlet has a split personality, which makes it difficult for him to put revenge into action.' Discuss

this statement, considering whether Hamlet's personality is split into two, or whether there are more sides to him. To what extent is he a typical revenge hero?

◆ In Denmark's corrupt world, Hamlet is too naïve, too full of the better sides of human nature, to survive. Discuss.

◆ Write an essay on the links between the private and the public in *Hamlet*, focusing on one or more of the main characters.

◆ The prevailing imagery of the play is that of confinement, prisons, chains and the physicality of the human body. This suggests the play is essentially about the struggle between the mortality of the flesh on the one hand, and the desire for freedom of the spirit and soul on the other. Discuss.

◆ At the core of the play is the struggle between free will and fate. But fate is divided into two kinds of determination: divine intervention and the machinations and deliberations of a corrupt political state. Is this a fair reflection on *Hamlet*?

◆ Write a study of Gertrude and/or Ophelia that argues that, far from being victims of circumstances, they have a power and self-determination that often goes unrecognised in commentary upon *Hamlet*.

◆ *Hamlet* is principally a play in which language dominates. It charts the interior life of a central character, and is more suited to radio than to television, film or the stage. Discuss.

◆ Is the plot of *Hamlet* secondary to a) the characterisation, and b) the creation of a fictional world of despair, gloom and corruption?

William Shakespeare
1564–1616

1564 Born Stratford-upon-Avon, eldest son of John and Mary Shakespeare.

1582 Marries Anne Hathaway of Shottery, near Stratford.

1583 Daughter Susanna born.

1585 Twins, son and daughter Hamnet and Judith, born.

1592 First mention of Shakespeare in London. Robert Greene, another playwright, described Shakespeare as 'an upstart crow beautified with our feathers'. Greene seems to have been jealous of Shakespeare. He mocked Shakespeare's name, calling him 'the only Shake-scene in a country' (presumably because Shakespeare was writing successful plays).

1595 Becomes a shareholder in The Lord Chamberlain's Men, an acting company that became extremely popular.

1596 Son, Hamnet, dies aged eleven.

Father, John, granted arms (acknowledged as a gentleman).

1597 Buys New Place, the grandest house in Stratford.

1598 Acts in Ben Jonson's *Every Man in His Humour*.

1599 Globe Theatre opens on Bankside. Performances in the open air.

1601 Father, John, dies.

1603 James I grants Shakespeare's company a royal patent: The Lord Chamberlain's Men become The King's Men and play about twelve performances each year at court.

1607 Daughter Susanna, marries Dr John Hall.

1608 Mother, Mary, dies.

1609 The King's Men begin performing indoors at Blackfriars Theatre.

1610 Probably returns from London to live in Stratford.

1616 Daughter Judith, marries Thomas Quiney.

Dies. Buried in Holy Trinity Church, Stratford-upon-Avon.

The plays and poems

(no one knows exactly when he wrote each play)

1589–95 *The Two Gentlemen of Verona, The Taming of the Shrew, First, Second* and *Third Parts* of *King Henry VI, Titus Andronicus, King Richard III, The Comedy of Errors, Love's Labour's Lost, A Midsummer Night's Dream, Romeo and Juliet, King Richard II* (and the long poems *Venus and Adonis* and *The Rape of Lucrece*).

1596–99 *King John, The Merchant of Venice, First* and *Second Parts* of *King Henry IV, The Merry Wives of Windsor, Much Ado About Nothing, King Henry V, Julius Caesar* (and probably the Sonnets).

1600–05 *As You Like It,* **Hamlet***, Twelfth Night, Troilus and Cressida, Measure for Measure, Othello, All's Well That Ends Well, Timon of Athens, King Lear.*

1606–11 *Macbeth, Antony and Cleopatra, Pericles, Coriolanus, The Winter's Tale, Cymbeline, The Tempest.*

1613 *King Henry VIII, The Two Noble Kinsmen* (both probably with John Fletcher).

1623 Shakespeare's plays published as a collection (now called the First Folio).

Acknowledgements

Cambridge University Press would like to acknowledge the contributions made to this work by Rex Gibson.

Picture Credits

Produced for Cambridge University Press by White-Thomson Publishing
+44 (0)843 208 7460
www.wtpub.co.uk

Project editor: Alice Harman
Designer: Clare Nicholas
Concept design: Jackie Hill